For Heather

GOD, GHOSTS AND INDEPENDENT MINDS

Very best wishes,
A.R. Utting
aka Newton Green
8-6-2011

en Press

Copyright © Newton Green 2011

All rights reserved

No part of this publication may be reproduced,
stored in a retrieval system, or transmitted
in any form or by any means, without
the prior permission in writing of the publisher,
nor be otherwise circulated in any form of binding or cover other
than that in which it is published and without a similar condition
including this condition being imposed on the subsequent
purchaser.

All paper used in the printing of this book has been made from
wood grown in managed, sustainable forests.

ISBN 978-1-78003-134-7

First published in Great Britain
Pen Press is an imprint of Indepenpress Publishing Ltd
25 Eastern Place
Brighton
BN2 1GJ

Printed and bound in the UK

A catalogue record of this book is available from
the British Library

Cover design by Jacqueline Abromeit

Observations

"The mind is its own place, and in itself
Can make a heav'n of hell, a hell of heav'n."

(Milton; *Paradise Lost* Book I)

"Under our control are creativity, choice, desire, aversion. If you think only what is your own to be your own, you will blame no one, nor is there any harm that can touch you."

(Epictetus; Stoic philosopher, c AD 55–135)

"If matter cannot be destroyed
"Then living mind can never die;
"If e'en creative when alloyed,
"How sure is immortality."

(Sir Humphry Davy, 1778–1829)

"To be frank, if your name were Beckham I'd sign you up on the spot, even if I then had to sit down and write your book for you."

(Candid British publisher, who had better remain anonymous)

Foreword

It is many years now since I retired, after a career pursuing science and technology, and returned to the Welsh Marches. I eventually found a church that celebrated Holy Communion using the 1662 rite – a rarity then, as now.

At the end of the service the priest asked me what I had done with my life, and when I told him he said I must meet a very good friend of his from his university days at Bristol, where they had both read history. I quietly shivered internally. I was well used to people of the cloth, and also people of faith, equating science with heresy at best, and more often with Hades – in their minds my future home! I need not have shivered, for this friend of the Rector was Newton (Tony) Green.

Tony was, and still is, the most unlikely polymath. He is a perpetual student!

Our first meeting was invigorating and enlivening, for me anyway. This was not a polymath anxious to demonstrate to me the width of his knowledge; this was a perpetual student keen to assess whether I had anything useful to say that could be added to his already breathtakingly wide field of achievement.

Equally I had problems with my faith, and particularly some aspects of the Old Testament. My science background would not permit me to accept, without question, some of the many things told in it. In Tony I had found a companion from whom I could continue to learn, but we needed a common vehicle.

It is written, "Ask, and you shall receive." The vehicle turned out to be the Parish Magazine. I was asked to edit it. It was agreed that this would not be the ordinary run-of-the-mill Church Magazine, but a little different. For one thing, we were not *only* going to preach to the converted, but to others as well; 40% Church, 40% secular, 20% advertising. I say 'we' because Tony had been asked to contribute a monthly article "about anything". In twelve years he has contributed 144 articles, each of about 2,000 words, totalling nearly 300,000 words in all. His view of life has found favour equally with the converted and non-converted. During that time he and I have, from time to time, journeyed together, not physically, but intellectually.

This book is a continuation of that journey, and I invite you to join Tony on what may become your particular 'Road to Emmaus', or 'Road to Damascus', depending upon from where you set out.

I commend this book to you.

Derek Embrey OBE
Industrial Professor Emeritus
Loughborough University

Foreword

It is many years now since I retired, after a career pursuing science and technology, and returned to the Welsh Marches. I eventually found a church that celebrated Holy Communion using the 1662 rite – a rarity then, as now.

At the end of the service the priest asked me what I had done with my life, and when I told him he said I must meet a very good friend of his from his university days at Bristol, where they had both read history. I quietly shivered internally. I was well used to people of the cloth, and also people of faith, equating science with heresy at best, and more often with Hades – in their minds my future home! I need not have shivered, for this friend of the Rector was Newton (Tony) Green.

Tony was, and still is, the most unlikely polymath. He is a perpetual student!

Our first meeting was invigorating and enlivening, for me anyway. This was not a polymath anxious to demonstrate to me the width of his knowledge; this was a perpetual student keen to assess whether I had anything useful to say that could be added to his already breathtakingly wide field of achievement.

Equally I had problems with my faith, and particularly some aspects of the Old Testament. My science background would not permit me to accept, without question, some of the many things told in it. In Tony I had found a companion from whom I could continue to learn, but we needed a common vehicle.

It is written, "Ask, and you shall receive." The vehicle turned out to be the Parish Magazine. I was asked to edit it. It was agreed that this would not be the ordinary run-of-the-mill Church Magazine, but a little different. For one thing, we were not *only* going to preach to the converted, but to others as well; 40% Church, 40% secular, 20% advertising. I say 'we' because Tony had been asked to contribute a monthly article "about anything". In twelve years he has contributed 144 articles, each of about 2,000 words, totalling nearly 300,000 words in all. His view of life has found favour equally with the converted and non-converted. During that time he and I have, from time to time, journeyed together, not physically, but intellectually.

This book is a continuation of that journey, and I invite you to join Tony on what may become your particular 'Road to Emmaus', or 'Road to Damascus', depending upon from where you set out.

I commend this book to you.

Derek Embrey OBE
Industrial Professor Emeritus
Loughborough University

Preface

Look around you. Whatever you see, can you explain it, wholly, and in every part? The means by which grass is green, the atomic activity which keeps the Sun shining, the 'energy trail' which powers an electric light; all are familiar, yet what do we really know about them? "Nothing too detailed, but so what?" might be our reply. Do we actually need to know these things to get along from day to day? No, quite simply. We take them on trust. But if we had time, now and then, to have our world explained to us, would we perhaps find it more interesting?

Well, yes... probably. Most people are intrigued by new information. There is something in us which delights in finding things out. And there is a well-established and logical system for examining our world and our human role within it; it is called Science. Over the past three hundred years or so it has become ever better at explaining the entire universe, including the mechanics and chemistry of our bodies. Translated into technologies, it enables us to dominate just about everything upon the planet, bar major acts of nature like earthquakes – and the weather, of course. We are, in fact, fast approaching the stage where anything which occurs unexpectedly, and not as part of some foreseen or pre-planned human arrangement, will seem a culpable failure by humanity to control its environment. And yet some subjects are still very mysterious indeed and, worse, seem almost off-limits to organised enquiry.

These are 'the spooky bits', the 'psychical phenomena', which do not perform to order or conform to common patterns of cause and effect. They worry us when we encounter them because we know that something is going on which we do not understand, and which is out of our control. We accordingly feel a bit shy of mentioning it. One legacy of the eighteenth-century Enlightenment which, broadly speaking, ushered in our present intellectual approach to life, is an unspoken assumption that everything around us is either fully understood, or has a rational explanation which it merely requires a bit of thought to reveal. Yet if things move – and nothing we can detect is moving them, or if we hear noises – and nothing we can find is making them, or if we see someone – who disappears into thin air, or are called by a voice which issues from the same element, we cannot explain these things. And we feel as much ashamed of our ignorance as uneasy because of the experience itself. "There are more things in heaven and earth, Horatio, than are dreamt of in your philosophy…" as Shakespeare has Hamlet express it. Which is true; but it is we ourselves who feel inadequate, and are troubled accordingly.

Someone over-confident in his stock of knowledge may deal with such matters by denying them. Perhaps he will then ridicule those who refer to them. For example, he will happily explain – scientifically – that the active ingredient chemical in a bottle of homeopathic medicine is so diluted that it is possible that not a single molecule of the original substance remains in the solution. Therefore, there is none of the chemical there, so the solution is just water – QED. Which is perfectly true, upon those terms. He may then see nothing odd in following up this fact with a reference, again in its proper context, to quantum entanglement, whereby two atoms, having once been closely associated, stay 'in contact' in crude terms, even if one of them is subsequently moved very far away. Might not this have something to do with the claims of homeopaths for the efficacy of their solutions? Are they really 'just water'? I do not know, but could there possibly be a connection to consider here? Perhaps all the types of experiences which are broadly called 'telepathy' have something to do with quantum entanglement, too? But where can one find out? Has any research been done? It is not good enough simply to ignore what does not appeal to one's world view. It may take courage to admit ignorance about something, but this course is more honest than pretence, or making slick assumptions and just hoping they are about right. Asking questions gets answers.

Naturally the view we have of our world changes from day to day. New news, new discoveries, new political, social, economic, legislative, or community demands are made on us, and we react to them as we feel obliged to do. Even the weather affects us. What we tend to forget is that we still live in a culture – a way of doing things – which has to be acquired from our parents, our teachers, and all those from whom we learn in one way or another. This also evolves, naturally enough. However, we do not reinvent our culture when we get up every morning. It is a basic 'given' of our existence, and in the Western World it consists essentially of the respect paid to each citizen as an individual. Its origins lie in the city-states of Classical Greece, and the teachings of Christianity. Certain outlooks, attitudes and types of behaviour are valued and preferred accordingly.

We all refer to someone who is kind and helpful to others in sudden need as a Good Samaritan, someone who puts himself out to right wrongs and restore the status quo. His origins are Biblical, but he is part of our general culture, and if he is only a vague concept in someone's mind, his story can be told in terms which destroy his true significance. For example, I have come upon an American book by a psychologist who states that the Good Samaritan intervened in a fight between some robbers and their intended victim, helped drive off the robbers, and was then rewarded by the man with gifts of 'gold and livestock'. Thus his intervention was motivated by a 'reciprocal altruism', implying that he saw no point in intervening beyond consideration of what benefits he might later get out of the incident himself. Now let me set out the original story:

"A teacher of the [Religious] Law came up and tried to trap Jesus [in debate]. 'Teacher,' he asked, 'what must I do to receive eternal life?' Jesus answered him, 'What do the Scriptures say? How do you interpret them?' The man answered, 'Love the Lord your God with all your heart, with all your soul, with all your strength, and with all your mind'; and 'Love your neighbour as yourself.' 'You are right,' Jesus replied; 'do this and you will live.' But the teacher of the Law wanted to justify himself, so he asked Jesus, 'But who is my neighbour?' Jesus answered, 'There was once a man who was going down from Jerusalem to Jericho when robbers attacked him, stripped him and beat him up, leaving him half dead. It so happened that a priest was going down that road; but when he saw the man, he walked on by, on the other side. In the same way a Levite also came along, went over and looked at the man, and then walked by on the other side. But a Samaritan who was travelling that way came upon the man, and when he saw him his heart was filled with pity. He went over to him, poured oil and wine on his wounds and bandaged them; then he put the man on his own animal and took him to an inn, where he took care of him. The next day he took out two silver coins [roughly two days' wages] and gave them to the innkeeper. 'Take care of him,' he told the innkeeper, 'and when I come back this way, I will pay you whatever else you spend on him.' And Jesus concluded, 'In your opinion, which one of these three acted as a neighbour towards the man attacked by robbers?' The teacher of the Law answered, 'The one who was kind to him.' Jesus replied, 'You go, then, and do the same.'" (Luke 10. 25-37)

It is worth noting that Jews in Jesus' day viewed Samaritans as being not only heretics, but vaguely less than human, definitely not the sort of neighbours they wanted moving-in next door. A Levite was one of the contemporary 'Establishment', an organiser of society, someone who 'set the tone' – just as his present day equivalent is the individual who sits on all sorts of councils and committees.

Would we prefer to live in a world where the Good Samaritan sets the standard of behaviour, or to take our chances with 'reciprocal altruism'?

Our civilisation presupposes the former, yet the psychologist could not have known the story, or he would surely never have blundered publicly and in print. So, in his case at least, one of the underpinning assumptions of our civilisation was missing because, I assume, he had never heard of it beyond a vague notion of 'public goodness', which he himself discerned as self-interest. I hope someone told him the full story. If we do not pass on our essential inherited culture properly from generation to generation, it seems to me that we lose something of value which has taken years to evolve, and which has become part of our way of life because it has proved beneficial, and also defined a strand of our humanity.

For how do we see ourselves, and what do we make of the world around us? What are the mechanisms by which we do so? Why did they evolve that way? And what happens next?

In this book I have set out my own views of the world and humanity's place in it. Hopefully, I have come up with some interesting information and ideas. In the end, what I have written applies to me… and to you…and to everyone we have ever known, know now, and have yet to meet.

Newton Green. January, 2011

About the Author

Newton Green is a fidgety sort of person. Every so often he stops in his tracks and asks the sort of questions which can annoy people. Even if they come up with a good answer he is still likely to respond, "Fine – but…" And off he goes again to try and pin something down more exactly.

Born during World War II, his first formal education was in the care of the Sisters of Mercy in the ancient garrison town of Colchester. In addition to the three Rs, he acquired from them a wonderful universe of God, Saints, angels, devils, leprechauns, and magical old Irish folk tales. It lifted his spirits way above the drabness of the era, and opened to him a wider view of life than most of his contemporaries even guessed at.

From such beginnings later came a BA in history from the University of Bristol, and a post in Her Majesty's Senior Civil Service. Thereafter he should have made his career in the corridors of power, but poor health and an increasing dislike of the London environment decided otherwise. Accordingly, he passed a rather eccentric working life in the provinces until, 'trouble-shooting' for the Post Office, he hit more targets than were supposed to be visible. The embarrassment was resolved by a profitable early retirement with full honours.

In the meantime he had married, helped raise the resulting daughter and son to independent adulthood, and continued to satisfy his curiosity by probing some of the cloudier frontiers of knowledge. This led him to become a member of The Society for Psychical Research, a scholarly body which investigates the 'paranormal' and the anomalies of human experience to the very highest academic standards. Such interests occasioned him a few askance glances from sections of the Anglican Church, for his Christian convictions had also prompted him to become licensed as a Lay Minister. In both these capacities he has been able to help and reassure many people.

Countless small incidents encountered over the years confirmed his suspicion that anomalies in many areas of human experience were being brushed under the prevailing cultural carpet, simply because they did not conform to the 'acceptable opinions' held by various academic and professional authorities. Whilst such worthies could get along very well in their careers by not bothering about them, these 'spooky bits' of life still kept cropping up and upsetting people. "So why don't we set out what we think we know about them, admit our lack of overall sound knowledge, and suggest ways by which we might find out more?" he asked quite a few people who turned instantly deaf ears to him.

But pinning down exactly what takes place when individuals experience anomalies to the normal run of life's events has bedevilled philosophers, physiologists, and psychologists for centuries. Although he makes no claims in this book to have solved any psychical problems by some sort of magical process or dazzling insight, he has set out some areas of human experience which seem to offer prospects for progress in future investigations. Focussing firmly on the business of what it feels like to be human, he suggests that 'mind', as opposed to the purely material brain, underlies all our perceptions of the material universe, and perhaps interacts directly with it.

This book deals with what it says in the title, therefore, and it is the author's hope that it may prove helpful to everyone who, like him, wonders from time to time about such of life's questions for which there are no entirely satisfying answers. It will give the reader much to think about, and may hopefully inspire new lines of research work in capable quarters

Contents

Foreword		v
Preface		vii
About the Author		xi
1.	Ourselves and the Universe	1
2.	Mythology of the 'Book of Genesis'	11
3.	The Limits of Materialism	19
4.	The Beginning – and Development	28
5.	Laws of Nature	39
6.	The Evolution of Selfish Genes	49
7.	God	58
8.	God Speaks	71
9	Discarding the Deity – Philosophy not Requiring a God	78
10.	Christianity's Roots	86
11.	Inside Our Skulls	93
12.	The Independent Mind	101
13.	Consciousness – a Product	110
14.	The Mind at Work	121
15.	Mind – Synaptic Science	129
16.	Out of Body Experiences	138
17.	Near Death Experiences	144
18.	Reincarnation	154
19.	Hypnotism	161
20.	'Telepathy'	170
21.	Poltergeists	179
22.	Apparitions	189
23.	Spiritualism	199
24.	Post Mortem Minds – Evidence	208
25.	Cultural Ignorance – A Barrier to Progress	220
26.	The Ten Commandments	229
27.	The Curse of 'Political Correctness'	238
28.	The Necessity of Truth and Toleration	247
Index		259

1. Ourselves and the Universe

I have written here about God, ghosts, and our independent minds. I have also included a potted history of the Universe, plus some science and the way in which it is done. My aim has been to deal with all of these in one package, along with the sort of things which we half sense are somewhere at the back of the business of being human, but which we never really get around to thinking about. Now and then these 'spooky bits' ambush us, and we are puzzled for a while. Life goes on, of course, but there remains an uneasy feeling that nothing has been settled properly, and we may later wish we had made time to look into questions about them in more detail.

Our lives, though, are not exactly undemanding. We find ourselves at the top of the evolutionary tree. We have evolved huge brains to give us the edge over all other species. We ought to be sitting pretty, masters of our universe. Yet there is so much going on in the world around us that we cannot keep track of it all. Nor do we feel very much in control of even those things which affect us directly. Then there are those times when everything seems to bear down upon us all at once. We call the result 'stress', and it upsets us out of all proportion to the irritants which cause it. It is, in the end, not being in control of these irritants which is the main problem, in fact. And there are those 'spooky bits', which we may not really believe in, God included, but which still make themselves felt in odd ways. What are they all about? It might reassure us to have a better understanding of them. And when we have had 'one of those days', don't we feel like yelling,

"Help! I want a break from all this. And what am I doing, stuck in the middle of it, anyway?"

This reaction can come unprompted at any time, often in the middle of the night when we are safe in bed and our mental defences are down. It forms part of that '3.00 AM feeling', when we have turned over in our sleep, half woken, realised it is not time to get up, and then vaguely thought, "But get up for *what?*... To go on doing what I have to do, and more of the same after that... *How* shall I cope with it all? ... Much as I always do, I suppose... And *why?*... Because that's life. Heigh ho!" And back to sleep we drift.

The world 'out there', full of all the essential humdrum stuff which fills our lives, has broken into the privacy of our sleep, but has been put off again until we are ready to deal with it once more. We mildly resent it, because whilst we are asleep we feel we are ourselves and not what our life in the wide world obliges us to be. Indeed, sometimes we might reckon that life would be easier if everyone else took a holiday and left us to get on with our own bit of it for a while in our own way. That would be nice. But it won't happen, of course. Then in the end we must die. So what is the point of it all? Is there a point at all, in fact?

This just about sums up the '3.00 AM feeling'. Perhaps someone getting it a couple of hundred years ago would have had a stock of pat, ready-made, hand-me-down answers to the sort of questions it brought with it. His thoughts might have turned, from habit, to God and the Devil, Heaven and Hell, Angels and Demons, a whole spiritual world and landscape in which he knew his place – as a mortal man, a sinner in need of God's grace, but with hope of salvation. Still, lying half-awake in the dark he might not have felt any more secure or comfortable for that. But he would still have had, for what it was worth, a grasp of the options as he had been told them. He might, perhaps, have feared he had been roused from sleep by a ghost in the bedroom, an agent of the Powers of Darkness. For what God had not specifically made according to the *Book of Genesis* must logically have had its origins somewhere else. And since the Devil was the only option then available, he might then have fancied that there was an evil spirit in the darkness of his room. People can still get very upset by ghosts and things-that-go-bump-in-the-night. For they exist, whatever may be asserted to the contrary.

But nowadays if the '3.00 AM feeling' won't leave us alone, we can reach out and turn on the bedside lamp. In its light we can wake up properly, see our familiar bedroom, reassure ourselves, and rouse our thoughts from whatever sub-nightmare frame of mind has started to unsettle them. Having taken stock of our surroundings and found that all is well – I discount a house full of burglars – we can go back to sleep again and wake when the alarm clock goes off. The '3.00 AM feeling' is then well and healthily behind us and we are ready to face life with all our usual spirit and vigour – such as these may be at whatever time we must get up.

Therefore it should follow that just as an electric bedside lamp is superior to flint, steel, tinder-box and candle, our present knowledge and ways make us better, wiser, more accomplished, and happier people than our ancestors were a few centuries ago. Can we add 'QED' to this statement?

Probably not, if we are honest. What has changed is the technology. We are just the same *Homo Sapiens* species as we were in past ages. We go back more than 90,000 years, in fact, but this is a mere eye-blink in the scale of time. Both physically and in our mental equipment, we seem to have changed scarcely at all since we appeared on Earth. Nor should we wonder at this. Evolution is a slow process. We are part of it, as is every other living creature, but we won't notice it happening. In fact some localised population of another animal species may, even now, unknowingly be adapting in ways which will equip its descendants to branch off and take over Earth when we have had our day, some millions of years hence. A betting man might back the octopus as our successor, for example. At that time the Earth's environment will certainly be very different from its present state, and this other animal may find itself able to cope with it better than we can. It does not have to be a perfect creature in order to do so; just better fitted to prevailing conditions than the opposition proves to be. And the opposition would be us, presumably. We are in charge at the moment, but have no eternal right to remain so. This is the way Creation is organised.

At present we dominate the Earth because we have evolved to possess the highest level of consciousness – so far as we know – and the most intelligent brains – according to the terms in which we measure intelligence. Thus we have come to understand our environment quite well by a logical process which we call Science, and we can manipulate its resources to our advantage by means we refer to as Technology. To date we have prospered so well as a species that there are far too many of us for our own good, when we compare our food, water, and energy needs with what Earth can keep on providing. The resulting problem can be solved by logical means – i.e. everyone agrees to have fewer children; or by more natural and haphazard ones – the 'apocalyptic' sequence of wars, starvation, and disease, resulting in the death of multitudes. Given the lessons of history, we may have our own views about which course will prove the more likely. But it is up to us, in the final analysis.

What seems to me self-evident is that Mankind currently rules the Earth, and has a consciousness and intelligence which allow us to ask the essential *What? How?* and *Why?* questions. These floated quite naturally into our '3.00 AM feeling', remember, and underlie pretty well all types of questions we are likely to feel like asking about ourselves and about our environment. Our Christian / Classical civilisation has embraced a culture of technology, the use of which has enabled us to make our material lives ever more comfortable is every way – better health, better access to all forms of knowledge, better means of transport and distribution, better agricultural techniques and improved livestock and seeds, diverse forms of energy provision, instant communications… make your own list. As the 1930's popular song put it, "Things are getting better, better, better every day…" There is an assumption that they will continue to do so, too, and that any little worries about 'where we are going', as it is sometimes expressed, are only temporary, local, and capable of being resolved.

We are accustomed to thinking in terms of evolution, by which 'the best fitted' to prevailing conditions triumph and so 'improve' species, ourselves included. We assume that it follows that our culture, technology, institutions, standard of living, and expectations in all areas of human experience will likewise evolve and be 'better' for us. But there is no natural law which says that this must be so. Before the Enlightenment and the Industrial Revolution, no one thought that there was. Each age had its fashions, but 'getting better every day' was not the expectation or perception. There were discoveries, certainly; metallurgy and writing were terrific benefits to mankind. But there are no inevitable natural processes which will make our lot better. Our assumption of 'Progress' as an automatic state of things is no more than an assumption. We need to remember that.

So what? Is our world about to vanish? How will it all end, come to that? Why did it start in the first place? *What? How? Why?* That awkward trio turns up again. And somehow we sense that we cannot answer all the questions that they suggest to us. Nor, more alarmingly, can the ubiquitous *They* – as in '*They'll* sort it out. *They* deal with these things'. Our knowledge of our circumstances in Creation is better than it was even a few years ago, of course, but there are many things about which we are entirely ignorant or only semi-informed, pending more research and information. The unsettling aspect of all this is that if *They* don't know something, or can't do something, what sort of chance have we?

For there are many parts of our lives where our knowledge is basically sound and reliable, but still lacking in the depth and detail which would show us the whole picture. For example, what happens when we sleep; how do we change our consciousness into a state we call 'sleep' and then return it again to full wakefulness? And why can't we do without sleep? What are dreams, how do they arise, why do we have them? What is hypnotism? How is it done? Why do *They* seem to fight shy of trying to explain it? Then there are life's really 'spooky bits'; ghosts, poltergeists, reincarnation, telepathy, spirit-messages, crisis-apparition, wraiths, fetches, and all the rest of it. What are they all about? Hosts of scientists, eminent in their own fields of work, may foam at the mouth at the very mention of 'the spooky bits' and say things to the effect that they are all delusions, effectively all-in-the-mind. Which is great; what *is* the mind, exactly? Ah! *They* are working on that one, too. "At last!" I would add, with a mixture of exasperation mingled with thankfulness that serious investigation is at least under way. For all the things I have just mentioned relate to us; they are part and parcel of what it is to be human, and we don't know overmuch about any of them. Given that they now and then make an impression upon us, and so upon our self-knowledge and our outlook on life, we might all be happier if we did.

Of course, way back in Ye Olden Tyme religion was held to have all the answers people needed. With greater knowledge, education, and sophistication, though, everyone's cultural horizons have widened. Nowadays people tend to look to science for answers about life. We want to feel sure of things. We want certainties. We are only interested in what works. We want instant satisfaction of our needs. We want it all here and now. And, also, we only want what seems right in the light of our own experience; we don't trust Authority too much these days because it has often proved deceitful. What we can actually see is what we want to get. And the product must live up to what it says about it on the packet, too. Science, through all its derivative technologies, can usually meet such expectations consistently – delivery guaranteed. We do not need to worry ourselves about how *They* do it. Therefore it makes sense to rely on science – as we perceive it – to sort out our lives. That way we know what's what; or do we?

To an extent we do, of course. Otherwise what I have just written would look stupid. Science and technology have improved our material lives right across the globe. The 'developed' or industrial culture is the benchmark against which living standards are often compared, and consequently in some social surveys poverty may mean not owning a television set and a washing machine. (My own early years were passed very agreeably in 'poverty' of this sort. How fatuous this definition is!) This is, however, a cultural perception and not an objective evaluation by science, and neither does it say anything about science in relation to religion. There is a vague idea around that somehow science and religion are mutually exclusive, and that there is a war to the death between them. This is nonsense, as shall become apparent, but we may as well try and suggest how this idea has arisen.

Our culture of late has been tolerant of the expression of all views. This may baffle or dismay the dogmatic, but enquiry, discussion, examination, and open debate form part of the foundations of our civilisation. We undervalue them at our peril. Thus it is that the opinions of many worthy and capable scientists openly dismiss religion. They regard it as an ignorant superstition, and perceive those who are religious to be deluded and unable to face demonstrable facts about the world and about life generally. This is, broadly, their point of view and they are properly entitled to express it. Other scientists of equal integrity and accomplishment, though, are convinced adherents of a religious Faith, and feel rather affronted when apparently deemed by some of their colleagues to be less than adequate people on this account. They may say so from time to time, and uphold their right to believe in God, or their Gods, if they so wish. Religious belief, they maintain, has nothing to do with their capacity to undertake correctly the methods and rigorous procedures of science.

As is often the case in these affairs, it is the more excitable disputants who make most of the noise. The broad difference of opinion between those of Faith and the unbelievers appears to become polarised as a result. At all costs the yelling bigots on both sides must project the perception that the 'other group', seen from whichever side one is on oneself, is bent upon depriving one's own group of all the things that are worthwhile. This might apply to such matters as pay, funding, promotion, publication of results, professional esteem, and the opportunity to work at high level. Thus distrust of the 'other group' arises, and a mythology is concocted to justify it. Those in the 'other group' are demonised, their motives decried, and their work wilfully misunderstood and misrepresented. Both groups may then view the normal run of inadvertent inter-personal errors and social slip-ups between individuals from the opposing camp and themselves as undoubted evidence of the most terrible conspiracies directed against them, personally. Bitter suspicions get voiced accordingly.

But it boils down to no more than a difference of opinion, proceeding along customary and very human non-scientific and irreligious courses. And that's all there is to it.

For there is no necessary and inevitable conflict between religion and science. Neither approach to understanding Creation embraces all the answers, and it would be bad science and religion, not to mention intellectual dishonesty, to claim otherwise. So let us look at what religion and science actually are.

The word 'religion' has its origins in the Latin, *Ligare* – to bind. This is the same linguistic root as the 'ligaments' that tie our joints together. Concerning religion the Oxford English Dictionary states; "1 the belief in and worship of a superhuman controlling power; especially a personal God or gods. ➤ a particular system of faith and worship. 2 a pursuit or interest followed with devotion." It goes on to give the derivation from the ancient French *religio(n)* 'obligation, reverence'. Here we should remember that by the time the word got into French, as opposed to 'Gaulish', it was already 'Christian' in context (few outside the Church could write it down, for a start) and the idea of being bound up in a reverence of God follows naturally from this. As a system which applies to the spiritual needs of Mankind religion is universal, too. It ties together and / or bundles up all the various bits of life and our experience of it, hopefully making some fair sense of it all in the process. It is in the sense of 'bundling-up' that I shall use the word.

'Science' also derives from the Latin, *Scire* – to know. The OED yields the following; "1 the intellectual and practical activity encompassing the systematic study of the structure and behaviour of physical and natural world through observation and experiment. 2 a systematically organised body of knowledge on any subject. 3 *archaic* knowledge." It seems to me that the key words here are 'systematic study' and 'observation and experiment'. We start to understand things when we work at examining them methodically. We can give this process three distinct phases; Observation, Repetition (of the experiment / experience), and Interpretation (of the results / our conclusions).

I want to add Philosophy to this outline consideration of Religion and Science. Back to the OED; "1 the study of the fundamental nature of knowledge, reality, and existence. ➤ a set of theories of a particular philosopher. 2 the study of the theoretical basis of a branch of knowledge or experience. 3 a theory or attitude that guides one's behaviour." This time the derivation is from the Greek, *Philosophia* – the love of wisdom. It will be noticed that Religion, Science, and Philosophy all overlap in their fields of activity. In fact, the old term for a scientist was Natural Philosopher, i.e. a philosopher who specialised in matters appertaining to Nature. Then came the modern classification of science into, broadly Physics, Chemistry, Biology, Medicine, Astronomy, Engineering. This tends to be broken down still further, e.g. Astro-physics, Radio-astronomy, Tropical-medicine, and so on. Whilst these sub-classifications are self-explanatory and justified by the work done under their headings, I rather mourn the loss of the Natural Philosopher as someone who knew enough, for all practical purposes, to be able to talk to laymen about science as a whole, and not simply about this or that sub-section amongst its component parts. Perhaps I idealise such a person too much, but I feel that the over-specialisation of the sciences does not work readily for a wide understanding of them. Maybe we would all have more reasonable expectations of science if such a general understanding existed.

For, I repeat, I see no conflict between religion and science. They both deal with what is there, what is around us, what is perceived by our senses, what is conceived by our minds or imaginations. In short, religion and science deal with the universe, Creation (I shall use the capital C to distinguish between 'the whole lot' and the 'act of creation'), and "...all things visible and invisible..." as I recite in the Nicene Creed when it forms part of my worship.

I write as a Christian, of the Anglican denomination. Science is also part of my 'heritage', for I was born in England and brought up in a Christian family which earned its living from science. In maturity I made a different career for myself, but I can claim from childhood onwards a working knowledge of the essentials of science and the physical aspects of Creation. When I refer to science I am not contemplating a mystery or simply using a word, therefore. I have some clue as to what I am talking about.

Science, of course, could also have been part of my heritage if I had been born in similar circumstances in Amman, say, and grown up professing Islam. Similarly if I had been born in Madras, my Faith would presumably now be Hindu; in Bangkok, Buddhist; and so on around the globe. However, a common factor in my being, regardless of my Faith, would have been my knowledge of science. My natural-philosophical musings during quiet moments would still, no doubt, have allowed me to appreciate that I, myself, am one consciousness, of one species, in one Creation, the origin of which I would shamelessly attribute to the activity of One God.

Science, however, should stand outside Faith, and provide a universal, culturally neutral, disciplined method of viewing material Creation. It properly concerns itself with the *What?* and *How?* types of question. The *Why?* questions are more generally the province of religion and philosophy.

Possibly these last three paragraphs will have alienated me from fundamentalists of all Faiths, and from those of the self-proclaimed 'objective' science community, too. Never mind; they have their beliefs and I do not want to interfere with them. What I am setting out to do is to say, "Here is Creation as I have come to view it, Faith, science, and 'the spooky bits' all in one package – *religata,* 'bundled up together' as I might try putting it if I were writing in Latin. (I am not, thank goodness!) I am setting out a view – my view – of much of Creation, in the hope that anyone who may wonder which way the world is going may find a few helpful ideas among what I have dealt with to use as signposts on what is often termed 'life's journey'. The rest is up to the reader.

Let us start with The Universe – (as presently known).

2. Mythology of the 'Book of Genesis'

We are told that about 95% of our universe is missing. I had better clarify this statement a little; 95% of it is currently undetectable by any instruments we have yet devised. Its existence relies upon inferences drawn from the behaviour of the 5% we can observe, for the remaining 95% does not show itself. Its extra bulk is evidently there, somewhere, somehow, providing the gravity which makes the detectable 5% conform to existing scientific laws. This much is not in dispute. However, no one has yet seen it, or come up with any incontrovertible suggestions as to its nature. So the universe is currently described as:

Matter = 4.6%
Dark Matter = 22.4% (an as yet unexplained force of gravity)
Dark energy =73% (an as yet unexplained anti-gravity force)

Reassuringly it is all distributed throughout space in accordance with Euclidian geometry. What this means is that it is spread out in the normal three dimensions, which permits us to draw imaginary geometrical straight lines through it without having to make allowances for twists and turns which are at variance with common mathematical logic. It does not appear to behave capriciously or have pockets of random behaviour anywhere, in other words.

This Euclidian aspect has been confirmed within the last few years by the Wilkinson Microwave Anisotropy Probe (WMAP), a space vehicle containing appropriate instruments which was launched specifically to test this aspect of what is around us. The Wilkinson it is named after is the Rev. Dr David Wilkinson, an internationally renowned astrophysicist who is also a Methodist Minister. He looks at God and Science with a mind fully informed about both, and finds them compatible. Which need not surprise us, for both deal with human experience, but concern themselves with different aspects of it. Both Religion and Science depend upon the perceptions of the human mind –

what else? There is, after all, no other species to conceive the *What? How?* and *Why?* questions and try to find answers to them.

In his book *God, Time, and Stephen Hawking,* Wilkinson sums up the matter neatly. *What?* and *How?* questions are well suited to probing material Creation, but *Why?* questions best lend themselves to human affairs such as decisions, motives, and priorities. So, to continue in astronomical vein, we might ask, "<u>What</u> is a telescope?" "An optical instrument designed to make distant objects appear nearer to the observer," would be a satisfactory answer. "<u>How</u> does it work?" "It refracts rays of light by means of lenses or concave mirrors to focus the magnified image of whatever is in front of it at a point accessible to the observer's eye, or directly upon a photographic plate," gives the general principle of its working. But "<u>Why</u> do we make and use telescopes?" Ah! Why, indeed? Why do we put ourselves to the trouble?

From a utilitarian viewpoint, science can in fact help us answer such 'why?' questions by changing them slightly to ask, "What's in it for me? What is the use of it? How can I exploit this knowledge?" The emphasis is placed upon our own needs, desires, hopes and fears. We ourselves then become the standard by which we judge something. This was the way that Galileo thought when, in about 1608, he heard rumours of the primitive telescopes which had been invented in the Low Countries. He worked out how they had been constructed, and promptly made a better one. His telescope, when it was mounted on the top of the Campanile in Venice, could make out returning ships when they were still 20 miles or so from the city, say four hours' sailing away. This gave the merchants on the Rialto information which they could turn to their profit. Therefore, "What's the use of a telescope?" Answer, "Getting advance information denied to your telescope-less business rivals, making money, and growing rich to your greater personal comfort." Not unnaturally, every Venetian engaged in overseas trade soon wanted his own telescope! But then Galileo looked at the heavens.

What was the point of doing so? The only thing of worth which drops from the sky is rain, and that is not traded by merchants on the Rialto. So his star-gazing resulted from simple curiosity, *human* curiosity. Why does the Moon look rough? Why does Venus appear to wax and wane like the Moon does? Why are there spots on the Sun? These are three of the questions he asked, and since no one had at that time come up with acceptable answers which fitted the observable facts (indeed, the phases of Venus and Sun-spots were then unknown) he used his brains to work out answers. Falling foul of papal politics he then got himself into trouble, as we know. But by the very fact that he was asking 'Why?' questions, he was going to the roots of enquiry into Creation.

It all started with Eve. Now, clever and sophisticated people that we are, we know that there was no such person, don't we? As children, perhaps even at our mothers' knees, we hear the myth – I use the term in its proper and non-pejorative sense – of creation as recorded in *Genesis*. We learn that the first man was called Adam, and that he lived in a garden given him by God in a place called Eden, where there grew the Tree of Knowledge. The fruit of this tree gave to whoever ate it knowledge of good and evil, and God warned Adam that he was not to eat this fruit upon pain of death. That was the sole condition for leading a care-free life in the garden of Eden. Next, perceiving that Adam was lonely with only animals for company, God put him into a deep sleep and took out one of his ribs. From this he fashioned Eve, the first woman. So far, so good; they had it all.

Because small children are preoccupied with what is agreeable to themselves and rather lazy concerning other matters, they can identify with a happy and untroubled Adam and Eve with ease. But, of course, we adults who have learned some science and know all about evolution (don't we?) cannot seriously go along with a word of this infantile piffle. It is all a bit embarrassing, isn't it? So when Eve encounters a talking snake which strikes up a conversation with her, we mentally withdraw from any consideration of what they actually said to one another. Accordingly we lead our children, by the age of 9 or 10, to appreciate that evolution is the true account of the development of life upon our planet, and give them the impression that 'The Bible' is just a lot of old stories. Nor do we consider it odd that we tend to view the whole Bible as consisting of just the first few chapters of *Genesis*. To our shame we may never progress further in the formal spiritual consideration of our inherited culture. Since so much of Western civilisation derives from it, this neglect is greatly to our disadvantage.

Let us be clear about one thing at the outset. For a Christian, God is the Ultimate, Total, and Absolute embodiment of Truth. In the context of the development of the universe and of life upon Earth, science, which includes the theory of evolution, embraces the material truths of Creation. Therefore by seeking out and telling these truths, we honour God. To adhere literally to *Genesis* simply because it is part of The Bible, is to uphold a falsehood – a myth, as we have said – and speak falsely of God and his Creation. Certainly the theory of evolution has its rough patches. There are aspects of it which require a spot more research and refining. But it is undoubtedly and demonstrably right overall. Evolution is a truth of Creation, and it is backed up by rational science. *Genesis*, in its day, was not a bad shot at accounting for Creation. There is no reason to suppose that philosophers and theologians in the Levantine Bronze Age, or earlier, were any less intelligent and able than we are. They did, however, lack the means to gather, sift, and examine evidence about the world in which they lived. Darwin and Wallace were not so constrained, and they hit upon the principles of evolution as the truth of the matter. They did not invent evolution, but they did discover the evidence that was already there awaiting formulation into a theory.

It is important to grasp that to discover something is to find, examine, classify, and detail what already exists as part of Creation, but which has not previously been examined, classified and described according to scientific disciplines, properly applied. By analogy, the American continent was always there within the evolutionary span of mankind. But it was unknown to Europeans until the Vikings, or Columbus, or St Brendan, or Prince Madoc, or Bristolian or Breton fishermen, or some hapless voyager blown way off course and likely scared out of his wits, came upon it and returned to his home port to tell the tale. None of these people gave rise to America, but any of them could have been the first Europeans to come upon what was already there, and then speak of it. The same applies to Creation. Science explains it in terms of scientific concepts and constructs, but does not create it. Science investigates, examines, publishes its findings, and so expands our knowledge. This is its process of discovery. It does not make anything out of nothing, but undertakes investigations and experiments in order the better to understand Creation.

Eve, in her little world of Eden, was trying to do just that. She knew about what was around her, but then a fascinating snake came along and told her that there was rather more to life. If she disobeyed God in the matter of not eating the fruit from the Tree of Knowledge, she would "…be like God, and know good and evil." This was a speculative idea worthy of experiment. By telling Adam that he would die if he ate the fruit, the snake reassured her, God had merely been coercing him into obedience to laid-down dogma in order to keep his monopoly of knowledge. But Eve was rather cleverer than Adam, wasn't she? And if she ate the fruit she could be as wise as God. Experiment, therefore… That was the bait, and she took it. Who would not? We have evolved with large brains in order to use them to explore and exploit our environment, and prosper thereby.

With one bite she had gained this knowledge, the myth continues. But by that self same act she had put humanity into the position of having to make moral choices – deciding what is right and what is wrong, and why – in all that it did ever after, and having to take responsibility for the outcome of those choices, moreover. The concept of human free will was thus explained. Of her own free will Eve had chosen to eat, and the consequences were the moral result of her choice. Moral dilemmas have been facing us ever since. At the same time, however, she was in a position to use her brains for herself. She did not have to rely upon hand-me-down wisdom. She could ask the first "Why?" question, which probably went something like, "Why on earth can't life be more straightforward?"

She quickly embroiled Adam, too. Repetition is essential to the experimental method and, after all, two heads are better than one in the consideration of observed results. Discussion is very useful in seeking to unravel truth by methods of science and philosophy, too. It also needs to be well-informed and wide in scope. I see, perhaps wrongly, a tendency amongst scientists these days to over-specialise, as if they were a child who has been given a box of 'Lego' or 'Meccano' which will allow just so many structures to be built and 'inventions' to be made but, by virtue of a lack of parts, imposes a limit upon expanding into greater things. I sometimes wonder if a certain type of specialist scientist is not perfectly happy to sit in a box marked 'Physics' or

'Biology', or whatever his discipline may be, and not bother to look over the box's rim at what else may be out there in Creation. Perhaps this is merely prejudice upon my part, but I harbour the notion that a Natural Philosopher might seek to view and draw a fuller and more coherent picture of what is all around him – and not only within the scope of science, either. Specialists could then pursue the most interesting areas he had described, and add their observations to his. The whole lot, once duly published, would join up to other areas of knowledge and so provide a broad and readily understood picture. This would inform more people, to wider benefit, than many jargon-riddled publications which the Media usually do not understand but feel obliged, regardless, to turn into sensational pronouncements – often to the general confusion.

Eve and Adam, though, ceased to be God's pets in Eden. So the myth continues, for our consideration and instruction. Once they had disobeyed God they had taken upon themselves the need to make the moral choices he would formerly have made for them. They could no longer be in blissful ignorance of even the need for such things. They were thrown out of the 'Innocence Theme Park', and had to fend for themselves in the material world as it had evolved by the natural laws governing Creation. These same natural laws now applied to them, too. So they needed their superior brains very much indeed, just as our ancestors did when they trotted out of Africa via Suez, ambled around Europe and across Asia, and found a land bridge – or boat passage – across the Bering Strait to reach the Americas, all in the space of about 50,000 years. This is the latest idea on the subject, at least. It looks plausible. Mankind was at large in material Creation and so, by its own efforts, it would have to sink or swim on Creation's terms. God might be blamed when there was trouble; just look at the responsibility-dodging that goes on in *Genesis 3. 8 ff.* How well the myth-makers knew human nature! But the sons and daughters of Adam and Eve had their own ways to make in the material world. And we are their descendants, of course.

Would our lot be more agreeable if we resided in some mythical place like Eden where there were 'Mangoes and bananas you can pick right off the tree…' as the song from *South Pacific* puts it? Old wisdom would not have it so. In the Sumerian *Epic of*

Gilgamesh, which dates from at least the third millennium BC, the hero Gilgamesh visits the Sumerian version of Noah, a chap called Utnapishtim. He alone (apart from Mrs Utnapishtim and their household) escaped the flood sent by the gods when they could bear the noise made by the human race no longer. When the gods found that Utnapishtim was not dead, they shipped him off to the magical land of Dilmun to live amongst all those free-gift mangoes and bananas as an ageless mortal, for ever and ever. By the time Gilgamesh came upon him he was near terminally bored. It would seem, therefore, that our huge evolved brains need the stimulation of a bit of adversity provided by life's little problems, just to keep our wits sharp. For God has made it so.

Why? We are in Creation, not molly-coddled in Eden. We must deal with life as we find it. We know what to expect by experience – e.g. drop something, and it falls – and observation, such as is made by scientists. But being at the top of the evolutionary heap grants us no privileges. If it rains, we get wet. If we fall over, we hurt ourselves. If we don't – or cannot – breathe, drink, and eat, we die. And so on, upon much the same terms as apply to all other living things. We are made of the dust of stars (of which more, later) just like everything around us. We are not materially something special and set apart by God as a sort of masterpiece of his work. Now and then, indeed, this very fact is used as an argument against the existence of God. It runs roughly, 'If there were a loving God he would look after you, if you believed in him, wouldn't he? Yet children fall ill and die, sometimes in appalling pain, and people treat each other in ways that any God who cared about them would never allow. So there cannot be a God, or horrible things like this would not be permitted by him. Thus there is no God. Q.E.D.'

Those who adopt this line of reasoning have mentally not yet left Eden, a place whose very existence and attributes they would doubtless vehemently deny! They yearn for something better than the world as it is, but do not seem able to reconcile themselves to there being no tangible 'quid pro quo' in return for believing in God. It is as though they see God as some unusual sort of politician who actually can and will keep the promises he makes in order to amass votes at elections. In return for a vote duly cast for God, they would expect a cushy existence here and now, delivered immediately. It would 'show that God *really cares...*

assuming he exists, of course. Only a mug would get fobbed off by hazy promises of a better life for this world's goody-goodies when they die. We want our *entitlement* now!'

In material terms they have a case. If merely to take the trouble to be born entitles one to all sorts of material delights provided by a superior power, then there is an obvious advantage in being in that power's good books when the hand-outs are given. Many a politician would like to have a permanent client constituency which would support him in return for its being kept in material comfort without any effort on its own part. Some have even tried to achieve something of the sort through 'welfare' systems, or straight-out corruption. But 'there is no free lunch', as the saying goes. Someone has to labour to produce the hand-outs, for they are not to be had for no effort. Even the mangoes and bananas in the song need to be picked from the tree; they don't simply drop into the mouths of passers-by. If we want a 100% material existence, its component parts are all around us in Creation, and what we make of them is up to us. There are no hand-outs. Which does not prove the non-existence of God. It merely shows that this is the way material Creation works. The laws for its ordering are discovered, formulated, and put to use by scientists, but have not been invented by them. Natural laws exist, and have done right from the beginning, as part of Creation's material package. Mankind is subject to them, but alone – so far as we know – in Creation has the ability to conceive God underpinning it all. How God is conceived we shall consider later.

Let us first look at the way we view our own environment and some of the oddities within it.

3. The Limits of Materialism

Whilst considering Creation and mankind's free will, coupled with its attendant moral responsibilities, we had better recall that we are dealing with a material Creation which is just 4.6% of what is supposed to be there. This does not mean, as is sometimes argued, that God has made his abode in the remaining 95.4%, (the God-of-the-gaps idea) and will be unceremoniously evicted and sent searching for new accommodation once science has found out what makes up this great bulk of missing matter. It does mean, however, that there is an awful lot about which we are currently ignorant. Worse, science is often so 'boxed' in its various disciplines and concerned with the limits of the natural laws it has teased out of Creation, that anything which does not fit a particular view of what science would acknowledge to exist is denied altogether. Science has come to hold certain facts to be inviolable, e.g. the attraction of gravity, and although scientists will acknowledge as a matter of principle that all scientific conclusions are 'provisional', in practice there will be certain phenomena that most of them would never dream of entertaining as even remote possibilities. For example, H G Wells' anti-gravity metal, 'Cavorite', essential for travelling to the Moon in the story 'The First Men in the Moon', would come within this category because all rational scientists know that it cannot exist, and therefore there is no point in wondering about its composition.

Whilst this may be common sense outside the context of fiction, like Superman's X-ray eyes, it is seriously wrong morally. Cavorite and X-ray vision are certainly very remote possibilities which can be discounted for all present *practical* purposes, but to write them off as beyond all rational possibility is arrogant and unjustified. Science is quite happy to contemplate the possibility of there being 'parallel universes', and in one of these Superman may in fact float around in a Cavorite car, and see through walls as he proceeds. Remember, science does not create natural laws;

they are already there and working, keeping Creation running. Science simply discovers them, which means that they are a perception of the human intellect. We have not yet perceived 95% of Creation adequately, even though ideas about it abound. Thus we should refrain from writing off odd or anomalous occurrences when they are experienced and reported. They might merely be the result of bad observation, illusion, mental illness, supposition, or fakery, but until conclusions about them have been teased out and proven, they ought to remain on the scientific 'case open...' files. Five hundred years hence our present science will look quaint and unsophisticated enough. We are not superlatively knowledgeable, and we overlook this fact to our intellectual and moral detriment.

In fairness science generally accepts that its 'models' of Creation are capable of refinement, and occasionally may have to be abandoned in favour of better ones, the formulation of natural laws being modified accordingly. Good science acknowledges that its perceived version of universal laws represents only the current thinking about them, the 'status quo' which could change in the light of more evidence. Trouble usually arises when some new concept, or the report of an anomalous experience, remains so tremendously at odds with established scientific thought that science is tempted to dismiss it without further consideration. For example, the evidence for plate tectonics and continental drift was available, and argued, for decades before anyone of sufficient status in the scientific establishments of the world was prepared to pronounce it respectable and valid. This slowness harmed no one, but it is a sobering comment upon the way science sometimes works.

Matters get even trickier when science enters the field of human experiences. There is so much about ourselves which is simply not understood and classified by any system used by present-day science. For example, sleep, dreams, and consciousness itself are presently occupying some of the best brains in the neuro-scientific field. Not overmuch is presently understood about them. Yet do we not all know that we are ourselves, and not something / someone else? Do we not all sleep for some portion of each day? Do we not dream? Indeed, do we not exercise what we call our imaginations, in terms, say, of conjecturing what might happen in the future, or to conceive how a picture might look if hung upon a particular wall as opposed to some other place? Do we not undertake creative activities from time to time, for the sheer pleasure of self expression and the delight in achievement? Or consider Time; what is it – just one-darned-thing-after-another? Or is it 'God's way of stopping everything from happening all at once' – a tongue-in-cheek explanation which rather appeals to me because it sums up what is self-evident, and yet encapsulates the basic uncertainty about time's nature. Do we fare a lot better with gravity, even? We would be in a mess without it, but we do not need to calculate variable masses and curves in space-time if we wish to pour ourselves a cup of tea. We have evolved to cope with it without effort, but our understanding of it is slight. Science, however, is prepared to consider these matters.

Alas, science is often not so keen to engage with even stranger areas of human experience. They do not easily fit the present scientific 'boxes' – paradigms – and are accordingly often disparaged as observational errors or human aberrations. I am referring to the really anomalous areas of experience, matters like ghosts, 'telepathy', reincarnation, 'spirit possession', hypnotism, and much more. (Again, we shall consider such phenomena later.) Some scientists will classify them as 'anomalous – i.e. not known to existing disciplines', which is fair enough. Others, more dogmatic in a purely materialist approach to them, regard them as an insult to their intelligence – like the concept of the existence of God. Indeed, it probably does not help level-headed consideration of these anomalies for them historically to have been associated with God – and the Devil. In times past, anything that was not obviously material was seen as necessarily being 'spiritual', and so into the realms of religion it went. This made sense enough in its day, but in our more rational and enlightened age anomalies should be the subjects of investigation, and not dealt with by automatic resort to established dogma, religious or scientific.

Thus a report of a ghost, dressed in the clothing of a bygone age, which has walked along a corridor and then passed straight through a locked door at the end of it, may offend the beliefs of someone who has concluded that any such report cannot be true because, *a priori*, ghosts do not exist. So far as such a person is concerned, it must necessarily follow that anyone who reports having seen this ghost is either mistaken, deceived, mentally ill, or a liar, Q.E.D. But the *a priori* type of argument, that is, an argument "**1** relating to or involving deductive reasoning from a general principle to the *expected* facts or effects. **2** known to be true *independently of experience* of the subject matter." (Collins Concise Dictionary, *my italics*) is not an honest approach to such cases.

A human being has reported having seen a ghost in a specific location, and proceeding in a particular way. This is that person's experience. As such it is real to that person, who attests the subjective truth of it. It is from this point that an open-minded careful investigation should start. To pronounce judgement on the matter to the effect that, 'It is inconceivable that a visible body should move purposefully and pass through a locked door. Therefore the experience is delusion or fabrication', and thus dismiss it without further consideration is to be totally prejudiced and blinded by dogma. The experience requires the best investigation possible, and if the result is inconclusive it should be recorded as such. To dismiss the experience *a priori* as an account of the impossible is simply not a valid or scientific way to proceed.

Investigation of the anomalous is not helped by dogmatism of any kind. Writing in the *Paranormal Review* (Issue 37. January 2006), two experienced investigators of the *Society for Psychical Research*, Montague Keen and Prof. David Fontana, expressed the frustration of many an investigator; "The challenge... is to advance credible alternative explanations for so many effects investigated under careful conditions and reported in appropriate detail. We are often told that the inability of critics to explain how a convincing piece of evidence can be explained by conjuring [i.e. stage magic] in no way detracts from the fact that those reporting it must, nevertheless, somehow have been deceived. But if this argument is taken to its extreme limit it permanently precludes accepting anything as paranormal, because it merely arises from the *a priori* view that nothing can be paranormal because paranormality contravenes the rigid laws of normality. Those who subscribe to this view resort all too often to postulations of fraud or self-deception on the part of the investigators or those they have been investigating – fraud or self-deception on a scale and to a degree that frequently affronts common sense. Alternatively, they may insist that the critic has no duty to explain by normal means how phenomena could have occurred, or to replicate them under the same conditions, on the grounds that it is the responsibility of the paranormal claimant to prove beyond all doubt that all conceivable normal explanations have been exhausted. And if and when they are exhausted, the same people can always fall back upon the argument that although normal explanations have so far eluded everyone, they will doubtless turn up one day."

In short, a reasonable person cannot argue to any purpose with a bigot.

The experience of ghosts and similar anomalies is common to all mankind. Thus, somehow, these are as much part of God's Creation as the elements in the periodic table. At present we are not able to account for them satisfactorily. But this does not mean that they may be rejected out of hand. In some scientific quarters, unfortunately, such rejection is encouraged as legitimate. The search for truth is impaired accordingly. This cannot be honest and, by the same token, cannot be God's purpose.

Just because some subject does not fit into a pre-conceived 'box' of ideas, it does not mean that it cannot be part of Creation. By way of illustration let us consider the question, 'What is a motor vehicle?' We might answer, 'A self-propelled vehicle, powered by an engine which causes the vehicle's motion and consumes energy, producing heat, waste products, and noise as by-products.' Very probably a physicist or engineer would shoot holes in such a definition, but it will serve its purpose here to illustrate the limits of science as it is sometimes done. Any domestic motor car will fit this definition well enough. Let us pretend, therefore, that an over-specialised scientist has no knowledge of any sort of motor vehicle other than a domestic car. How would he react if someone rushed into his study shouting, "Hey! I've just seen a bulldozer!"? "What's that?" he might ask. "What does it look like?" Well – let readers provide their own description… Could our over-specialist recognise it as a motor vehicle, though? How many wheels does it have? Well… How easily accessible is the spare wheel? How many passengers does it carry, and what is its luggage capacity? Are child seats fitted as standard? How fast will it go? What is the cc of its engine? What is its mpg? Is the roof solid, or does it fold away for fine weather? Does it have a heater and air-conditioning? What anti-theft devices does it boast? With his over-specialist mind firmly fixed upon the attributes of a domestic car, our scientist might quickly conclude that no such motor vehicle as a bulldozer could exist. Therefore, *a priori,* the fellow who had just rushed in with the report of one was either deluded or lying. Q.E.D.

Yet the bearer of the bulldozer report still insists upon what he has seen, because he knows that he has seen it. In fact there are many sorts of motor vehicle, even if the bulldozer 'discoverer' and the domestic car fixated scientist do not know this. For example, most run on petrol, diesel or LPG. But some are electrically driven, or, increasingly these days, hybrids. Some fork-lift trucks and tractors required in the very specialised environments of explosives factories and flour mills are even converted to run on charges of compressed air, thereby eliminating any possibility of a fire-starting spark. In size motor vehicles can range from a single seat racing car, via 90-seat double-decker bus, to specialised giant quarry truck; these by way of just three examples. Some are designed for speed, others for brute power. Some are manufactured for extreme environments, e.g. polar exploration or military operations, others start out as a basic chassis on to which all sorts of adaptations may be bolted. Some occasionally take to the water or even fly. Perhaps the over-specialised scientist has heard, and dismissed, stories of such vehicles.

"So," he sneers, "just show me a bulldozer which fits the known and proven attributes of a motor vehicle, or really make my day by producing for me a Formula One electric bulldozer to examine, and I'll believe such things exist. If you can't do this, don't waste my time. I'm not in business to listen to fantasies." Some of his colleagues would applaud him in taking his no-nonsense, evidence-or-nothing stance, moreover, because if whatever is perceived and reported as existing in the world cannot be, as it were, carried home in a plastic bag they don't want to be bothered by reports of it. So out of the window go God and a myriad 'Why?' questions which their disciplines could well be capable of addressing to some extent, but for bigotry and prejudice.

Proper scepticism in evaluating evidence is good scientific method, long established. And there is wisdom in such caution, for we all know that if we are 'out of sorts' – tired, stressed, suffering the latest 'bug' which is doing the social rounds, or afflicted in some other minor context – we are not apt to view things quite as sensibly as we otherwise might. This is undeniable, and scientists suffer these maladies along with the rest of us. Yet the sheer amount of anecdotal evidence that exists for the anomalous should give even the most convinced and committed materialists among them pause for thought. There is too much of it for it all to be the product of various human failings and afflictions.

We need to consider how we can be sure of the evidence of our senses, too. We shall deal with this a little later on, but it is sufficient here to acknowledge that if our remote ancestors had not paid attention to the rustlings of predatory animals stalking through the undergrowth we would not be here now. The evolved ability to perceive not only stimuli – the rustling sound – but to make connections in our imaginations with what it possibly represented, although invisible, and to choose our actions accordingly – 'fight or flight' – has served us well, along with countless other species. The 'fight or flight' choice is fundamental to animate life, and is made in the oldest and most early-evolved parts of our brains.

So where does God fit into all this? God is a concept of the human animal. Only humans can conceive God, so far as we can judge, and why (note the 'Why?' question) we do so should interest us. The materialist might argue that the concept of God is just an extension of the trust a child has – or ought to have – in the care and wisdom of its parents. The child is 'neotenic', that is, it takes a long while to grow up to full adulthood; its brain does not cease developing and settle into adult modes of working until it is about 25 years old, in fact. Because of this the youngsters of our species will be dependent, albeit to a diminishing extent, upon their elders for about a quarter of their lives. Bodies, including brains, can go on adapting even then. This is purely in biological terms, and quite apart from the learning of the culture which will form, or deform, them as they grow up. The human animal with its great brain to be developed and informed culturally, cannot simply be born and then get up and start running around like a gazelle on the plains, largely independent within a couple of hours of birth. Still less can it hatch, like a turtle or salmon, and swim off to fend for itself for the rest of its life by sheer instinct.

With high intelligence and allied complex needs, the human being has the longest period of dependency upon its parents and elders yet identified. Does it therefore create God to act as an invisible parent, like the 'pretend friend' which most children seem to invent for a while when very small to try out various ideas and behaviours upon?

So a materialist may argue. He would probably add that some psychological inadequacy in the child would require it to cling to the invisible 'God elder' for security, as a comfort-blanket in adulthood. Thus God, in this view, becomes a projected compensation for the insecurities the individual feels in his dealings with life. So far, so plausible; but, as we have noted, God does not give a material quid-pro-quo for belief. There is no cause-and-effect pay-back. Thus, if this psychological compensation idea is to carry weight, every individual of every culture who has conceived God has necessarily lived a life based upon a delusion. Can the cultural achievements of whole civilisations be entirely the manifestations of the collective imagination compensating for personal psychological insecurities over the course of millennia? This is a point of view. We can adopt it if we choose – choice, again – but it seems to me to leave unconsidered a vast range and wealth of human experience and accomplishment.

Where did it all start, for one thing? A materialist will, at the moment, refer to 'The Big Bang' or 'a spontaneous temporal fluctuation in a quantum singularity', if he wants to appear erudite about it. Press him a little, though, and he must honestly admit that for his 'spontaneous fluctuation' to have worked out, as it obviously has done, certain physical laws which did not come into being until *after* this 'spontaneous fluctuation' had occurred must be invoked in order to allow it to have taken place. Then there is a little matter of 'imaginary time', several states of which are necessary for this process to have started and achieved a universe. To an advanced physicist the process, incorporating all these elements, does its job and allows the outcome we see around us. But so, in their day, did Earth, Air, Fire, and Water. The materialist is proving Creation by reference to itself alone. He can also invoke quantum theory to demonstrate that effects do not need a cause – as things stand at present. But this offends common sense, which is the sum of our basic culture and ready experience. We can argue plausibly that before there was *something,* there was, presumably, nothing. Thus we are still left, common sensically, with the need for a prime cause, an initial momentum, a bringer-about of things. In short, we want a Creator. We may as well call him God; All-powerful, All-knowing, Total, Absolute, and Ultimate. And, apparently, seeking a relationship with us, as we with him, in whatever form we perceive him.

The idea and implications are unquestionably staggering. To consider them more fully, we had better get the fact of Creation out of the way.

4. The Beginning – and Development

'And God said, "Let there be a Big Bang." And it was so. And God heard the bang, and it was very big…' There is a natural temptation to parody the opening chapters of *Genesis* after this fashion, but we should take care before we go overboard with such whimsy. The Big Bang is currently our preferred creation theory, and it has a lot of evidence in its favour. But it does not have the field all to itself, and it is at least possible that another way of viewing The Start of Everything Around Us – the 4.6% of it that we can detect, that is – will come along one day. Perhaps it will then be something like A Different Loudness Of Big Bang, or possibly A Big Bang That Went Off A Little At A Time. We shall just have to wait and see. However, even then it will still be our starting point for the Everything that we can examine.

Although quantum theory can pronounce otherwise, Creation would common sensically seem to need a Creator. God can fill that need very well, and simply, too. But one can have all things come from 'a spontaneous temporal fluctuation in a quantum singularity' if this formula is preferred. It sounds far more erudite, certainly, although it rather begs the question as to how such a quantum singularity was constructed in order to experience its temporal fluctuation in the first place. Then the fluctuation would seem to have needed to know that matter, entropy, and, thus, linear time were to be the acceptable outcomes… and acceptable to whom? But does this matter, in fact? They are acceptable to us because we are the evolved result of them. They are what we are used to. Let us bear in mind, though, that there might be all sorts of other options existing in parallel universes we know nothing about, and which would horrify us even if they were pleasing to whoever might live there – Superman with a Cavorite car, for example.

We tend to assume that what we know about is all that there is, but there is no demonstrable reason why this should be so. And what about other types of matter, such as 'anti-matter'? Why did not the whole universe annihilate itself just as soon as it got going, matter and anti-matter reacting violently with one another and wiping out any sort of material universe in the process? Perhaps the Large Hadron Collider at the CERN installation near Geneva will shed light upon such questions. Meanwhile, we may still wonder how we find ourselves here at all.

Physicists cannot take the whole universe back into the lab to run tests on it, obviously. Thus all investigation has to take on a rather forensic aspect, with evidence being adduced and interpreted as it is perceived and discovered. However, what is examined when seeking the process of creation is not *exactly* the Big Bang. We can try to work backwards and take a look at what happened, but a minute portion of a second after the Big Bang boomed out is as near to it as we can go. If we imagine a second split into 0.0 followed by 42 zeros with '1' at the end of them – 10^{-43} – we have the picture in arithmetical terms. It is an almost inconceivably minute flash of time, but before it there is just 'fuzz', impenetrable by maths or instruments. Is this important? Yes; very important, for it stops us from examining the Big Bang as it took place. Consequently we cannot say how it happened. We must deduce and theorise, hopefully correctly, but without demonstrable certainty. Our theorists tell us that just after creation our whole universe was infinitely hot, dense and just big enough to pass through the eye of a needle. To develop into anything worthwhile – into us, for instance - it had to spread and cool, as does the gas compressed in a fire extinguisher or the coolant in a domestic fridge. After roughly 10^{-35} seconds our universe had cooled, 'depressurised', and consequently expanded enough to allow Quarks – the sub-atomic building blocks of all matter – to emerge from the cosmic soup. After one whole second, recognisable protons and neutrons appeared.

Theoretical physicists are almost dealing with a fossil record of matter by this stage, but why did energy / matter actually have to form in such convenient and universally occurring little packages, all with their own built-in rules and natural laws of behaviour? They are there; but is there any prime necessity why they should be as they are? Could there not have been something else instead? And why is it all so observable, testable, and understandable? Why not have an infinitely varied and capriciously behaving universe? The one we have makes it easier for us to deal with and understand, but is this logicality factor of any necessity in its construction? The material building blocks which comprise it, and the construction blueprints which govern the way it is put together, are effectively one and the same thing. Why is this so? Note that 'Why?' questions flood in after only one bare second's worth of creation. We may ponder them and arrive at answers of our choice. However, the material sub-atomic blocks had no choice in the process. They evolved in the first second of creation, their properties are governed by built-in blueprints – natural laws – and they have been behaving regularly and according to type ever since. This seems to me inexpressibly wonderful.

These facts force us to consider questions of consciousness and free-will, both of which are human attributes which we employ to examine natural laws and to draw our conclusions. Matter must govern itself according to its built-in blueprints, but our mental processes are not restricted in this way. Yet our brains are made of matter. It is what our consciousness employs them to do which takes them beyond the rigid material grip of predictable natural laws. Here is another intriguing aspect to Creation, ...which we will think about later.

Our universe is now three minutes old. It has cooled to an atomically tolerable $1,000,000,0000^0$ K, moreover, just cold enough for the nuclei of hydrogen and helium to form. Which, straightway, by virtue of their built-in blueprints, they duly do. Thus we have a universe which is measurably composed of 76% hydrogen and 24% helium, with a few slight smears of lithium and deuterium thrown in. It has a life history to date of these mere three minutes, but because it is proceeding rigidly according to its own laid-down and in-built laws, *no other outcome could by this time have occurred.* Surely this is staggering to contemplate? Nowadays our scientists can scan the vastnesses of space with spectroscopes and confirm these proportions for hydrogen and helium. It is the fossil record all over again. By using very large telescopes to look to the edges of the universe we can even 'time-travel' back to within about 2,000,000,000 years of the Big Bang (the universe is currently reckoned to be about 13.7bn or so years young) and still find that these elements occur in the same proportions in stars whose light has taken some 10bn and more years to reach us. This confirms the work of the theorists who predicted that it would be found to be so. The universe is capable of being analysed and understood. We can work out its in-built laws. Why, though, did these same laws arise as matter developed from pure energy? Why were they there all along in some form to guide the universe's evolution?

Such questions need not strictly be viewed as scientific. Any answers to them are necessarily speculative at present. Therefore it is in considerations such as this that the narrow divisions of the sciences may usefully yield to the wider scope of natural philosophy. The universe is both an entity and a unity, and it is useful to regard it as a whole and not simply as a collection of minute parts which just happen to inter-act in specific ways.

One million years on, and expansion and cooling have allowed electrons to associate themselves with the atomic nuclei. One can almost imagine the critical point being arrived at and a universal – literally – 'Clang!' being heard as the electrons, floating around aimlessly, cried, "This is it! Here we go!" and grabbed the nearest atomic nucleus. But, again, in the right numbers as laid down in the built-in blueprints. Is this not something to wonder at? The result was a scattering of light throughout a still rapidly expanding universe, making conditions for astronomical observation everywhere akin to those of our Sun's photosphere – too bright for individual bits to be detected and analysed. This constitutes another very effective block to our having a look at the Big Bang in progress. Clouds of hydrogen and helium now start condensing, pulling themselves together under the force of their own gravity, to form stars. The Hubble space telescope has spotted galaxies – i.e. star groupings – which are 10bn years old, as we have noted. The fossil record, again; beyond doubt it was so. There is no argument about it. We reckon the earliest stars started up their thermo-nuclear burning within 200 million years of the Big Bang, in fact. And the whole universe was, and still is, expanding and cooling. How long before we 'chill out', therefore?

There are various opinions. But none needs worry us, or the human race at all, in fact, if evolutionary processes continue. We are talking in terms of billions of years. We shall have evolved into something else entirely by the time we note that our sunshine is not quite so bright and warm as it once was, and have to move urgently to new galactic lodgings to be out of harm's way before our local star swells and engulfs us. Or, more likely, we shall by then have been supplanted by some other species now lurking among us, and evolving quietly to take over the Earth once we have brought ourselves to extinction and are no more. I rather favour the Octopus, reigning over an oceanic civilisation after mankind has multiplied, over-populated, consumed, plundered and polluted itself to death on land. Time will tell. However, since the Big Bang is still only the current 'best guess' scientific theory for the start of Creation, the fate of the universe may evolve in accordance with a completely different set of circumstances. In fairness we should acquaint ourselves with some of the possibilities.

'Big Bang' began, in fact, as a term of derision voiced by Prof. Sir Fred Hoyle. He likened the idea of a 'one-off' act of creation to a cabaret girl bursting from a cardboard cake at a banquet for boozy businessmen. At the time (he later modified his views in the light of evidence, for he was a true Natural Philosopher and something of a Renaissance Man into the bargain) he preferred the idea of a Steady State Creation, whereby the 'loose' sub-atomic bits and pieces floating about in the void bumped into each other and created one single Hydrogen atom per cc of space about once in 10,000 years. The maths will bear him out. The material is there, and its gravity and electro-magnetic attraction could do the job as suggested. But the idea rather ducks the question of where it all comes from in the first place. There is no God or 'Spontaneous temporal fluctuation…etc. etc.' to produce this matter. His idea is not entirely rejected, though; it will be found a-simmering upon most astrophysicists' back-burners, just in case. Elements of it, e.g. what *does* happen to sub-atomic debris in space, are needed and useful still.

In addition to the Steady State view of the universe there are several which rely on various forms of perpetual recreation. These are quite like the Steady State idea, in that the universe has no actual beginning or end, but feeds upon itself and re-cycles its essential parts in a fashion which keeps the whole in being. The awkward fact that the Big Bang has a good deal of evidence going for it is explained away piecemeal by finding alternatives for its various features, or by blaming bad observation and flawed interpretation. Some of the points put forward by the perpetual creationists are tricky to ignore, too. There will be much more debate and experiment to do over the course of the next several decades, or perhaps centuries, before anything is half-decently settled. Which is exactly how good science should be done and intellectual enquiry conducted.

Even the Big Bang idea began with a hiss. In 1964/5 two radio astronomers, Arno Penzias and Robert Wilson were using an old Bell Telephones 'ear trumpet' type of antenna for their work when they became annoyed by a pervasive hissing noise interfering with their observations. They tried various expedients to get rid of it, even evicting a flock of pigeons which was in the habit of roosting in the apparatus and covering its lower surface with the inevitable consequences, but still they were hissed at. Then the light dawned; they were actually hearing the background radiations of protons and neutrons combining into hydrogen atoms in the very earliest stages of the universe following the Big Bang. Also, whichever way they pointed their aerial, the noise was the same. They had found a 'universal'. In a paper entitled "Infra-red measurement of excess antenna temperature at 4080 Mc/s" they published their findings, and the Big Bang idea had a spot more evidence in its favour. Their data, in fact, confirmed the amount of helium found by spectrographic observations as being that predicted by the Big Bang mathematics of the theorists. Which was all nice and satisfying. In this way the Big Bang became the favoured idea for creation. The final fate of the pigeons is unrecorded.

But let us not lose sight of the fact that we are dealing with only 4.6% of what needs to exist in our universe if the mathematics describing its functioning are to be borne out. The maths work. Our space probes go very much where they are supposed to go, and travel to time, too. (It must be mentioned, though, that there is currently concern about the 'Voyager' probes. They have travelled through the solar system and are now far out in interstellar space, but still bleeping away about what their instruments find there. They are reckoned, however, to be nearly half a million miles askew of their predicted trajectories. There could be many perfectly normal reasons for this anomaly, but it is causing a certain concern in the offices of NASA. Are the Voyager craft showing us something about the universe's continuing expansion which was not predicted by the mathematicians, or have they simply received a bit of a tug from the gravity of a passing meteor or two which no one happened to notice at the material time? There is, rightly, some careful work being done to try and find out.) Therefore there ought not to be anything seriously wrong with our perception of what is around us – apart from the fact that we have no idea what the great bulk of it may be!

This ought to interest us, for we are entirely creatures of star-dust, composed of the ashes of creation. What applies to the stars may apply also to us in ways we do not readily appreciate. So let us have a look at the life cycle of a star.

The Hubble Space Telescope, our first primitive attempt at such an instrument, has supplied us with pictures of stars condensing out of huge clouds of hydrogen. The pictures are in themselves breathtakingly beautiful; why do we find them so? ('Why?' question, again.) More to the point, they can be viewed as almost a comic strip of the stages of star-birth. First comes the young, bright hydrogen star, collapsing upon itself under its own gravity. This causes the internal gravity-induced 'pressure' which, by the in-built laws of atomic processes, fuses hydrogen atoms together into atoms of helium. The energy released in the process 'powers' the star. Here on Earth we have been trying very hard for decades to replicate this fusion process, in the interests of generating cheap electricity. At a temperature of a mere $10,000,000^0$ K this 'cookery' is well established, and the heavier helium sinks to the centre of the star where its energy supports the star's lighter hydrogen covering. All is in balance; the star may vibrate or wobble in and out a little, but its size is pretty well constant. Our Sun is at this stage.

The drama occurs when the hydrogen fuel is all used up. The helium core of the star contracts inwards under its gravity. This increases the 'pressure' and, therefore, the temperature. At $100,000,000^0$ K the helium atoms themselves start fusing, and 'medium heavy' elements such as carbon and oxygen are the result. We, and all living things, reduce to carbon, and we depend upon oxygen to breathe and combine with hydrogen to form water. The size of the star is important in this context. If it is rather large, the gravity will be greater at this stage and the atoms will crunch together into 'heavy' elements like iron. The outer layers of the star expand to compensate for this increased internal pressure, and a 'red giant' star is formed. The Sun will go this way, swallowing up its planetary system as far as the Earth, and probably beyond. If our evolved Octopus has not perfected interstellar travel by then he'll be roasted, because all water will have boiled into vapour long before this stage is reached. Such upheavals cannot last, though, and eventually the outer layers break away, drifting off towards alternative centres of gravity – other stars – whilst the heavy mass that is left contracts still further to become a 'white dwarf', brilliant, fierce, and deadly.

This white dwarf is roughly planet-sized, but at least 1,000,000 times denser. It is dangerously unstable, and becomes more so as it cooks up all the main elements in the periodic table. Eventually, it explodes as a supernova, hurling gaseous matter out into space at over 1,000km per second – Land's End to Lerwick in about one swing of the pendulum! What remains is a super-dense 'neutron star', perhaps twenty miles in diameter. In the 'shock' of the explosion, that is, the compression which travels inwards towards the star's centre before rebounding and flying out from it again, the 'really heavies' such as gold and uranium are formed. These, likewise, get flung off into space. In time they mix with more hydrogen, helium, and other star debris to form clouds of molecules which, come their hour, will condense into another star and accrete into discs of material swinging around it. As individual lumps of this material in the discs bump into each other they fuse together, and become yet bigger lumps which then have enough gravity to do some serious attracting in their own right. They tidily sweep up all the other bits and pieces in the plane of their disc, which is now their established orbit, and collect any passing meteors and comets that they can grab. They have become planets.

So, materially, we are creatures of star-dust. Every atom larger than hydrogen or helium in our bodies has had a history which incorporates the birth, life, and death of at least one star. And most of the hydrogen and helium has probably been compounded from the same source, too. Did bits of us once comprise other conscious, sentient beings? Did they live their lives and die in peace over the millennia knowing, as we do, that their star had a finite life? How did those who saw their sun dim a little and then, quite rapidly, start to expand itself in a growing, red, baking menace across their sky react? Had they the knowledge to say, 'Well, this is it!' and make their peace with each other and with

God, as understood by them? I doubt we can ever know, but it is distinctly possible. We shall hand on our personal atoms in our turn. This is certain. They were created in the Big Bang, and there is no way of destroying, as opposed to mutating, them. In fact, if we have about us articles with gold in them, we are probably carrying mementos of at least a couple of supernova events. For this to have come about, the 'medium heavy' elements of Star One would have had to have settled at the heart of Star Two, and so had a head start in their promotion to 'really heavies' via that route and sequence when Star Two blew up as a supernova. Its built-in blueprint would have required such a course for these incorporated elements, even if its mass was by itself too slight to have created them on its own.

This is what stars do. The processes by which they do it were built into them at creation. They have no option or choice in the matter. All stars will do it, or some variation upon the theme according to their size, again and again. But we must remember that the universe is expanding and is, therefore, getting cooler. That means that there should, logically, be an end to all things, just as there was a creation at the outset. This is our experience in our short lives. It is also written in our histories, in the fossils in the rocks around us, and in the stars about us. Consider, too, that there are popularly said to be as many stars in the universe as there are grains of sand upon all the beaches of this Earth; i.e. rather a lot! Must it all end? We have mentioned the Steady State and the Recreating Universe lines of thought. They, or something like them, may finally turn out to be true. Lucky old us; until we ponder the stresses and strains involved in moving house – to another star system. If we want to carry on much as we are used to doing, this will be the only option. It will be 'Do or die' come the day when our radio astronomers confirm that the Sun is making grumpy noises, and its Red Giant phase is only a comparatively few years off. We know this. No words of man can 'spin' it differently.

By that time our technology may be so 'magical' – to our present limits of expectation – that it may be possible to 'recharge' the Sun in some way, perhaps by stripping accumulated energy from a black hole for the purpose, or to cocoon the whole Earth and Moon for a quick flip through space-time to start orbiting a suitable star in another part of the universe.

Or, if we (or the Octopus Empire) can by then manipulate Time itself, why not 'isolate' the Sun in time, and send it back to behaving as it did when quite a young star? In such terms we could then have a 20bn-year-old Earth and a 10bn-year-old Sun. Nice trick, eh? And there would still be a few unaffected stars for lovers to gaze at, though obviously not quite as many as there are now. Which would seem a pity.

Are we justified in speculating that in the future mankind will have the technology to bring about such manipulations of nature? I cannot tell. But, in mitigation of raising the speculation, I would call to mind that in the days of the dear old *Eagle* comic which sustained the sci-fi fantasies of my early youth, I occasionally envied Dan Dare – Space Pilot of the Future – the 'communicator' which now and then occupied his lapel to assist the story line. I never dreamed that I would one day carry something much better in my pocket as a matter of course. In fact present day mobile TV phones are far beyond anything Dan Dare's creators dared to draw upon a page. Thus what is now in common use seemed in the 1950s to be simply too 'impossible' for inclusion as part of a comic-strip hero's kit, even for his adventures in 'the future'. The same goes for Dick Tracey's 'two-way wrist radio', to recall another wonder from that era. If this can be the case in terms of electronics, what might be achieved in other fields of technology? We can only do the science, put the knowledge gained to legitimate use, and wait and see.

But back to the End of Everything. There are three main lines of thought upon the subject, I find.

First, there is the Infinite Universe, which expands (into what, I wonder? It takes its own Time with it, presumably) forever, cooling all the while. Logically this ends up with each atomic nucleus of hydrogen being many light-years distant from its electron, which seems silly and impossible until one reflects that, if the whole universe is like this, who might notice the difference? Does scale rule it out, or is distance merely a relative factor in the consideration? I leave answers to science.

Another line of thought is the Oscillating Universe, in which there is just enough matter in existence for the laws governing it to put on the brakes when expansion has gone as far as they permit. They then throw all Creation into reverse, so that there is a Colossal Crunch as opposed to the original Big Bang... from which matter promptly rebounds as another Big Bang. Does Time also go into reverse during the Colossal Crunch phase, I wonder? If so, how would our species read its records written in the natural context of our present forward-running linear time? Would fossils slide from their rocks and come to life again? Would a pencil note written just before the turn-around re-absorb itself into the pencil, and leave the writer quite placidly watching the written lines leaving the page to become the material of the ever-growing pencil in his hand, as he unconcernedly knew himself to be a few minutes nearer to his own inevitable birth? It is hard even to conjecture such phenomena. Nor do I, in my forward-running-linear-time-prejudiced frame of mind find them at all pleasant. A friend who is a bit of a gourmet finds them distinctly alarming!

Finally there is the Many Worlds line of thought, which relies upon the universe's sub-dividing every time a 'quantum measurement' of it is made. With regard to this type of universe anything would seem logically possible at any time, if one goes along with the basic idea. Knowing little beyond basic physics, and not even pretending to an adequate grasp of quantum ideas, I would merely point out that St Augustine of Hippo annoyed some philosophers with talk of 'worlds without end' – which is possibly the same concept – in the fifth century AD.

So, there must be an end of some sort to present arrangements, it seems, and sentient beings are going to get caught up in it somehow. The experience might not be particularly pleasant, either. How does this square with the master-plan of a God of love who cares about his Creation? The better to explore questions such as this let us consider how the material world works, having once been created, and how – and if – God may act within it.

5. Laws of Nature

Matter, we have noted, is constructed of various basic particles each acting as dictated by its built-in blueprints. A hydrogen atom in a laboratory here on Earth has exactly the same properties as any other hydrogen atom anywhere else throughout the universe, – so far as we know. In this way natural laws are universal. This very unity of Creation is one of its many wonders, it seems to me. Further, the attractions of gravity, electro-magnetism, and strong and weak sub-atomic forces (plus, perhaps, other forces which have yet to be isolated and described by science) will cause our hydrogen atom to associate with another atom and form a molecule. This also is universally true.

Or so it seems at present. There is always the possibility that we are ourselves in an atypically stable and understandable portion of the universe and, in consequence, we make the mistake of applying the conclusions we have arrived at from observing the – to us – ideal environment in our own cosmic vicinity to the universe as a whole. Perhaps it is only a few galaxies which conduct themselves according to the natural laws we have perceived and come to regard as universal. Perhaps what we perceive as the rest of the universe's behaving in accordance with these laws is an illusion. Perhaps we ascribe to observed events – for example, a supernova in a distant galaxy – behaviour which agrees with our understanding, but which has its true cause in processes unknown to us. Perhaps it is merely the observed effects and properties of this supernova which appear to us familiar and in accordance with the laws we have teased out from our observations and experiments.

Yet, if they appear to correspond with what we expect of a supernova, how might we find out the truth? For example, it is just about possible that some part of the universe is composed of 'anti-matter' and therefore behaves according to laws which are the mirror image of the ones we know. How might we find this out, being far from it in distance of space and time? Can we be sure that what we observe is the truth as we have come to know it, in fact? Such possibilities should urge us to caution in forming our intellectual models of Creation. Hubris, that well-tried ancient Greek sin, is not exactly unknown to other long established civilisations. It is all too easy for the over-specialist researcher to fall into its embrace. The OED definition of 'hubris' in fact, goes thus; "excessive pride or self-confidence. (In Greek tragedy) excessive pride or presumption towards the gods, leading to nemesis." Nemesis, for her part, was a conceptual goddess whose inescapable retribution ('nemesis' means 'retribution' in Greek) brought back to earth with a nasty bump those who had got too far above both themselves – and it. For although we speak of universal laws we must always remember that they are nothing greater than our own perceptions, or working models, of what takes place around us in the universe. Occasionally they may have to be modified in the light of better data or new insight, and it is we who perceive these laws who must decide both upon their intrinsic truth or the possible need to modify them. We cannot appeal to matter to justify itself in relation to itself. Our own judgement is necessary for the purpose. We, of course, are only human and likewise fallible.

In such considerations we are entering upon the province of the philosopher. The sort of questions which we are asking are like the anxious ruminations of generations of philosophy undergraduates who have asked, "What is the nature of knowledge? Can we know anything? How do we know that we perhaps truly know what we think we may know…?" And so on, in ways which are good intellectual training but scarcely make light conversation for social occasions. Yet, if we are to consider universal matters we must be aware both of the way our minds work and of their limitations. Whilst not needing for our present purposes to formulate a 'theory of knowledge', we must remember that we should take nothing as certain or settled.

So, returning to matter as it has been created, we think that its properties are universal and understandable. We can choose whether we want matter to have been created by God; by God working through a Big Bang; to have appeared as the result of 'a spontaneous temporal fluctuation in a quantum singularity'; or by any other process which satisfies us intellectually. We have the choice. We cannot value choice too highly, either. It is a wonderful off-shoot of consciousness. It is fundamental to all intellectual processes. Where it does not exist we are in the realms of dogma, which should always be kept under scrutiny, for dogmas are made by mere people – just like us.

It is sometimes claimed that everything about Creation is predictable. The argument goes after this fashion: – if there are two particles in Space, and we know their positions in relation to one another in Time at 'time A' and again at 'time B', we can predict where they will be and what they will be doing at 'time C', 'time D', 'time E', and so on, right along a time-line to 'time n', or infinity. Therefore, the argument continues, if there existed a computer large and complex enough to follow the courses through time and space of all the particles in the universe, it would be possible to predict where each of them was and what it would be doing at any time of one's choice. (In the absence of such a computer this idea obviously cannot be tested.) If we acknowledge God and credit him with being Almighty, i.e. all-powerful, we might assume that within the scope of his intellect lies the ability to do just this.

From this consideration, which is as old as religious speculation, comes the doctrine of Predestination, by which the fates of all humans are sealed even before birth. This idea denies choice and free-will to any creature, but it exists as a school of thought and belief supported by its adherents. Some of us are born to salvation and others to damnation, regardless of the moral quality of the lives we lead, this idea contends. It would have all sin permitted by God as a prime means of illustrating virtue in contrast to it. In this way a sinner may even be doing God's will by providing the morally wavering with an Awful Example to be shunned, and in this context not be guilty in God's judgement of the sin deriving from whatever wickedness he has committed. An extension of this strange thinking even has the committing of sin as a necessary prerequisite to sincere repentance and the earning of God's grace in return. Such ideas are odd, convoluted, and not supported by the main streams of Christian thought, however.

Strangely enough, a series of psychological / neuro-scientific experiments conducted by Dr Benjamin Libet in 1983 seemed to suggest that we really had no free-will after all. Libet asked his subjects to place one of their hands upon a table, and then lift a finger whenever they felt like doing so. At the same time he monitored their brain waves and found that the motor neurons required to lift the finger were active *before* the subject reported making his decision. Thus the finger movement seemed to be predetermined by some other agency than the subject's will. This caused some excitement for the next twenty years or so but led nowhere, because Libet subsequently found that the subject could cancel the unconscious anticipation of the finger movement right up to the moment when it would have occurred. He withdrew his earlier speculations accordingly. It seems that conscious and unconscious features of an action are simply part of the questions relating to free-will which have taxed philosophers and scientist for ages – and no doubt will continue to do so.

Libet's idea is still dogging research, though. Free-will is again challenged by John-Dylan Haynes of the Bernstein Centre for Computational Neuroscience in Berlin. Whilst Libet uncovered the 'spark' (NB the terminology in terms of light; we shall meet this again) of brain activity in the brain's prefrontal cortex 300 milliseconds before subjects opted to raise a finger, Haynes suspects that this brain area may only consider the mechanics and implications of raising the finger in any prevailing contest, and set up an 'action plan' accordingly. It would not actually make the decision to lift the finger. FMRI scans showed that a part of the pre-frontal cortex in which it is considered that 'executive' thoughts are consciously created, registered on the scanner about seven seconds before the volunteers opted to press one of two buttons. In addition a slightly different brain pattern was revealed by the decision to press one button as opposed to the other. Apparently prediction of volunteers' choices could be made on the basis of the scan's indications with 60% accuracy. This is fine, but the experiment shows only what the brain is doing. I suspect that what we have here is evidence for decisions being taken in the mind, and the unconscious mind at that. I shall argue this point when considering brain / mind as being separate and distinct entities.

From a theological point of view we may state that when God gave his conscious creatures free-will he essentially put them on trust to behave properly according to his revealed requirements. It follows, therefore, that even God cannot automatically control the every action of his creatures, as he would if they were akin to puppets and he was pulling their strings. Therefore we have as background to our lives the terrible trio of free-will, choice, and responsibility for the outcome of our actions. We are free, but must bear the responsibility inherent in this condition. This is too often overlooked.

We find, also, that in the idea of an entirely predictable universe there are snags which would tax the functions of the greatest imaginable computer. Certainly the particles which comprise matter are governed by predictable and universal laws, but the matter they constitute may be arranged and behave according to 'systems' which interact in ways that make them highly unstable. Systems embrace the interaction of elements, and those involving liquids or gasses, or solids which at the time are behaving like liquids or gasses, are particularly unpredictable.

For example, we have a daily interest in the weather, a system which involves liquids and gasses which we call rain and wind. Attempts in the early 1960s to enhance weather forecasting by the use of computers came to grief upon the discovery of the fact that tiny variations in the data fed into the computer resulted in huge variations in the predicted forecasts. From such beginnings emerged the whole concept of Chaos Theory, whereby it is true that the beat of a butterfly's wings in Brazil really may set off a snow storm in Siberia. In such a system there is such terrific sensitivity to the initial conditions for the process, that a tiny change in input brings about a colossal change in the resulting output. The butterfly flaps its wings once – a snowstorm in Siberia begins. It flaps them twice; an impending thunderstorm breaks out over Paris. The system itself is unstable, and even though the laws governing the weather are known, the slightest change in the initial conditions for a forecast will produce a tremendous, and largely unpredictable, difference in the outcome.

Therefore the elements remain predictable according to their built-in blueprints, but once they start interacting this predictability breaks down for the system as a whole. So much of the universe is governed by Chaos Theory that any hope of predicting future events in detail in its systems must be abandoned. Certainly, the broad sweep of events remains predictable. The Monsoon will continue coming to India every year, but where each raindrop will fall, and how each resulting trickle of accumulated water will flow are beyond calculation. Predestination in Creation is ruled out accordingly.

Does this mean that God is not all-powerful? Both 'Yes' and 'No'. We do not see God tampering daily with the physical processes of Creation, but occasionally we may perceive a miracle. Note that I write "*perceive* a miracle". Just as we can only make sense of Creation by applying our observation and intellect to its attributes, so from time to time we may perceive an anomaly to the customary course of events which strikes us as particularly wonderful and to the advantage of some part of Mankind – which is probably the only part of Creation which can differentiate between the 'normal' and the 'anomalous'. How we then proceed is a matter of choice, again. We could say, *a priori*, "There is no God; therefore there cannot be miracles; therefore this anomaly merely serves to illustrate our ignorance of the universe; therefore at some stage in the future we – or the inhabitants of the Octopus Empire – will understand such anomalies and laugh at us for even having considered miracles." Or we might say, "This event is so extraordinary that even the scientific experts consulted cannot account for it. Whilst there may conceivably be a rational explanation for it which dawns upon somebody at some stage in the future – or not, as the case may be – in the present context its nature, timing, and outcome suggest this event to us as a miracle. Such things we attribute, again *a priori*, to God. Praise be to God for his goodness and mercy." So we have a choice in what we may perceive in such cases. That is the essential point.

It is difficult to hit upon the level of consciousness which could be said to give rise to the prospect of a conscious choice's being made, but it must be fairly low down the evolutionary tree. A barnacle fishing for its food might pause in sweeping its tentacles to and fro, and so let a nutritious morsel escape it. This morsel's escape could not have been foreseen. Therefore it floats free, perhaps to feed another barnacle, or to become a constituent part of the seabed. Neither outcome would seem to have been predictable even a couple of seconds before the event, never mind having been lined up to occur just a short while after the Big Bang. Similarly an earthworm might push to the left-hand side of an obstructing stone rather than to the right and, by so opening a channel to water, allow grains of earth to be washed away from one side of the stone as opposed to the other. Once more the theoretical idea that this could have been predicted almost at the moment of creation must be rejected. By the time mankind comes upon the scene and starts mining, building, hunting, fire-raising, farming, and transporting matter around, any idea of a detailed, predictable, and predestined universe is clearly wrong.

Likewise, the theory of Quantum Mechanics, for those who understand its working, undermines an entirely predictable universe. Given the amazing complexities of quantum theory itself, this fact is all that needs to be mentioned here. It has been said, probably with truth enough, that anyone who claims fully to understand Quantum Mechanics obviously does not! For my own part I despair of trying to pick my way through its intricacies and write about them for those who, like me, prefer a Creation that works according to common sense principles. Certainly Quantum Mechanics 'work' very well, otherwise the technologies which give us small computers and mobile phones, for example, would be out of the question. That is the fact of the matter.

So we have a universe which may not all be exactly what it seems to be. Nor let us forget that we are referring to only about 5% of what we have to assume to be there. Yet we are used to living in our own little part of it. Indeed, we become quite skilled at coping with the bits of it that affect us for good or ill, and, hopefully, emerge from our experiences of life as abler people. A little verse entitled 'Advice for Young Vikings' by a poet whose name escapes me but whose insight I gladly acknowledge, puts it thus; "Here is a fact / That will help you to fight / A little longer. Things that don't act / ually kill you outright / Will make you stronger." Mankind is coping well enough, in other words.

But, and this is a big 'But…', if all is for the best in this, the best of all possible worlds, (I tip my hat to Voltaire's wilfully blinkered Dr Pangloss), how does it come to be that God allows suffering of every conceivable kind? It may inspire our awe when we behold Chaos Theory at work in hurricanes, tsunamis, and earthquakes, but such events kill people and cause all kinds of misery besides. Then there are awful accidents and illnesses, too. Why has God built his Creation this way?

We might just as usefully ask ourselves why we should expect our world to be different from the one we know. Do we see God as nothing more than a pusher-around of building blocks of matter? Do we require him to slave away for mankind's exclusive advantage and comfort, as though he owed this to us as his due obligation? We touched, at the outset, on the question of suffering, and suggested that once mankind had become aware of its moral responsibility for its actions, it had necessarily abandoned its mythical status as God's pets in the 'Garden of Eden' theme park. Mankind had to face the world as it was.

We added that the Garden of Eden myth was devised to illustrate the moral aspects of the business of being human. We can also consider whether or not we *choose* to acknowledge God, even as a possibility. If God were always popping up like some sort of nanny-policeman to stop us hurting ourselves or being hurt by the material world, what would be the effect upon our choice and, by extension, our free-will? What would we be in these circumstances but God's puppets? How could we then question or speculate about the existence of a God who was forever making himself felt by pulling our strings? Would we, in fact, truly appreciate and welcome his ceaseless benign attentions, forced upon us? Recall that Utnapishtim – the Sumerian Noah – was materially secure and immortal in the happy land of Dilmun... and at the same time bored to despair. He was an 'ex-mortal' man in a state of being that the gods had reserved for themselves, and it did not suit his material nature. Such was the price his *material* security had cost him. These myths well understood the human condition a good 4,000 and more years ago, and essentially we are no different today.

Could there be some way, though, whereby God could let the universe work in accordance with its built-in laws, yet at the same time keep mankind safe from their effects? If we grant that God is omnipotent, it follows that this is a possibility. But again there is a problem. Are we not also material beings made of stardust? Do we not eat, drink, and breathe it? How then might we be made differently from the rest of Creation around us, if this were our desire, yet still breathe, nourish ourselves, and live? The ancient Greeks explored the abuse of material laws in the story of King Midas, to whom the gods allowed the ability to turn all he touched into gold ... and who ended up thirsty and hungry, and finally transmuted his daughter into a golden statue when he kissed her.

So we are materially a part of material Creation, and however horrible a disease might be in its effects upon us, if we are susceptible to the microbe which causes it, we are at risk of contracting it. Pretty well daily our scientists come to understand more about the mutations of DNA, how they occur, what effects they potentially may have, and the laws governing the process. The cumulative effects of mutation produce great changes in organisms, thereby creating species. These things we know. In the context of DNA we may alter artificially patterns of molecules in order to produce specific results. This constitutes a bio-chemistry which affects the basis of life forms themselves. Normally chemistry applies itself to the composition of compounds of elements which are inanimate, but the same laws apply. So if the results of chemical changes in specific material contexts are injurious to our own material selves, we are potentially at risk of being harmed by them. Which is a long-winded way of saying, "If there is a 'bug' going around, we are as likely to catch it and suffer from it as to avoid it." It is matter – bug, acting upon other matter – us. By similar processes science may be able to mitigate the effects of the 'bug' – inoculation – or contrive a cure for its effects upon our bodily systems. Material systems and their manipulation are involved. There is nothing special about mankind in this context.

So God does not force himself upon the human consciousness, and his choice not to do so is an interesting insight into God's conduct. For God himself makes choices, it would seem. Consider; we conceive God as Almighty, that is, there is nothing God cannot do. This being so, it should follow that God is capable of doing evil as well as good. Yet our revelation of God is of a God of love who wishes to establish and maintain a loving relationship with his Creation. Therefore it would appear that God *chooses* not to do evil. We see no evidence of outbursts of a divine bad temper, for example. Bits of Creation are not stricken down or raised up capriciously. Only natural laws and processes apply. This ought to give us food for thought and, accordingly, underline the importance of choice in human consciousness, not overlooking the moral responsibility which necessarily accompanies it.

What we term evil is necessarily our perception of wrong conduct by mankind in relation to Creation, and the basis upon which we make this perception is of course influenced by our culture. Since our 'Western' culture is based upon Christian and Classical concepts, it follows that Judaeo-Christian thought and spiritual revelation – for example, the Ten Commandments – underpin our basic views of right and wrong. These moral concepts obviously reflect the social needs of mankind as an evolved species, for we do not stand apart from Creation, as we have noted. But if we believe that God wishes to have a special and loving relationship with us, we may suggest that he has influenced, indeed, inspired the free-will of our spiritual teachers and leaders at the material psychological moments of our history to bias their insights, pronouncements, and decisions in ways which have tended to further God's will and presumed purpose for us. In this way we can argue that we are able to have our free-will 'cake', and yet 'eat it' by virtue of God's prompting within the mechanisms of free-will to keep us upon a righteous course of life. Arguably God has not thereby intervened directly and unmistakably in Creation, but has nonetheless influenced mankind's moral perceptions and conduct. The materialist will object that that there is absolutely no demonstrable evidence that this has ever happened, and that our spiritual teachers and moral philosophers have proceeded throughout history by their own efforts in order to regulate the social wellbeing and effectiveness of our species. Our free-will, again, allows us the choice between these, and allied, points of view.

However, what means do we choose, individually and socially, in order to live our lives as we think right? Will just any old means do so long as they work, or should we choose means which work but also bring about a certain quality of outcome? If we opt for the latter case, what sort of outcome should this be? We had better look at such questions.

6. The Evolution of Selfish Genes

Good answers to questions about the social organisation of species come from Prof. Richard Dawkins, whom I can only describe as a brilliant biologist but also a 'crusading atheist' of the most blinkered materialist persuasion. He is to materialism what primitive, unyielding, fundamentalist Bible-thumpers are to Christianity. Dawkins is apt to refer to them as 'blind' bigots – which is a point of view, and his own choice. Dawkins himself long ago came up with the concept of 'the selfish gene', his basic idea being that every gene will fight to survive, reproduce, and pass itself on to subsequent generations. This may be at the expense of other genes which are less 'selfish' and, therefore, less reproductively successful. So be it – for survival in order to reproduce and proliferate is the name of the game. Anything goes in the process, moreover. Genes not well adapted for survival in whatever conditions prevail shall be eliminated by those that are better adapted to them, because more of these will survive them. These successful genes are termed 'best fitted' to reproduce in such conditions, as they duly do. Such 'fitter' genes accordingly transmit their 'fitter' characteristics to the next generation, which is thus given a head start over all other genes competing with it to breed, and so pass these 'best fitted' traits on in turn. *Cumulatively* this step-by-step building up of advantageous characteristics will, if continued, result in a new and superior species, fittest for the prevailing conditions in which it lives. This process is one of the insights which gave Darwin and Wallace the understanding of the processes of natural selection, formalised in the theory of evolution. It is straightforward enough, and well supported by evidence.

Obviously the gene's fight for survival does not depend upon the gene itself, but upon the possessor of that gene, which must necessarily be the parent. So far, this is quite in line with Dawkins' arguments; all [normal] parents would wish their offspring a good start in life and success thereafter. So parental choice very often means the choice made by a mother of a mate who appears suitably strong and able to pass on a good set of genes in mating. Or the female's choice of whether or not to mate at all becomes a key factor in reproduction. Crudely, this is why species usually go in for courtship and not rape. Choice is the lady's natural prerogative. Characteristics of the father which appear desirable to the mother ought to be inherited by the offspring. Thus they are perpetuated in the species, cumulatively over the generations. The quality of the outcome has been anticipated prior to mating. By extension, choices made in other social contexts likewise have their outcomes. The 'best' result in the given context is sought.

For example, if I saw someone collapse in the street as I walked through my home town, I would (I hope) feel obliged to go to help him and use such first aid techniques as I know until the ambulance with its crew of experts had arrived and could take over life-saving efforts from me. Dawkins would argue along the lines that I did this because I am quite often walking round my home town and, if at some time I were to be taken ill there myself, my selfish genes would benefit from being first-aided by a fellow citizen. In this way I, the gene-bearing organism, should survive and continue in the struggle to ensure the proliferation of my selfish genes at the expense of other people's. Therefore, he might continue, it would make perfect sense for me to set a good social example of helping others in order that this should become a cultural trait which, in the event of my own necessity, might likewise help me. There is a certain cynical wisdom in this argument. The essential principle involved is not unknown in other species, either. One feels reassured if one knows that one's social environment is basically well-disposed towards one.

But should I bother to offer first aid to someone who collapses in my sight if I am visiting a far-off town where I have never been before and may never go again? What's in it for me? Is it worth the risk to become involved, and possibly catch some awful infection from the casualty in the street, if I am never likely to be in a position where he or his fellow citizens might help me on some future occasion? Logically, my selfish genes could benefit in no predictable way from my involving myself in this particular case and, the better to safeguard them, I should take care to have nothing to do with the casualty. This is the logical conclusion; 'Not of my tribe – therefore not my concern'.

But Christianity flies in the face of such logic. We see a unity in Creation. We are all made of its stardust. Therefore we are all God's creatures. Therefore we all stand in an equal relationship with God, our creator, 'Our Father...', as we express it in the Lord's Prayer. Thus, we have a responsibility to consider the outcomes of our actions, or lack of them, in relation to Creation as a whole, not just to our 'tribe' or locality. We try to behave accordingly, which is contrary to the built-in promptings of our selfish genes and consequently often very difficult to do. What we are seeking is to conduct ourselves in line with the perceived love of God, by his own choice, for his Creation. The quality of our choices of means directed to that end is important to us accordingly. We in our material lives seek to practise, universally, God's precepts in our dealings with his Creation. This is expressed through Christianity's own moral system which, in terms of the universe, is a very recent innovation. For its own part the selfish gene has a perfect material history going right back to the Big Bang and the elements, with their built-in blueprints, behaving as the laws governing their constituents require them to do. The selfish gene's natural law is to proliferate itself as widely and as often as possible. Its activities are dedicated to achieving this outcome. All its conscious considerations are aligned to it. It has no choice in the matter, logically.

But Christianity is founded upon choice – to believe, or not to believe, in God and his revelation. Its outlook is universal, and it views its responsibilities in that light. Its believers have every choice open to them, and they strive to make the right choices in every aspect of their lives according to their understanding of God's will. It is on these grounds that Christians consider outcomes when choosing means. It is consciousness, in fact, which raises all the religions above the built-in blueprints of material Creation's natural laws. It is consciousness at a level apparently unique to mankind which allows us to conceive God. For whilst we accept God as a matter of faith, the way in which we conceive him is necessarily unique to each of us, and derives from our culture, experiences, circumstances, temperaments, and so forth. This makes each of us a unique individual 'child' of

God, complete with free-will, as opposed to a uniform 'unit' in our particular species. We are made of matter, but in our consciousness we are something more.

Faith, meanwhile, begs questions along the lines of, "By what means are we here at the top of the evolutionary tree, and equipped with consciousness? Why, in short, are we set up in a perceived relationship with God?" Here we must unashamedly resort to faith to try and find answers, for we do not know what set off the Big Bang, nor how the built-in blueprints next appeared in order to organise matter. Faith says, "God did it." Materialism argues, "It happened spontaneously; yes, it was all an accident, if that's the sort of language you want to use. There was nothing *before* the Big Bang, because that event created Time as well as everything else. So there can have been no period 'before' the Big Bang to consider. Concepts such as 'before', 'then' and 'now' can only have meaning in relation to Time. Therefore it all came out of nothingness, anyway." 'Steady State' theories also arrange themselves without reference to God. Materially, God cannot be proved or disproved; therefore God does not exist in materialist dogma.

God is not necessary. It is that simple, materially. How hard it is, by contrast, to argue for faith founded upon a personal and subjective consciousness of God. Yet this is what religious faith demands of our consciousness. If we were to say that everything exists essentially as the result of a cosmic accident and emerged from nothingness (but is equipped nonetheless with constant and intelligible laws which allow us to plot its processes and conclude that the universe is most unlikely to pop back again without warning into nothingness) we may at least wish to consider how we, as Creation's highest conscious part, should view its laws.

These laws are built-in, as we have noted. Otherwise we could not perceive and understand them at all. Elements combine to build up complex new forms. Some of these forms, the amino-acids, came to replicate themselves spontaneously and so form the DNA essential as the building blocks of life. Life evolved, becoming ever more complex in the process. Prof. Dawkins advocates what he conceives as a 'speculative picture' of the primaeval Earth, in some part of which mineral crystals had evolved in such a way that they were able to replicate and, in the process, pass on their essential individual properties. This would have constituted a primitive type of heredity, including all necessary elements of multiplication, inherited characteristics, and the possibility of mutations occurring, both advantageously and detrimentally. Some sort of system would have powered the process and kept it going, once started. In effect, this would have been the beginning of evolution. (Prof. R. Dawkins *The Blind Watchmaker. Peters, Fraser, and Dunlop Ltd.*)

He also points out that a number of assumptions need to be made in support of the evolution of life, using as his example the fact that the arch of a bridge cannot be built without a supporting scaffolding first being erected under the arch as it is constructed, and then removed upon its completion. The finished arch necessarily proves the one-time existence of the scaffolding in this case, he states, even though it has all been taken away and no one knows any more exactly what it looked like, what it was made of, or how it was joined together. Which is a fair enough method of arguing a case, but is far short of the sort of absolute proof that he, and others, would loudly demand if considering phenomena they do not support, 'ghosts' being an obvious example. To give Prof. Dawkins his due, he does in fact refer to a '*speculative* picture'. So whilst the theory of evolution may have its critics, there is such overwhelming evidence for it as a broad and all-embracing process that it has to be essentially correct. Quibbles about small parts of it are unlikely to change it very much, once resolved.

So is life to be all about grabbing what one can, and devil take the hindmost, as the selfish gene would seem to demand? In this way, logically, the 'superior elements' of mankind, i.e. those at the top of any particular heap, will have the advantage in passing on their selfish genes. Those at the bottom of the heap will fail to breed, starve to death, or otherwise die off, leaving the field clear for the 'superior elements'. Compassion or mutual aid, as in helping someone taken ill in the street, should be solely in relation to the perceived logical benefits to a particular set of selfish genes. Possibly a modicum of deception would advance the cause of the selfish gene in such a context, too. So a pretence of help might be made in order to impress as many dupes as possible in the expectation that they, in their turn, might prove helpful one day in circumstances where it would be useful to have them in one's support. Thus, if the audience of dupes is large enough, and only if it is, one should help the casualty, conveying the message 'Look at me being *good* (and thus worthy of your support),' in the process: "Be prepared, and be careful *not* to do / Your good deeds, if there's no one watching you..." (*Tom Lehrer* – sung advice to the Boy Scouts of America). This business of the selfish gene's putting on an act of false 'goodness' to manipulate dupes to its own advantage is the essence of the behaviour we have come to know as Political Correctness, and is a great sin of the present age. PC has nothing to do with true and loving goodness, as I shall make clear later.

Appeals to science alone for the resolution of all questions are another necessity of materialism. To apply the truths revealed by science is right and proper but, as we have suggested, there are limits upon what science can be expected to do. Science is good at answering 'What?' and 'How?' questions. We depend upon it for insights into the material world, and suggestions for technologies deriving from them. Its methods cannot penetrate the 'Why?' queries with anything like the same authority, however. Yet, despite this, materialism often promotes a narrow philosophy which has been termed 'Scientism' because of its dogmatic exclusiveness and rigidity in rejecting anything which cannot be carried back to the lab for examination. Scientism, at its worst, would tend to view a great painting as just an application of certain minerals upon a netting of vegetable fibre, or describe a symphony as a series of oscillations within the auditory range. This view looks silly in print, and is so in practice. However, let us recall our equally silly imaginary example of the narrow-minded scientist who could not bring himself to contemplate the existence of any form of motor vehicle other than a domestic car, and demanded to examine a 'Formula One electric bulldozer' before he would be prepared to change his mind. There are, unfortunately, bigots in the sciences just as in any other walk of life, and they give science a bad name. For scientists are as human as the rest of us, and do not have any special claim to moral or intellectual superiority because of their profession.

Another unfortunate by-product of dogmatic 'Scientism' is that in some scientific circles there is a culture of unspoken prejudice against any facet of human experience which cannot be replicated in the lab. This is not without its effects upon what a student may risk being seen to take an interest in if he wishes to pursue a scientific career. It also affects the allocation of funds to researchers, whose research projects must conform to the dogmas of 'Scientism' or be rejected when the cash is allotted. The selfish gene is busily at work here. In such a culture science must be exclusively materialist or remain undone. Even a profession of religious faith might ruin a young scientist's career, for how can he be 'scientifically objective' if he believes in 'fairies'? Pass him by for promotion and / or funding, therefore.

A fairly small number of the Science community seems to support a general undercurrent of strange assumptions about religion. For example, if we judge from the correspondence columns of scientific magazines, all Believers worship a 'sky fairy', a shadowy god-of-the-gaps (in current scientific knowledge) who will cease to exist when enlightened science has explained subjects such as consciousness, and laid bare the 95% of the universe in which the said 'gaps' must be located. In the meantime Believers – especially Christians, the fact that God is also worshipped by Jews and Moslems is either unknown or overlooked – are in effect contaminating the planet by pedalling fantasies, referring to 'daffy publications', distorting facts, and corrupting public perceptions with an hysterical insistence on myths and unjustifiable ancient folklore. Our God is an 'adore-me-or-be-damned genocidal megalomaniac' who incites his worshippers to kill people. Since we are all 'lame-brained lunatics' we may rise at some time and start a universal massacre, it seems! Apart from being discourteous as an approach to debate, the intolerance of this vein of expression should give rise to concern in anyone who values truth and seeks to understand the lot of humanity as a whole, whilst seeking to improve it. Automatic intolerance of viewpoints differing from one's own, especially if born of remediable ignorance, is an unhealthy outlook on life.

We know something of about 5% of Creation. Have 'Scientismists' truly nothing in common with Believers ... stardust ... consciousness ... a shared cultural background...?

To a Christian, God, the 'sky fairy' just mentioned, created the universe by means known to him but presently thought to be the Big Bang. Thus there is a unity in Creation, as we have argued. The grimly predetermined nature of matter can vary somewhat when behaving according to systems where chaos theory and quantum mechanics operate, again as we have argued. Then consciousness, acting through the medium of autonomous creatures exercising choice in various ways, further reduces the predetermined, predictable and predestined behaviour of Creation. We can show that this is so, basing our facts upon what is perceived by our sciences. Other insights are founded upon our subjective experience of what is around us, and by our reaction to it. If we allow such experience as evidence of anything, even as evidence of experience itself, we may classify this experience as 'anecdotal evidence', i.e. what people say about how they have reacted to what their senses have told them. A scientist describing his experiment and its findings would be doing neither more nor less. If we wanted to embarrass him, we might just ask him to *prove* to us what occurred in any dream he dreamed last night!

Such is the Creation we consider, and the sciences, philosophy, religion, and a host of other professions and disciplines have their own perceptions of it and their own ways of describing it. What they are all viewing is a unity, a whole, nonetheless. No individual profession or discipline can arrive at any worthwhile truth about our universe without reference to at least some others. To go seeking in *Genesis* an answer to all questions relating to the universe would have served very well a couple of millennia and more ago, when few people (and there were indeed some, even then, as we now know) would have been able to argue against its myths by producing facts suggestive of evidence to the contrary. In view of truths discovered since those days, however, it would be dishonest now to look upon *Genesis* as a history of creation. God is a God of truth, not of make-believe, and each time we reveal a demonstrable truth we reveal something of God. So let us not debase God by immersing ourselves in out-of-date explanations of Creation, or by becoming dogmatic about the approaches to knowledge enshrined in 'scientism'.

Religion and science are not incompatible. They never have been so, and will not benefit mankind by being separated, narrowly defined, and confined in 'boxes'. If this view of Creation is adopted there will be a tendency for people to look only into one box, and even be unaware of all the others, let alone what is in them. This is akin to seeing the world only through a strongly coloured filter; much of it appears in its wrong colours or disappears altogether. What is then perceived is not the true view of the world. Decisions made about it would be to some extent wrong or harmful as a result. There would also be a diminished quality to the life of the individual who looked at the world only through the filter.

There is a wicked little story told of a scientist who sought the River of Truth. He came upon it, and followed it up into the hills until it was just a little mountain stream. He pushed on, right up into the snows which fed this stream, and finally came to the summit of the Mountain of Truth where, to his amazement, he found a large number of philosophers and theologians of all faiths and persuasions, enjoying a leisurely picnic. They welcomed him, refreshed him, and asked him if they might accompany him on his descent and have him explain, as they went along, all the interesting but incomprehensible things they had seen around them in the scenery on their own routes up the mountain.

This is the essence of our human condition. We need ways of understanding the material world, and also ways of understanding the subjective world of our consciousness. Science, or more ideally 'natural philosophy', will help us in our viewing of the material, but it will fall to philosophy and religion to guide us in our dealings with the subjective attributes of our own consciousness.

Since everything, in the Christians' view, derives in the first place from God, let us consider how we may conceive God and build our relationships with him.

7. God

When we consider God we have a very simple choice to make; does he exist or not?

God cannot be proved. Neither can he be disproved. Therefore our own opinion about him is essential to what we do next. Do we say, "Yes, God does exist," or "Well, I'll go along with the general idea of God in the absence of anything more specific to account for my feelings about this and that"? Or do we say, "No. There's no God. In his day he inspired a lot of good architecture, painting and so on, but he's run his course. I'm not going to bother my wits with a lot of old historical myths about him"? Or might we say, "I just don't know what to think. I'll wait and see if anything about him suggests itself to me, sometime, somehow, at some stage of my life"? And there are many other possibilities, as many as there are people who consider the question, in fact. The answer we come up with will have direct relevance to the view we take of life and its purpose. God is either lurking somewhere in the background, or he is absent and we are entirely on our own, as material creatures living a purely material existence. We cannot, logically, have it both ways.

In *Genesis* we are told, "And God said, Let us make man in our own image…" Essentially we can take this to mean, "I give man the spiritual capacity to conceive me." Right from the outset the writer of *Genesis* sensed that Mankind has a special relationship with God. It is one of the parts of *Genesis* we do not need to reject in the light of better knowledge. Although in ourselves we cannot come anywhere near to God who, by his own choice, is the Total, Absolute, and Ultimate of all that we perceive as good, we can seek to know and emulate him. Man, though, is a very poor emulation, even when behaving well. Therefore the capacity to conceive and appreciate God for what he is, is about as near as we are likely to get to seeing God in terms of our own image. We lack the ability to do any better than this. God is God. We are just a part of his Creation.

To us, God is essentially a concept. We conceive goodness, and we attribute the very best forms of it that we can imagine to God as necessarily being part of his nature. We do the same for righteousness, justice, love, wisdom, and all other attributes that we have evolved to hold dear. That is all our brains can do. From what we conceive to be God we take our own bearings, and try to imitate God's totals, absolutes, and ultimates in the way that we live.

It is also the case that God is not necessarily perceived in terms of goodness. We have already seen opinions of him as a 'sky fairy' and 'genocidal megalomaniac'. Such concepts, whilst born of unbelief, are arguable in terms of various traditional views of God, deriving from certain passages in the Bible and Koran. In this respect we find, once again, that the concept of choice underpins human consciousness. The God we choose to conceive will be the God we know. If we know God, our knowledge is a matter of faith, plus – probably – some other factor, such as those life experiences which are personal to ourselves and which confirm that faith in us as individual believers. There is no detailed 'God blueprint' for the spirit, as there is in matter. The God known to his followers is known in an individual relationship conceived by each one of them. Each concept of God is entirely personal to the believer, and the believer's relationship with God develops from this point onwards.

The way in which we first come to know of God is likewise personal. If we are brought up in a household which is noticeably religious, God will be part of the culture, and he will first be introduced to us in the guise of a 'Big Daddy', address – 'Heaven'; occupation – 'Being Good, and Helping Us'. He gets presented as a sort of superior Santa Claus, in fact. This is a basic archetype (for those who delight in them) and God is depicted in this way in many ancient paintings and manuscript illustrations as a benign old fellow with long white whiskers, peering through a gap in the clouds at the humans on Earth below. This image is very powerful, even if the gap in the clouds tends later to become a sort of celestial radar room where God presses switches and pulls levers to keep his universe in order. Although good enough to convey an idea of God to a child's limited understanding, this general concept is often about as far as many people get. It is too superficial, of course, and in maturity people find it trivial and of no use to them. "Why doesn't God *do* things to sort out the nastiness of the world?" they tend to ask. Their wishes not being met by 'Super-Santa', they lose interest in God, and perhaps occupy themselves in some cultural or artistic form of 'spiritual activity' to add a necessary extra dimension to material life.

For every culture upon Earth embraces an awareness of this 'extra dimension', something which in itself is greater than, and transcends, the everyday experience of everyday people. Even avowedly atheist cultures set up an abstract concept as an ideal to be striven for and emulated. For example, the politicians of the French Revolution extolled 'Reason' as their guiding genius. (Their 'goddess' of Reason is still around of course, and is much worshipped in dogmatic materialist circles.)

At a more extreme level the same impulse is found in the 'Heroic Worker', like the Stakhanovite of Communism, who is held to embody certain characteristics dear to the regime. The idealised and heroic elements in such creations are central to the concept. They are to be upheld and emulated as essential to obtaining the desired results. As Cicero put it in his book *Concerning the Nature of the Gods*, "We Romans honour our gods because they bring us success." It is a fact that by virtue of a robust social organisation and a well-drilled citizen army, the Romans were able to create and maintain a civilisation lasting several hundred years. A firm religious sense and practice were part of their culture. One did one's duty to the gods and to the State. Thus, in their own eyes, material success and the practices embodied in the religious aspects of their lives were interlinked. Worship of the gods produced the required results. So it followed that the gods approved of the worship accorded them, and rewarded Roman policy with success.

The theology might not have amounted to much more than begging and bribery offered to the deities in various forms, but it worked. Therefore, "We Romans honour our gods because they bring us success." The good results reinforced belief in the efficacy of the practice. There is something of a psychological parallel here with that 'Scientism' mentioned earlier. The outcome is elevated to a status which is greater than the sum of its constituent identifiable parts. It is a matter of perception, from which a justified belief is derived by those who subscribe to it.

The perception of God is a personal business, as we have noted. No two people will have exactly the same outlook on life, the same history of personal experiences, the same cultural development, or the same DNA – in short. We are all individuals. Therefore the God we conceive will be individual to each one of us. Likewise God's personal relationship with every individual will be one-to-one with that individual. So God's activities will be perceived a little differently by each of his worshippers. Therefore where one person may see God very much in action, another may simply note some other force or factor at work, or mere chance, or coincidence. We are back to individual consciousness and choice again.

This being so at a purely personal level we need not be surprised that, collectively, people of broadly similar views about God will band together for mutual support and encouragement. In this way distinct sects and denominations will arise within the broad scope of a religion's beliefs. This is basically a temperamental or cultural sub-division in terms of belief. What comes easily and naturally to one group will be an embarrassment to another one. To illustrate the point let us contrast, by way of a caricature of strands in Christianity, the stolid Dutch Calvinist burgher observing his frugally sedate Sabbath, and the volatile Latin-American young lady bent upon enjoying the ecstasies of a Roman Catholic fiesta. What the one chooses by way of expressing Faith, the other would gladly avoid! Yet both are worshipping the same God. They simply conceive him in different ways, and offer their worship accordingly.

To extend this argument, until the later years of the nineteenth century travel around the world was a difficult and risky business. Therefore, although large numbers of people were surprisingly mobile in their day, it is only within the past century that we have been able to speak glibly of a 'global village'. Right up until perhaps the 1950s, very distinct strands of cultural evolution were the norm from region to region around the world. Each culture tended to have its own religious revelations, although a certain degree of interchange and adoption of ideas was discernible amongst some of them. The strange thing is that to a great extent the underlying impulse was to conceive one God as supreme. He might have had many aspects, many guises, many lesser helpers, but behind it all was essentially the Great Spirit – The One.

Anthropologists and religious historians will argue that this statement should be qualified at nearly every turn. But its basic truth remains. Mankind, it appears, needs a single 'point of departure' in spiritual matters.

In each of the main world religions of Hinduism, Buddhism, Islam, Judaism and Christianity, we may discern this concept of 'The One'. I do not intend here to make a foray into the considerations of comparative religion. This work is for the specialist, and I am not qualified to lay down the essentials of belief for any religion other than Christianity. I nevertheless find the shared belief in 'The One' significant, and worthy of comment accordingly.

The 'Bhagavad Gita' is deeply spiritual. Its contents are relevant across the religious spectrum, although couched in terms most readily recognisable to Hindus. Its eighteen short books contain enough matter for a lifetime's religious meditation. In Book 8 Krishna speaks, "[3] Brahman is the Supreme, the Eternal, Atman is his Spirit in man. Karma is the force of creation, wherefrom all things have their life. [4] Matter is the kingdom of the earth, which in time passes away; but the Spirit is the kingdom of Light. In this body I offer sacrifice, and my body is sacrifice." These statements will be clear to anyone of a religious persuasion, though uttered in the accents of a particular culture. Their essence is universal.

Buddhism derives from Hinduism, but the Buddha stressed that each individual is responsible for his own salvation. This is seen in transcendent terms as *nirvana*, a state of being free from craving, suffering and sorrow. Nirvana is attained by the Middle Path, a regime between the excesses of pure hedonism on the one hand, and the grimness of self-mortification on the other. Neither of these approaches to life will enable the individual to escape the miseries of the material world, but he may gain insight, knowledge, tranquility, and enlightenment by meditating upon the Four Noble Truths. These are:

1) There is suffering in the world, both mental and physical.
2) Suffering occurs because of the individual's over-great attachment to his desires.
3) By eliminating the cause – attachment – one can eliminate suffering.

4) There is a method to eliminate the cause of suffering called the Eightfold Path, which provides a guide to correct behaviour and thought. It guides one to Wisdom – (right views, right intentions); Virtue – (right speech, right conduct, right way of life); and Mental Discipline – (effort, consideration, concentration).

As in Hinduism those who progress spiritually rise through successive incarnations to a state where all desire, and the pains it brings, are absent, and union with The One is experienced. In a sense the very concept of God becomes superfluous, since the experience transcends all experience and is in itself perfection. It is the experience of a supreme concept, even so.

Islam, in common with Judaism and Christianity, is strongly monotheist. In Sura 4 (Women) 171 we read, "People of the Book [i.e. Moslems, Jews, Christians], do not transgress the bounds of your religion. Speak nothing but the truth about God. The apostle and His Word which He cast to Mary: a spirit from Him. So believe in God and his apostles and do not say 'Three'. Forbear, and it shall be better for you. God is but one God. God forbid that He should have a son! He is all that the heavens and earth contain. God is the all-sufficient protector. The Messiah does not disdain to be a servant to God, nor do the angels who are nearest to Him. Those who through arrogance disdain his service shall all be brought before Him." Also Sura 5 (The Table) 68–73, "Say: 'People of the Book, you will attain nothing until you observe the Torah and the Gospel and that which is revealed to you from your Lord.' That which is revealed to you from your Lord will surely increase the wickedness and unbelief in many of them. But do not grieve for the unbelievers. Believers, Jews, Sabaeans, and Christians – whoever believes in God and the Last Day and does what is right – shall have nothing to fear or to regret. We made a covenant with the Israelites and sent forth apostles among them. But wherever an apostle came to them with a message that did not suit their fancies, some they accused of lying and others they put to death. They thought no harm would follow: they were blind and deaf. God turned to them in mercy, but many again were blind and deaf. God is ever watching their actions.

"Unbelievers are those that say: 'God is the Messiah, the son of Mary.' For the Messiah himself said: 'Children of Israel, serve

God, my Lord and your Lord.' He that worships other gods beside God, God will deny him Paradise, and Hell shall be his home. None shall help the evil-doers. Unbelievers are those that say: 'God is one of three.' There is but one God. If they do not desist from so saying, those of them that disbelieve shall be sternly punished."

The theme of devotion to one God is clear from these two extracts. Islam is grounded upon six Articles of Faith:

Belief in Allah (the One and Only God).
Belief in all the prophets of God (more than 124,000 of them) with the Prophet Mohammed as the Final, or Seal, of the Prophets.
Belief in Angels.
Belief in the Divine Books, like the Psalms (*Zabur*) the Law (the Torah or *Taurat*), and the Gospels (*Injil*) with the Koran being the Final Revelation.
Belief in the Power of Allah in determining one's destiny.
Belief in the Day of Judgement and Final Reckoning.

There are also the Five Pillars of Islam:

Shahadah (Declaration or Testimony of faith).
Solat (The five-times-a-day prayers).
Saum (Fasting in the whole month of Ramadan).
Zakat (Charity, both obligatory and voluntary).
Haj (the annual Pilgrimage of Islam).

Some of these Articles and Obligations clearly differ from the traditions of Christianity and Judaism, but are not incomprehensible to them. Essential to Christianity, however, is the Divinity of Christ, which Islam does not accept. Neither do Christians view the prophecy of Mohammed as God's final word to his Creation. Judaism likewise does not recognise the primacy of the Revelation of the Prophet Mohammed. This much established, there is a deal of common ground among the three religions of The People of The Book which, courteously respected along with the differences, can encompass worship of one God Almighty as perceived by them all. The idea that there is a natural and inevitable conflict simmering amongst them derives as much from misunderstanding of the true nature of their beliefs as from a gory history of intolerance and persecution. It is to be regretted that the politics associated with some adherents of these religions entrench the stereotypes of the 'enemy – infidel' as perceived throughout the centuries. As with all politics, however, assertion and presentation take priority over truth, courtesy, and a proper tolerance of differing points of view.

It is, of course, the Christian who says "Three". Not three gods, nor a single God chopped into three, but One God viewed from three different aspects, Father, Son, and Holy Spirit. This is not necessarily an easy concept to grasp if one comes upon it anew. Originally the Trinity was preached as 'One God in persons three...' when the audience of first-century hearers would have been accustomed to the actors of the time appearing upon stage behind masks – *personae* – to represent the essence of the characters they were portraying. We still retain this convention today in the 'heraldry' of the theatre, a laughing mask to represent comedy, a grief-stricken one to indicate tragedy. According to the *persona* worn, early preachers explained, so God presented himself to us in the role of Father, Son, or Holy Spirit.

Beyond the Roman Empire, though, St Patrick found a simpler illustration of this idea in the shamrock. "Look," he expounded. "Here we have one leaf, but with three obvious lobes upon it. They are all joined together and form the one leaf. None of the lobes is more important than any of the others, and the leaf would not be proper and complete if we took any of them away. They are all part of the one leaf, and whichever way you look at it they make up the whole undivided leaf. In just the same way we say that God is, at one and the same time, Father, Son, and Holy Spirit. These are the three different ways of looking at him, but he is still the one God regardless of which name you call him by. Sometimes it is easier to view him as being Father, or Son, or Holy Spirit, than it is to see him as God alone. That is why we say he is Three-in-One, whilst we know just as well that he is also and at the same time One-in-Three. Like the three lobes of the one shamrock leaf, there are three aspects to the one God. It is just a matter of how you look at him."

And the world also sees each of us in different aspects, depending upon what we are doing at the time. For example, I am a husband, a father, a son (or I wouldn't be here), and if I could claim any siblings, I could also be a brother. I might likewise be known by the titles of any jobs I did or functions I undertook; Lay

Reader, Churchwarden, Bellringer, and so on. Yet there is only one of me; like everyone else I simply have different aspects to my one identity. This is the way we view God.

God the Father is, frankly, too great and wonderful to be conceived. We may speak of him as Creator, Sustainer, Judge, Almighty, Omniscient, Ultimate, Absolute, Total and much more along the same absolute and superlative lines. He has historical titles, such as The Ancient of Days, given him by the Jews in Biblical Israel. He existed before the Big Bang, and he alone knows why he brought the universe into being. He is to be found in no one place, or at any specific time. He is everywhere, always, and aware of everything. He has a special one-to-one relationship with his worshippers, and with all the human race if its members choose to acknowledge and develop it, and that relationship is based upon an altruistic love that is too pure to be conceived, far less practised properly by his worshippers. His power is infinite, yet he uses it consistently for the benefit of his Creation, and in accordance with the natural laws he has called into being. Given that an all-powerful deity cannot, logically, be constrained by anything other than himself, it appears that God works for the benefit of his Creation by his own choice. We should view this attribute of God with due humility, indeed. He is, in the end, too immense to contemplate comprehensively, and we may find it easier to grasp him in human aspect as God the Son.

The Son we know as Jesus. He is an historical figure, and the Incarnation of God; "The Word was made flesh and dwelt among us," as St John puts it. This is central to the Christian's belief. The Jew regards Jesus as, at best, a heretic. Islam acknowledges him as a great teacher and prophet, but will not countenance his divinity. Hindus can incorporate him within the scope of their spiritual pantheon without difficulty, although the result can be troubling for strictly orthodox Christians. The materialist considers any view of him as being more than a limited first-century moral teacher as bunk, pure and simple. Therefore he carries with him his own baggage of perceptual difficulties. We are not sure of his historical dates, even; late 7BC or early 6 BC to the Spring of AD30 seems to cover the probable span of his earthly life well enough. (We have to thank the monk Dionysius Exiguus, writing in 625, for forgetting that the emperor Augustus ruled as Octavian the Consul for four years, in order to account for the Nativity's occurring 'BC'. He has been confused by the traditional date for the foundation of Rome in relation to the date of Herod the Great's death in 4 BC, too.)

For about the final three years of his earthly life Jesus roamed Palestine, healing, teaching the largely rural populace, and correcting the Judaism of his day. This did not endear him to the religious authorities at Jerusalem, who contrived with the occupying Romans a political arrest, trial and execution to get rid of him. 'Et resurrexit tertia die…' and on the third day he rose again, as Christians believe. There is no hedging on this point; one either believes it or one does not. He appeared, and was touched by 'doubting' Thomas to confirm his physical presence to his immediate followers. He ate, drank, conversed, reassured, and steadied them to go and proclaim the Good News – 'Gospel' – of God's 'Kingdom' (i.e. God's way of having mankind enter into relationship with him) to all the world. The rest is history, down to and including our own day, plus all our tomorrows. He is termed 'Christ' or 'Messiah'; both words, respectively Greek and Hebrew in origin, mean 'the Anointed One', that is, the man expected by Judaic tradition to be set aside by God to settle the chosen people of Israel in the territory supposedly covered by King David's realm, and there allow them to live correctly and worship God forever.

If they were expecting an all-conquering, miraculous superman, one can see why the Jews were disappointed by Jesus. To be told, "Love God with all your heart, with all your soul, with all your mind, and with all your strength, and your neighbour as yourself," was not what they wanted to hear, especially under Roman occupation. The requirement is hard enough in any case. We are still trying to live up to it. However, it is in Jesus' person that we can see how God can embrace both matter and spirit, and reconcile the needs of both in the context of human life. Jesus is God in human form. As such we may more readily identify with him and grasp his teaching. It is therefore by seeking to understand the message given by the Son, as shown in the Gospels and subsequent New Testament writings, that we can approach godliness in the conduct of our own lives and, we believe, behave as God requires us to do.

The Holy Spirit provides the inspiration of God in our lives. In this form God works directly upon our (unconscious) minds and gives us insights, courage and conviction, empathy and understanding to extents greater than we would consciously achieve. He also nags and cajoles us to proceed in unaccustomed ways to unusual goals. We cannot be God, but we can strive to do his will. The Holy Spirit can make us God's instruments in this context. In ways of which we are unaware the Holy Spirit may co-ordinate the efforts of numerous people to meet some special need or to bring about some humane result. We are spiritual beings, we believe, and therefore susceptible to the Holy Spirit's prompting, regardless of whether or not we know or wish it. God is with us in this way. The materialist will not be able to reconcile himself with the likelihood, never mind the truth, of such a concept, however. It is a matter of choice and faith once again.

Faith, as a matter of belief, presents terrible difficulties for many people. It is all very well, they say, for Jesus to have told us that unless we accept God and believe in him with the uncritical acceptance of little children we shall not make much spiritual progress. But how, in all intellectual honesty, can an intelligent, educated, responsible and sophisticated human being sign up to a faith that is fine by infantile standards but cannot be proved in the same way as one can, for example, prove the attraction of gravity? The point is fair in purely material terms. If one wishes to demonstrate gravity, one drops something; if one wishes to prove God, one cannot do so. Neither can one disprove him, of course, and it is at this stage that arguments can quickly degenerate into philosophical word-games of the 'lack of proof of non-existence does not constitute proof absolute of any existence...' type. If one explains Creation in terms of 'a spontaneous temporal fluctuation in a quantum singularity', there is no need for God to have been on hand to light the blue touch-paper for the Big Bang, let alone to have looked after his Creation subsequently. Any quest for God runs into a short cul-de-sac on these terms.

Recall, though, that God is a concept. We conceive him, or he reveals himself to believers by the Holy Spirit – if we wish to put it that way – in a personal relationship with us. We can describe as best we may what God means to us – or does not mean to us – but we cannot go out and buy a packet of him, or a bottle of his Holy Spirit. (We *can* buy his instruction manual, which is known as The Bible.) Our concept of God is entirely individual to each of us. There is a vast amount of it we conceive in common with other believers, of course. This is the cultural aspect of Christianity, collectively known as 'The Church'. God is worshipped, collectively, by 'The Church' (in some sort of building of the same general name) but each worshipper will have a slightly different perception of him, as we have already noted. Each believer has a unique relationship with 'Our Father, who art in Heaven...', and upon the perception of God in that believer's life the relationship will develop. If it flags at some stage, quiet meditation – i.e. sorting out one's motives, planned actions, and the integrity of one's actual style of life – is likely to put that relationship back on to a firmer footing with God. It is, inescapably, the childlike faith turning to a greater power.

But power is known as energy, in the real world. In physical terms it is generated, and in social terms it means getting one's own way. How is God's power demonstrated under either of these headings? Possibly by the work done, through God's grace, by this or that individual? Of course, the work might have been done anyway, without reference to God; but here faith kicks in again. One may choose what one believes about the matter in question. Even in more 'scientific' subjects one has to take an awful lot of life on trust; trust in the validity of the evidence or experience, trust in the accuracy of observation, trust in the exactness of measurement, trust in the correct interpretation of data, and trust in any judgement made upon its significance and implications. Modern psychiatry can cure all kinds of mental distress, but where in the lab can one see a Subconscious in a pot of pickle, or view an overactive Libido leering from a jar of formaldehyde? We talk glibly (far too glibly, usually) of such concepts as the Self, Ego, and Id. We understand them but hazily, unless they are part of our daily work, but when we go seeking them we find that they are unprovable. They work well enough as concepts in specific contexts, but where and what are they discretely? But for those who work with them they are real. And for those who know God, God is real. Yet God and the Subconscious are both concepts. One cannot lay them out and label their parts in a museum display. They still remain well known to those who deal with them and relate to them, however.

Is this a bad analogy? Quite possibly, but it is about as close to an understanding of God as one is likely to get from a cold start. Perhaps we should have a look at the history of God's revelation to mankind, as viewed from a Christian perspective.

8. God Speaks

The way in which God, as conceived by the People of the Book (i.e. Christians, Jews, Moslems), has made himself known to mankind – or the way in which they have perceived God in relation to their cultural development – is a fascinating history. For a start, from earliest Biblical scripture there has been only one God. In terms of the ancient Levant this is a unique concept. All other civilisations of the Middle East and Mediterranean lands had departmental gods for every aspect of life and human eventualities. The Egyptians, in particular, numbered them by the hundred.

It was the Jews who succeeded in conceiving and adhering to their single deity. From time to time some of them tried seeking a little variety in the gods of other folk that they came across. The prophets got very cross about it, too. But such lapses can be attributed to a nomadic pastoral people's settling to agriculture, and intermarrying with the children of farmers. Peace in the home, and in the community, could have demanded a little flexibility on this score. At any rate, in the end God still remained unique.

What did his early worshippers call him? Moses asked his name, and was told 'I am who I am'. So there was no name to conjure with, or use for other magical purposes. This holiness, or 'otherness', of God, is the very facet of his nature which set him apart and made even his name holy, too holy to be written or pronounced. The nearest we get to it is JHWH. Ironically, this was later taken up by cabbalists and magicians, and as Tetragramaton (the four letters) used in their spells. These days we refer to it as Jahweh or Jehovah. Euphemisms such as 'The Ancient of Days', 'The God of Jacob', or 'The Lord God of Sabaoth' (Sabaoth means 'hosts', large numbers of people) also helped get round the problem. God, however, is in a class of his own.

This could make speaking of him, to him, or with him a tricky business. In his most primitive form – which was essentially that of a tribal juju – God was seen simply as the protector of the twelve tribes of Israel, a sort of good luck charm to have around if they went into battle. With more enlightened sheikhs / patriarchs – for example, Jacob and Moses – God did deals to reinforce their faith. These 'covenants' were mutually binding upon God and the other contracting party. To God were owed faith, obedience, and good conduct; for his part God undertook to advance the affairs of the sheikh / patriarch and his followers. The result was a prospering group of shepherds and dwellers in trading towns who, when they conducted themselves well and honourably, set a good example to their fellows. They were God's chosen people, and would thrive for as long as they observed their obligations under their covenant with God. Upon this basic and rather idealised idea the first five books of the Old Testament are founded. The moral element apart, this concept is essentially the same as "We Romans honour the gods because they make us successful…" It is scarcely a developed foundation for a personal relationship with God which includes an individual moral outlook upon life and Creation.

Something more was required of mankind by way of understanding God and responding to him. Certain Jewish rulers had, or claimed, converse with him, and their deeds reflected the inspiration so obtained. Moses, David, and Samuel spring to mind in this context. They confirmed and extended the relationship between the Jews and God. Through Moses the Jews acquired the Ten Commandments, a pretty good guide to life by any decent standards, but couched in terms of the sort of political treaty which was current in the Middle East in the second millennium BC. The principles are eternal and universal, but their expression derives from its epoch. The Ten Commandments are the basis of what is known as The Law, which is usually linked with The Prophets. It is the prophets who made clearer God's purposes to the culturally developing Israel as it settled down and evolved into its own individual civilisation.

I do not think I have ever come across a better explanation of the role of the prophets than that given by a wise and worldly teacher… (Westminster Choir School, 1937 Coronation, Cambridge Footlights, VIIIth Army, composer, jazz pianist, and pillar of the local amateur operatic society) who taught 'religious knowledge', as the subject was then termed, at my primary school. Towards the top of the blackboard he drew a large circle which he labelled 'God'. Near to the bottom of the board he drew another which he labelled 'mankind'. He then drew a number of wiggling lines from the God circle towards the mankind area, but only one or two of them touched the circle around the label. "This is God trying to talk to people," he explained. "He's shouting away, just like someone standing on top of a mountain, but he is not getting through to them very well. You see that most of the lines aren't reaching the 'mankind' circle, let alone going into it. People aren't hearing him and getting the message. What is he to do?" At this point he drew a number of smaller circles about half way up the blackboard, and labelled them 'prophets'.

"To get over this difficulty," the canny man continued, "God chose a number of people to be prophets. He chose them because they understood a bit more about him and what he wanted people to do than most people did, and he told them exactly what they were to say to the rest of mankind on his behalf." With a piece of bright yellow chalk he drew some good thick lines between God and the individual prophet circles. "The prophets could hear God nice and clearly," he continued, "so, once they had heard God's message, they could go and tell other people what God wanted them to do, and how they were to live their lives in ways God approved of." The yellow lines were extended from 'prophets' to 'mankind' accordingly. "Of course," he added, almost as an afterthought, "people didn't necessarily like being told how to behave, and a few of the prophets came to sticky ends. Buckets of blood!" (We were immediately highly interested in the prophets.) "But on the whole, God got his message through to mankind. Let us look at the prophets and what they did... and what happened to some of them." (In anticipation of the 'buckets of blood' we stayed awake for the rest of the lesson. Nor were we disappointed.)

This is the essence of the prophets and their role in relation to The People of the Book. We may speculate on just where their inspiration came from – as a Christian I attribute it to the activity of the Holy Spirit – and we can be terribly sophisticated and talk of 'projection' of aspects of individuals' personalities in abnormal states of consciousness, and try and explain away all prophecy as personal 'compensation', 'externalised complexes', 'sublimation of desires', or plain wishful thinking. What we actually think about it comes down to a matter of choice once more. What is undeniable is that there is a development of prophetic thought / revelation which evolves to become increasingly in tune with the teaching of Jesus, God the Son, during his Ministry. Jesus inherited their revelation to date, of course. This was his starting point. We are too apt to forget that Jesus was a Jew, and that his ministry in the first instance was to 'the chosen people' – who rejected him.

The idea that the clear evolution of the prophets' revelation is attributable to the record's having been written after the event by the 'victors', will not stand scrutiny. The prophetic record was made over the course of upwards of 400 years whilst prophecy was still in progress. Equally, the message that was being passed on by the prophets was not what the Jews wanted to hear; Jesus' teaching was likewise unacceptable for the same reason. This aspect is particularly clear from the Christian viewpoint.

We need to recall, too, that prophecy in the Biblical context means 'revelation of God's will' rather than simply 'prediction' in the sense of political warnings and foresight. We know that there were also many 'false' prophets, most of them anonymous now, who were the 'spin doctors' and 'commentators' of their days, putting out the 'politically correct' line that would delight their contemporary elite. Yet whatever these false prophets were uttering as divine inspiration was so far out of touch with God as to be instantly forgettable once the purposes of its originators had been served. The corpus of prophecy that remains therefore, may be viewed as true inspiration, albeit uttered in terms consistent with the human quirks of the men who spoke it. It is approximately dateable, and can be read against the historical record of which it forms now and then a part. The message throughout is spiritual, not political, however. God is calling his people to behave better, not merely warning them of dangers ahead. The main prophetic voices are:

Elijah; c880–c850 BC. He is credited with heroic exploits and miracles (1st Book of Kings). For present purposes, though, his perception of God as a 'still, small, voice' is the most important point God has him make. It is entirely consistent with the prompting – or nagging, indeed – of the Holy Spirit within one's psyche, the basis of a personal relationship with God.

Elisha; c850–c795 BC. Succeeded Elijah. We sense that in their prophetic ministries they were considered rather 'wild' by the main priesthood, and not quite respectable in their approach to God. This is true of other prophets, and emphasises their *direct* relationship with God and 'non-Establishment' status.

Hosea; 750–715 BC. Grasped that the love of God for his Creation is absolute, and that mankind should seek God and increase its understanding of him, "…loyalty is my desire, not sacrifices, not whole offerings, but the knowledge of God."

Isaiah; 740–680 BC. Saw the need for a new covenant with God – the first stirrings of the idea of the Messiah. Dealing in detail with the Messiah, he foresees him as a servant who suffers for doing God's will. His world vision extended beyond the confines of Judah (roughly the New Testament Judaea) and grasped that the actions of other peoples and rulers also fitted into God's creation. He foresaw Cyrus, the Persian, as the instrument by which the Jews' exile in Babylon would be ended. Scholarship debates whether Isaiah is an individual or a 'college' of prophecy. He was killed, probably on the orders of King Manasseh, by being cut in two with a wood saw.

Jeremiah; 625–585 BC. A shy and retiring man, he was essentially forced into prophecy by God to cry out against contemporary moral and political trends. He saw that the mechanical daily round of ritual worship in the Temple at Jerusalem was a hindrance to spiritual development, and sought to establish a direct awareness of God in mankind; "The new covenant I will make with the people of Israel will be this: I will put my law within them and write it on their hearts. I will be their God, and they will be my people. None of them will have to teach his fellow-citizen to know the Lord, because all will know me…" (31. 31-34)

Jerusalem fell to the Babylonians in 587 BC, and the Jewish intelligentsia and skilled craftsmen were marched into exile. Jeremiah himself fled to Egypt, where the Jewish community killed him by stoning.

Ezekiel; 595–570 BC. Prophesied in Babylon. In the absence of the Temple the essence of 'Jewishness' in terms of religious belief and its various forms of expression, became of prime importance to the exiles. Religion becomes a more personal affair, and the concept of personal responsibility for one's actions as part of one's individual relationship with God develops. Jeremiah had spoken of individual accountability to God for evil done, but Ezekiel takes the same concept a stage further; " 'A son is not to suffer because of his father's sins, nor a father because of the sins of his son. A good person will be rewarded for doing good, and an evil person will suffer for the evil he does. If an evil person stops sinning and keeps my laws, if he does what is right and good, he will not die; he will certainly live. All his sins will be forgiven, and he will live because he did what is right. Do you think that I enjoy seeing an evil person die?' asks the Sovereign Lord. 'No, I would rather see him repent and live.'" (18. 20-23) This represents a major advance in individual relationships with God.

Daniel; 610–530 BC. Another prophet in the Babylonian captivity. He was also a 'civil servant' of influence in the Babylonian administration, where his insights were much valued. He spoke much rather apocalyptic prophecy, but his importance in spiritual development rests upon his insistence of the Absolute Holiness of God, the 'otherness' – a concept perhaps best grasped as 'other-than-worldliness' – of a constant and consistent God as opposed to the expedient ways of the world. He evolved the 'Son of Man' concept of the ideal Israelite, and this ideal was used as a title by Jesus.

Malachi; 460–440 BC. He advocates sincerity and integrity in life, which is to be lived as part of one's religious practice. As one's religious outlook is, so should one's life reflect it, in other words. This is a fine concept, but it became corrupted to a mere observance of certain practices and paved the way for the pseudo-righteousness of some of the Pharisees of Jesus' day – the sort who paid their tythes of 'mint and rue' but did nothing very much about loving their neighbours as themselves. The 'political correctness' of such Pharisees in their over-fastidious observance of the letter of the Law, believing they were thus doing all that was required of them by God, effectively prevented their attaining a healthy spirituality. 'The Law', as then set out in The Torah, had some 613 new and regulatory 'commandments'. These and the resulting complications caused by much Pharisaic interpretation, teaching and practice, incurred the censure of Jesus.

This summary of the influence on religious perception achieved by a few of the prophets can scarcely do justice to their revelations. Obviously a major part of the Old Testament cannot be summarised in a few hundred words. Any reader wishing to investigate further will have to deal with the original material, preferably in a modern English translation, and with an easily read explanatory Bible handbook within reach. The concepts the prophets raised are worth understanding properly. They are certainly not irrelevant to our lives just because they are over a couple of thousand years old. The human animal does not change much in the course of historical time. Our essential mental and spiritual equipment is just like that of the old Israelites. We are a little better informed about material Creation than they were, that's all.

In addition, we must never forget that the Bible – which of course includes the Old Testament – has done much to shape the world we live in, both by direct application of its precepts, and by the reaction of other Faiths and Philosophies to them. To know and appreciate the sources of its contents is important.

The importance of the Law and Prophets was in fact emphasised by Jesus; "Do not think that I have come to do away with the Law of Moses and the teaching of the prophets. I have not come to do away with them, but to make their teachings come true. Remember that as long as heaven and earth last, not the least point nor smallest detail of the Law will be done away with – not until the end of all things. So then, whoever disobeys even the least important of the commandments and teaches others to do the same, will be last in the Kingdom of heaven. On the other hand, whoever obeys the Law and teaches others to do the same will be great in the Kingdom of heaven." (Matthew 5. 17-20) There is to be no reinvention of God or his purposes. The call is to do God's will properly.

9 Discarding the Deity –
Philosophy not Requiring a God

One can, of course, live a perfectly good, socially responsible and useful life without reference to any god or god-substitute, such as The Heroic Worker. In fact, for the furtherance of some cause or scheme with which I might want to become involved, I would sooner ally myself with a rational atheist of integrity than with someone whose religious perceptions struck me as broad cultural ignorance allied with bigotry and grimly held superstitions acquired from heaven knows where in earliest childhood. In our talk during our more philosophical moments, the atheist and I would certainly find we had much of a common outlook upon many matters and, where we necessarily differed, we might well learn a deal about one another's beliefs which would dispel odd preconceptions and prejudice, to the benefit of our better work together. And we would both agree that, when the other one of us died, he would get a tremendous surprise!

Both of us, though, would have founded our lives upon something which was greater to us than a mere drudge for existence. Somewhere – possibly in Mark Twain, although I cannot find the source – I have seen religion defined roughly thus: 'a time-wasting purposeful activity which allows us to shirk our work with a good conscience.' I like it; it is true at a level it possibly never set out to plumb. To practise a religion, as opposed merely to subscribe to it in some generalised fashion, one has to make time for the undertaking. This in itself requires a purposeful self-discipline, and is undertaken as one's personal choice made of one's free-will. Yet one does not need to practise a religion to make such a choice.

I once arrived in Hong Kong in the very early hours, tired, jet-lagged, confused, beyond sleep, and perversely annoyed by the noise of the very air-conditioning which kept my hotel room habitable. On a little map I had gained along the way, I saw an open green area called 'Victoria Park', and decided that in this haven I would find fresh air, silence, solitude, and a degree of calm I had not enjoyed for a day or two. So, at about 6 AM, I passed the knowing gaze of 'Bell' at his post in the lobby, quit the hotel, and headed Victoria Parkwards beneath a sky greying with the advanced light of a dawn still breaking way out over the Pacific. The city's peaks stood in silhouette against it, their flanks staked by the high, lanky towers of luxury flats, filing cabinets full of mega-millionaires, striving up into the light of a coming day. Purposeful, roaring streams of traffic and I missed one another, and I gained the Park.

Clearly I was late on the scene. Apart from the tennis players, basket-ballers, and groups undertaking aerobics to rhythms blared from tape-recorders, the whole several acres brimmed with silent, disciplined activity, the timeless reconciliation of self and infinity. Meditators sat cross-legged upon the low walls bordering the shrubberies, eyes closed, their shoes neatly arranged upon the path before them. Men and women of all ages and conditions performed the slow-motion routines of tai-chi, either singly or in hosts. Some of them had chromium-plated sabres adorned with huge red or purple silk tassels to aid their actions. I traced a strange staccato clattering to a lady with an enormous fan, about two thirds her own height, which she flung open and snapped shut to the movements prescribed by her tai-chi practice. There was much purposeful activity, and none of it was work-shirking. Indeed, judging from the hold-alls near to hand – and my subsequent tactful enquiry of 'Bell' – most of those present were preparing mind and spirit before changing from track-suits into conventional attire, and going on to their work. Regardless of whatever Faiths those in the park may or may not have subscribed to, their activity was purposeful and directed at their innermost and most private humanity.

Since that day I have acquainted myself a little with the motivation, for in the absence of specific dogma I had better not refer to it as 'belief', of those whose activities I saw. Eastern religions seem always to have borrowed aspects from each other, and the personal attraction of features such as meditation and tai-chi is perhaps that they produce a spiritual fulfilment by their very practise. Buddhism itself can, quite properly, be viewed as a philosophy prescribing personal, purposeful practices to which Faiths, including Christianity, can be added. The Theravada branch of Buddhism has a practice of vipassana, translated as 'insight' or 'mindfulness', meditation, a discipline which is used to clarify the practitioner's What, How, and Why questions on a ruthlessly personal level where there is no hiding oneself from oneself. It is non-dogmatic, it allows measurable results in terms of one's progress in the achievement of its method, and its focus is entirely upon oneself. Above all, it requires tremendous self-discipline to do it, upon which self-discipline one must direct all the purposefulness of the Mind. One's brain may be full of brilliant thoughts, one's curiosity sharp and penetrating, one's understanding of one's particular environment and its demands quite faultless – yet all this is merely 'noise' which must be stilled as one takes control of all of oneself. It is not easy, and that is why strong and purposeful self-discipline – of controlled breathing, for example – is needed to undertake it. Even its result is what each individual makes of it – calm, 'sharper focus', relaxation, 'nothingness'… In the end it is all-in-the-mind, or Mind as I would ascribe it.

One way or another humanity has always known that the state of our minds has some bearing upon our general health and wellbeing. If we are over-wrought and stressed to the extent that we cannot sleep properly, our digestions go haywire. This affects the sweetness of our tempers and the response to us we may get from friends and foes alike, which in turn raises the adrenaline levels in our blood, and makes us even more prepared to take issue with everyone over everything. We have 'lost our sense of proportion', our common sense and humanity, all because we 'got into a state' to start with. To be burdened these days with mobile phones, BlackBerries and all the rest of the IT wonders which we allow to rule us rather than being usefully at our disposal when needed, does not improve our general stress levels. We never evolved to be at the world's beck and call '24/7' – we even have this short-hand term for our unnatural condition! – and it is not surprising that we resent being stressed and 'hot and cross', We want to 'chill out', often. It serves us right, then, if we do not put our Minds in charge, and adopt the disciplines that will return our humanity to us.

Science is on the trail of the 'negative emotions' engendered by our tendency to personal fecklessness in life as it is too often lived, and I have heard of work in USA at the University of

Wisconsin-Madison in which Tibetan monks, masters of meditation, have been helping Western science by putting the insights acquired over a couple of millennia at its disposal. Brain scans of people suffering aggravation from 'negative emotions' show activity in a particular region of the prefrontal cortex, whilst those who are relaxed and happy display brain activity in a different area of it entirely. Senior monks, when brain-scanned, proved to be in the latter category, essentially free of 'negative emotions', and contented, jolly old fellows. The inference is that long habits of meditation, and a calmer life lived accordingly, had served to reinforce their resulting cheerier view of the world, and had quite altered their perception of life – to their advantage. Many questions could be asked, and tests done – as they probably were; I only heard a brief account. But the monks certainly seem to have benefited by undertaking an activity which is very akin, arguably, to mind-over-matter. The university team apparently put some businessmen with 'negative emotions' through a course of meditation as prescribed by the monks, and found that a noticeable shift resulted in the position of brain-scan signals from their prefrontal cortexes. So perhaps people can cheer themselves up to order, if they wish to. If such is the case we are back to choice and free-will again, very much responsible in ourselves for ourselves.

'Negative emotions' are worth managing. I would be very cautious about eliminating or banning them from human behaviour altogether, though. How would we fare, for instance, if we could not be angry at injustice? Let me illustrate this. Long ago I worked briefly alongside an elderly and taciturn Polish electronics engineer. One very hot day he rolled up his sleeves, and there before me shrieked his tattooed concentration camp number. "You see," he said, "I'm one of the ones who made it, and dodged the Russians, too." Being young and silly I said something like, "God loved you and held you in the palm of his hand." I wince now at my smug tactlessness. Mercifully the response was a sardonic grin and not the sort of outburst which sometimes broke from him. "I don't know what God thought of me then – or now for that matter," he replied. "I *do* know that what kept me going was hatred, hatred for the Nazis, hatred for their system, hatred for what they were doing to me and to all of us, hatred of just the sight of them. I was going to live to get justice. And I lived, at least. If you're ever in a jam, don't forget the power of hate. I tell you!" It shook me then, long decades ago, but I can see all too clearly now the strength of his point. It was hatred which fuelled his personal emotional motivation to keep alive, to triumph over the evil assailing him, to get those responsible brought to justice. Hatred had suffused his mind to give him the will to live, no matter what befell him in the meantime.

Right at the beginning of this book I have quoted a little essential wisdom from the Stoic philosopher Epictetus, "Under our control are conception [we might now say 'creativity', I think], choice, desire, and aversion. If you think only what is your own to be your own, you will blame no one, nor is there any harm that can touch you." These are all attributes of the mind, and as such are entirely personal. Interestingly, Epictetus had started life as a slave, and I suggest it was possible that when all else had been taken from him, he still knew that his essential Mind, or 'Self', or inalienable 'Will' – it is a tricky concept to pin down, and it necessarily will vary among individuals – was still intact and functioning.

As a Stoic, his basic belief was that the universe is governed by physical laws of Nature, and that all people are, equally, subject to them as part of the universe. Therefore it followed that the purpose of one's life was to be obedient to the requirements of this natural law, and live with an unperturbed acceptance within it. He gave to Nature's working an aspect of an all-wise Providence, in relation to which everyone should refrain from the stresses of self-interest and promote the common good of all humanity.

Stoic philosophy bore in this way some resemblance to Christianity, and viewed from this perspective it is easy to see why St Paul came to grief in his well-intentioned foray on to the Areopagus in Athens (Acts 17. 16-33). But the snootily sophisticated Athenians would not *a priori* countenance the supernatural, whilst the rest of his message, as they saw it, was old hat and badly expressed. They hurried to get away from him, and even he had the grace to beat a retreat. Stoics did flourish in high places, however. The Emperor Marcus Aurelius AD 161–180, found himself in the wrong job "by a set of curious chances" as Gilbert has Koko express it, but, being at the head of the

Roman rat-race, he had nowhere else to go. He consoled himself with his version of Stoicism, and wrote his 'Meditations', full of considered thoughts such as, "Men live for each other; then either improve them or put up with them"; "The thing could have happened to anyone, but not everyone would have emerged unembittered"; "Yesterday a drop of semen, tomorrow a handful of spice and ashes... In the life of a man his time is but a moment... An empty pageant". He seems to me to have lived his life in the grip of a perpetual dose of the 'Old Man Rivers'. But he did his best, "Withdraw into your own self. Dig within. There lies the well-spring of good; ever dig, and it will ever flow."

This strength-from-within argument would, I am sure, be recognised as perfectly natural by the pre-dawn participants of all spiritual disciplines in Victoria Park. "Dig within," means "Work at it", and it is from the purposefulness of the activity that the Mind develops and becomes in control of its brain and, so, of the individual who owns both. In this way 'negative emotions' can be banished, and 'noise' from the brain's whirring gears blocked from one's Being by the sound-proofing of the chosen self-discipline. The result is stillness of Mind, an overall benefit in one's condition. The rather fashionably chic lady who once loudly announced to the company I was enjoying at the time, that she had bought a waterproof radio / CD player so that she could listen to the music of Bach in her shower, "...because I feel it is high time that I *did* something about my *spiritual* life! – (*smirk, pause for applause*)", would, I hope, have enjoyed some good music. If she had purposefully made time for working at it, however, I am sure she could have tapped some full and spiritual vein within her and then really got down to the business of spiritual improvement. I never came to know how long that radio lasted in her shower.

One cannot produce from within oneself that which is not already there. Yet by some evolved means which we 'know' about as a part of being 'us' – philosophers would speak of *qualia* in this context – we can experience within ourselves that deep calm, stillness, or 'nothingness' to which we have referred. Furthermore, we find this feeling agreeable in ways which are so individual to us that they are incapable of expression, save by metaphor, and which remain accordingly a colossal challenge to description and examination. Some indication of its experience is detectable in the brain's prefrontal cortex, as we have noted. Is it then with our brains or in our minds that we generate this 'nothingness', which may very occasionally come upon us in a stunning and brief 'flash', but more usually requires the slowly acquired disciplines which 'dig within'? If we knew that, we could add some sort of straightforward 'How to…'series of instructions to our cultural ideas on A Healthy Lifestyle, perhaps.

However, I have reservations about adopting such a consumerist approach to the benefits of disciplined meditation and similar practices. Unless the practitioner makes a deliberate effort, no benefit will accrue. Merely to go through the motions in a casual sort of way strikes me as akin to listening to Bach in the shower – a diversion, not a serious and focussed undertaking which is designed to bring about a specific state of Being. And from the inner mental calm, once achieved, the physical benefits of more restful sleep, improved digestion, reduced blood pressure, and a healthier heart are said to derive, all in a logical cause and effect sequence. Medical science can produce all of these by use of its pharmacopoeia, of course, but is this not matter acting upon matter, drugs upon the body's internal chemistry? If the body can achieve the same results without recourse to drugs administered from outside it, save in urgent response to disease deriving from specific pathogens, does it not seem more desirable to achieve good health by some process which is available within ourselves?

To a degree this question is rhetorical, for the way in which we approach our health is largely our personal choice. A 'quick fix' drug may suit our lifestyle far better than time set aside daily for meditation. And as we are persuaded – so shall we choose, I suggest. We seek physical good health by whichever ways suit us, and if we feel well we reckon we have achieved what we want. Which is why cunning old doctors often ask the question, "And how do you feel *in yourself…?*" – because we are not just physical mechanisms. We *feel* things about ourselves, and these feelings affect what we do day by day, which soon enough becomes habit expressed in a lifestyle – the way in which, subject to convention and social courtesies, we seek to go about being *us*.

Why, though, do we desire a healthy lifestyle? The question appears stupid; of course we want the benefits of good health. Aha! We have an objective in mind, a benefit, a concept that we will gladly pursue purposefully; 'desire' and 'choice' upon

Epictetus' menu. In 'management-speak' the psychologists would call this 'goal orientation', and I view it as being an important factor in the business of hypnosis, as shall be mentioned later. Is our 'digging down' within us to obtain, of and for us, the goal of the calm and balance in our lives that will allow us a good night's sleep, a contented digestion, and a generally agreeable personal life shorn as far as possible of 'negative emotions', a form of auto-hypnosis? And, if it is, how come it is already 'there' – but where? – within us, apparently just waiting to be called into action? It appears to be "Under our control...", Epictetus again, and I would classify it as Mind rather than brain. We shall look at this idea later; it is bursting with controversial aspects.

Meanwhile, let us recall that everything touched on above is part of Creation, and that we are right in the centre of the experience. Indeed, the experience itself may be uniquely human; we simply do not know. Is a desire for 'internal' calm a built-in means of preventing our huge brains from running amok? If so, what can we say in that context about other huge brains – in whales, for example? Let us muse upon the implications of that, and leave it there.

10. Christianity's Roots

What should we understand by the curious term 'The Kingdom of God'? For a start, it is not some sort of geographical area. It is better viewed as a state of mind open to perceiving and doing what God requires of us, and keeping ourselves spiritually in a condition to respond as required. It is part of the one-to-one relationship between the believer and God. In the Gospel of St Matthew (end of chapter 24 and in chapter 25) Jesus gives examples of the sort of conduct which is worthy of the Kingdom; – the Steward of the estate who keeps everything in order and ship-shape when the owner is absent; the bridesmaids who, in view of their essential task of lighting the night time wedding procession through the dark town, had taken care to have enough oil for their lamps (more likely torches) to do the job as expected, regardless of any hitches or unforeseen delays; the servants charged with keeping their lord's investments profitable during his absence and, in all but one case, taking trouble to do so. The message is clear – we are required likewise to keep ourselves up to scratch in our spiritual lives, and to ensure that our daily conduct reflects this as we go about our normal business. In this way the quality of our lives, and by extension the activities in which we engage or which we influence, take on something of the Kingdom of God.

Jesus himself – 'the Word [i.e. God, which] was made flesh and dwelt among us' – gives the commandment plainly enough; "Love the Lord your God with all your heart, with all your soul, and with all your mind. This is the first and greatest commandment. And the second is like it – love your neighbour as you love yourself. The whole Law of Moses and the teachings of the prophets depend upon these two commandments." (Matthew 22. 37-40). Expressed in a more negative way, i.e. "Love God, and don't do to anyone else what you would not like him to do to you," this same commandment was spoken before Jesus' time by the Rabbi Hillel, the father – or perhaps grandfather – of

Gamaliel, a 'teacher of the Law' (and rabbinic teacher of St Paul) who took the part of the Apostles when the authorities tried to silence them after Jesus' Ascension (Acts 5. 29-39). It is also known, in its same negative form, in Islam, Hinduism, Buddhism, amongst the followers of Confucius, and also in the philosophy schools of Greece and Rome. The idea is well established in God's Creation.

As we have already stated, the relationship between God and any individual is strictly personal – one-to-one. No two people are alike, and no two individuals conceive God in exactly the same way or perceive his role in Creation in identical terms. God loves us all, however, and in the person of Jesus suffered physical death by crucifixion for the sins of mankind.

This last statement causes difficulties for many averagely committed Christians, never mind the array of humanity without any particular Faith at all. How could God Incarnate make a sacrifice of himself, by being tortured to death in public, for all sin throughout all time? It surely cannot make sense.

It does, though, if we remember that the theology is in line with first century AD Jewish practice. We must not lose sight of the fact that Christianity derives from God's ministry to the Jews, or we risk missing the point. Certainly the Jews rejected Jesus. Their religious authorities were offended by him and handed him over to the Romans to obtain a dubiously legal death sentence, rather than resort to the morally awkward business of assassinating him. At that time only the Romans could inflict the death penalty in Palestine, and it was important politically for the Jewish Sanhedrin – the supreme religious authority in Jerusalem – to obtain a verdict which showed the populace that Jesus was criminally wrong and, so, justly condemned to death. By the same token, the Sanhedrin could then present itself as being in the right and above reproach. It followed that it accordingly had the undisputed religious and moral authority to stamp out any trace of Jesus' teaching as heresy, which was precisely what St Paul was engaged in doing before his conversion. Questions of orthodoxy, authority, politics and public-relations were the prime considerations of both the Sanhedrin and the Roman authorities in bringing about the Crucifixion. Calm, order, and the *status quo* had to be upheld by the Powers that Be. So far as they were concerned there was nothing holy about it.

It is against this background that we should view Jesus' ministry, and not in relation to the Apostles' subsequent evangelism. The Jews of the time understood Jesus' teaching in the context of the Judaism to which they were accustomed. What came to be Christianity arose out of this only later. After the Temple at Jerusalem was flattened, and remains so to our own day, by Vespasian and Titus in crushing the Jewish revolt in AD 69/70, Christianity was sustained by its own beliefs, set apart from any worship continuing after the Judaic fashion in what remained of Jerusalem. Therefore there was then a clean break between Judaism and the new Faith of Christianity. By this time St Paul had taken the Gospel to 'the gentiles' – i.e. people who were not Jews. The rest is history, and the process is still being worked out and refined, even in our own major civilisation that it, with the addition of Greek belief in the personal social value of the individual, made from God's love for his Creation.

So, in theological terms our sins are forgiven by Jesus in having taken upon himself the roles of 'paschal lamb' and 'scapegoat'. These terms relate to Jewish practice. On the Day of Atonement the Jews made sacrifices at the Temple to show repentance for all the sins of the past year which they knew they had committed, and also for those sins of which they were guilty inadvertently. In the former category would be the 'force majeure' sins of circumstance, for example, the rescuing on the Sabbath of an ox which had inconsiderately fallen into a ravine, pit, or well –according to one's preferred translation – and could not extricate itself. To have left it there for the day would have condemned it to a cruel death, as well as losing its owner the value of the beast. Thus, holy day of rest or no, the ox had to be rescued (Luke 14, 1-6). This sin, of knowingly doing work on the Sabbath, could be atoned for on the Day of Atonement when the High Priest sacrificed a lamb without physical imperfection. In this way the known sins of the past year were supposedly wiped away from God's records.

Inadvertent sins, such as taking one step too many in the course of a Sabbath day's journey, were dealt with differently. For the record, a permitted Sabbath Day's Journey was a distance of about 900m, although if one should have previously deposited a small meal somewhere within this distance, one could eat at the temporary 'home' so established, and then proceed a further

900m. This illustrates well how God's intentions, uttered through Malachi, were becoming corrupted in practice. Inadvertent sins resulting from such a minefield of formal devout practice were bound to be many. All these were loaded, as a purely 'psychic' or formal burden, upon the scapegoat. This was a poor old goat, on its last legs, which was sworn at, buffeted, ritually cursed, and then thrown out of Jerusalem by the north-west gate, to carry the sins heaped upon it to the demon Azazel who dwelt in the wilderness. As the goat staggered away from the gate, it passed a small rocky mound about fifty yards distant on the right. The name of this mound was Golgotha, the 'place of the skull' – and subsequent site of the Crucifixion.

The High Priest who officiated at this festival had to be, physically and morally, a man without blemish, just like the sacrificial lamb. If he was physically afflicted or blemished in any way, he was ineligible for the office of High Priest. We are told by the Jewish historian Flavius Josephus that some years before the Nativity, one Hyrcanus, of Jewish royal lineage and upon occasion King of Israel during the turbulent period in the region caused by Jewish civil wars plus the activities of Caesar, Cleopatra, and Marc Antony in the background, aspired to be High Priest. His rival, Antigonus, pretended to support his ambition, made as if to embrace him and then, having gripped him firmly, chewed off his ears. Thus rendered 'blemished', Hyrcanus was instantly ineligible for office. After a rather sad life, he was eventually murdered by Herod the Great – the same Herod who ordered the Massacre of the Innocents in order to try and kill the baby Jesus. In so far as he was ever religious, Herod was not too good at loving his neighbours as himself. I include this gory piece of history to illustrate the Jewish concern for due and exact form in their Temple worship.

Thus Jesus, as a man without blemish and the bearer of all sins, made the ritual atonement for mankind's sin in accordance with current Jewish practice, taking upon himself the combined roles of the priest and the sacrificial victims. This he did once and for all, for all mankind, past, present, and future – ourselves included. In brief, this is the theology of God's atonement for our sins, and it would have been understood perfectly, in principle, by a Jew in first century Palestine. Very likely he would have considered it blasphemous, but in Christian terms it illustrates God's love for his human Creation.

This does not make us sinless or incapable of sin. We are creatures of choice and free-will. What it does mean is that God perceives us as we are, incapable of perfection by our own efforts. Whatever we do, we cannot make ourselves sinless. By our very nature we are going to fall short of God's total, absolute and ultimate moral standards. This is logical; God alone is the Absolute, Total, and Ultimate of all that is good and right, and by *his* choice, as we have suggested. Therefore he has granted us 'grace' (Latin – 'gratia', a gift, as in 'gratuity') to have, as it were, the charges against us cancelled just so long as we have the faith to believe that he is able to wipe our slates clean if we repent of our sins, imperfections, and moral shortcomings, and try and do better for his sake.

St. Paul puts it thus; "Now that we have been put right [made 'at one' with God through the atonement – the at-one-ment of the sacrifice of the Crucifixion – the English language fortuitously helping to underline the point] with God through faith, we have peace with God through our Lord Jesus Christ. He has brought us by grace into this experience of God's grace, in which we now live. And so let us boast of the hope we have of sharing God's glory! We also boast of our troubles, because we know that trouble produces endurance, endurance brings God's approval, and his approval creates hope. This hope does not disappoint us, for God has poured out his love into our hearts by means of the Holy Spirit, who is God's gift to us. For… Christ died for the wicked at the time God chose… God has shown us how much he loves us – for it was while we were still sinners that Christ died for us. By his blood we are now put right with God." (St Paul. Letter to the Romans. 5, 1-11) "For I am convinced that neither death nor life, neither angels nor demons, neither the present nor the future, nor any powers, neither height nor depth, nor anything else in all Creation, will be able to separate us from the love of God that is in Christ Jesus our Lord." (Romans, 8, 38-39)

All of which, we might say, is good and fine if we happen to be convinced of the truth of it to start with. What is there in it, though, which would give a sensible person in the twenty-first century the least incentive to seek God and know and do his will as the basis for living a better and more fulfilling life? Exactly the same incentive as that which roused those who heard St Paul and the other evangelists in the first century.

"When so much is in flux, when limitless amounts of information, much of it ephemeral, are instantly accessible on demand, there is a renewed hunger for that which endures and gives meaning." (HM Queen Elizabeth II, November, 2005). There is a basic human need to believe in something which is the irreducible point to which all experience, thought and feeling ultimately lead and refer, 'and give meaning'. It is the 'digging down within us' of the meditator. It is the spike on the geometrician's compasses which anchors the fixed centre of his whole construction, and in relation to which the resulting proofs develop. This is true for individuals in every age. A materialist might place his faith in the reasonableness of scientific and mathematical proofs, demonstrable in their own context and by their own laws. Yet, as he will be the first to acknowledge, science develops, and today's knowledge can be exposed as tomorrow's error, as a greater truth about some aspect of Creation is discovered and proved. There is no Ultimate, Absolute, and Total aspect to this view of life beyond the logical belief that, one day, everything might be explicable. This future abstract hope is what endures. Thus the materialist pins his faith upon his own material brain and its capacity to satisfy him by his use of it. This is his choice. (Choice, again!) There is no reason why he should not live a personally fulfilled and socially constructive life on this basis. And when he dies he presumably expects his consciousness to die with him, and his end to be personal oblivion.

To any suggestion that there is a long and respectable spiritual tradition involving an eternal God, he might smile and say something to the effect that such a belief is harmless in moderation – and if kept well out of the lab – but that in reality it is just some sort of psychological crutch to enable the intellect to cope with what would otherwise overwhelm it. Our old friend the 'Sky Fairy' might be invoked again as a proof of the logical inadequacy of the idea. The ancient sin of pride could also put in an appearance, just as it did in the myth of Eve in Eden, where she decided that by disobeying God in the matter of the forbidden fruit she would be just like God, knowing good and evil, and thus able to go her own way on her own expedient terms. For the human to lay down the law about what is Total, Absolute, and Ultimate displays pride indeed!

We had better have a look at how we perceive Creation and our part in it; what is brain, and what is mind; what is death, and what is immortality; what is demonstrable experience, and what is anomalous to such experience; and where we stand in relation to it all.

Perhaps we can grasp it all in just a line or so!

11. Inside Our Skulls

We perceive Creation, i.e. the universe and the world about us, through the medium of our senses – sight, hearing, smell, touch and taste. They report via their proper channels to our consciousness about where we are, what is around us, and our personal condition in relation to it all. This begs the question of what consciousness may be, but for the moment let us concern ourselves with the way our brains work and how they handle the stimuli arriving continuously from our sense organs as 'sense data'. We build these up into a picture of our environment, and the bits and pieces we consign to our memories form our ideas – concepts – of the world as we know it. It all starts with sense data entering the brain.

Stimuli from our sense organs converge upon the Thalamus, a couple of grey, spongy areas at the bottom of our brains. The thalamus acts as a clearing house for the senses, sorting out what should subsequently go where within the brain for further consideration, processing, and action. First stop for it all is the Amygdala, an almond-shaped area found in each half of the brain, somewhat towards the front and a little above the eyes. The amygdala is linked with vigilance, fear, and pleasure, and its essential job when considering incoming information is to ask two basic scientific questions, viz; "*What's* all this?" and "*How* will it affect my selfish genes?" The answers it comes up with are often referred to as the 'fight or flight' choice. This means that on the basis of the emotional quality of the stimuli, the amygdala can start preparing the body's stress responses – through the extra production of adrenalin, for example – to take sudden and vigorous action in response to what might be either a feeding opportunity or a physical threat. It is a very ancient part of our brain, inherited from ancestors far back down the evolutionary tree, whence it has served all subsequent species well.

Furthermore, the latest research really does suggest that the amygdala works a little differently in male brains from the way it handles incoming information in female brains. All husbands – and, by extension, their wives – have known this for years, of course, but it is now scientifically proven and therefore respectable.

Nonetheless without it we probably would not be here. If we were in the primaeval jungle and our ears reported a rustling in the undergrowth, it is the amygdala which would at the outset decide whether the rustling was small and trivial and we could safely ignore it, perhaps to investigate it later with our next meal in mind, or whether it was big and threatening, and we ought to run for our lives. It would be a rough and ready decision. It might well be wrong in the light of further consideration, but it would get us out of the way of any potential danger for the time being. Our selfish genes would live to hunt or flee another day.

Whilst taking action on its own account, the amygdala also passes the information to the Orbital Frontal Cortex, a structure in the brain which looks after the integration of emotional and cognitive input. This reins in the amygdala's response to stimuli. In our jungle example it might ask, "Is that big rustling noise coming purposefully towards me, or is it getting out of my way? If it is moving off, do I need to worry about it? And why is it going away; is it avoiding me on purpose? If it is deliberately running off, is it because whatever is making it is scared of me? Would it be worthwhile fitting an arrow to my bowstring and following in case it represents an opportunity for dinner, in fact?" This evaluative train of thought takes place in the orbital frontal cortex, and also in other regions of the brain such as the Hippocampus.

The hippocampus acts as the brain's memory centre. All memories pass through it, but it is not in any way our archive for memories. It might be better viewed as a sort of intelligence-gathering agency, staffed by specialists in all conceivable areas of knowledge. It receives and notes the amygdala's reaction to the rustle, and enhances its quality as a memory for future, and better, reference. This is like a learning process. If there is a further alarm, the OFC and hippocampus may quickly override the 'run for your life' element in it if the threat is not judged to be instant or serious, yet they will not erase the neural pathways for the amygdala's response in such contexts. These will remain, just in case. And each case, once the initial shock of the stimulus is over, will be better considered upon its merits than was the previous one. The brain is forever making new neuron pathways in the light of experience.

We are here in the realm of memory, both short-term and long-term. The short-term can be very short indeed; the thalamus and amygdala sort things out in milliseconds, in fact. The OFC evaluates their work in three or four seconds, by which time all sorts of longer-term memory input about rustlings in the jungle is becoming available. A history of such events is springing to mind! We will try and deal with Mind when we tackle consciousness. For now, let us note and use a definition of memory as 'A stored pattern of connections between neurons in the brain.'

For working purposes we can describe a neuron as a stringy bit of brain tissue ending in a tiny 'clutching hand' called a Synaptic Connection, which engages with other synaptic connections on neighbouring neurons. When they are at work processing data, the synaptic connections 'fire' chemicals across the 'Synaptic Gaps' between neurons, a small electrical discharge occurring in the process. By scanning through the protective bone-case of the skull with electro-magnetic instruments, we are able to detect these discharges and form from them some idea of which parts of the brain are at work when dealing with specific situations or types of stimuli. This is a fairly new and exciting field for research. The chemical reactions across synaptic gaps need oxygen; the brain requires some 20% of the body's oxygen in order to function, in fact. If deprived of its oxygen supply for longer than about three minutes, it begins to shut down and die. We shall refer to this again. There are about 1,000 billion neurons in the average human brain, and each of them is capable of achieving between 5,000 and 10,000 synaptic connections, thus making 500–1,000 trillion (1 trillion = 1 million millions, or 10^{12}) synapses overall.

It is in the connections amongst the neurons that our memories are presumably stored, although the means by which the brain does this are not yet known. There may be more to it than just the brain and its workings. Moreover, memory is not 'set in concrete'; it is not immutable. Every time we recall something, every time we bring stored data back fully into our consciousness, the details of whatever we are remembering can be altered. It is a commonplace that 'Memory fades…', but perhaps we do not always appreciate that, quite unintentionally, we may subtly change emphases and nuances when we are recalling an event from the past. Exactly why we may do this is uncertain; probably we are altering, or editing, the memory in the light of experience gained in the meantime, or we are boosting our self-esteem to serve some present purpose by re-writing the past and our part in it.

'Old men are liars' – another folk truism! At any rate, once a memory has been recalled, when it goes back into storage it is filed *in its latest form*, which does not necessarily have exactly the same features that characterised it when it was last sought out and recalled to consciousness. If this happens often enough and there are no other sources to serve as a means of correction (or greater confusion), such as other people's memories, then the event as it has been told in its corrupted form goes unchallenged and the truth necessarily suffers. This is why we distinguish between the uncertainty of legends, and the greater reliability of history for which there is evidence. The owner of the memory will still stoutly maintain and defend the latest form of it in his mind, however. He believes what he 'knows'. Clearly there are implications for society as a whole in this aspect of memory, especially with regard to court cases or enquiries where much time has elapsed between an event and its examination by due Authority.

Possibly to confuse matters further, the same parts of our brains deal with both memory and imagination. This makes good sense in that we draw upon past experience in order to form plans that are likely to work out as we wish them to for the future. Accordingly we conceive Time as being 'linear', i.e. it 'flows' in one direction – from the future, through the present, and leaves a memory or record of itself as the past. Experience bears this out, too; we plant a seed, it grows into a plant, it forms its fruit, sets its own seed, and dies. We cannot send the process into reverse. It is one-way, 'linear'. However, thanks to Einstein and his theories of relativity, we know that we may also view time in relation to where we are and what we happen to be doing. If we are moving around at high speed, then our *experience* of time will be different from that of our friends who are sitting still. We may smile and wonder when we are told that relativity decrees that the vinyl (or, for us who are ancient, shellac) around the hole at the centre of a good old-fashioned gramophone record will wear out before the moving outer edge of the disc, which ages more slowly because it is in motion. But atomic clocks sent travelling on airliners – i.e. undergoing the experience of motion – have proved this to be true. So we are left with another scientific truth about Creation which disturbs our common sense. The real message may be that there is something odd about Time itself, or merely that our customary ways of perceiving and conceiving it are flawed.

If our brains were 'hard-wired' differently, would this perception vanish? If we did not draw upon the past, if we did not conceive the future in terms of what we have already experienced (or had the recorded experiences of others – *past* experiences, of course – to draw upon) might we possibly be able to live in our present consciousness of Creation at 'Time A', whilst being simultaneously perfectly aware of 'Time B', 'Time C', and various other states of time all naturally going on around us, as though we were looking down on them as we would if they were upon a map?

Let me try and illustrate this idea by offering for consideration the adjective 'uncompleted'. This word tells me three things: that some piece of work should be capable of completion; that its present state is incomplete; and that some work has already been done upon it. To perceive this information my eye has followed the course of the word along the line, and has drawn this information from it because the English language uses an alphabetical system of writing by which letters are set in sequence to build up words. Perhaps a different writing system, Chinese being an obvious guess, could convey the idea of the incompleteness of this particular piece of work-in-progress by a single ideogram which would be 'absorbed' by my eye at a glance, and would not require me to follow the *linear course* of the word, one letter at a *time*. I apologise to any Chinese reader who might wish to tell me that this example will not work in his language, but that he could offer me five-and-twenty better ones. I am simply trying to convey the idea that because something looks obvious, reliable, natural, and familiar to daily experience, "…it ain't necessarily so". This could be true of time, and perhaps other features of Creation which we feel are familiar, well understood, and accounted for. Our consciousness seems to be rather at the mercy of the way our brains work, and so much of Creation is merely what we conceive it to be, often by custom only, that we must be careful when thinking about it. Brain is not consciousness; it is the machine which handles the data for it.

We can no longer avoid entering this minefield called 'Consciousness'. What is it?

Consciousness is our sense of being 'us', as opposed to someone or something else, and of being aware of as much. It gives us our own being, our 'self', complete with our own history of thought, sights and sounds, sensed from instant to instant, and giving us the continuum of awareness, or wakefulness, which is often referred to as our 'stream of consciousness'.

I have, indeed, seen consciousness described very fully, aptly, and simply as 'How it feels to be you'.

This immediately gives rise to philosophical and scientific problems, because our feelings are entirely subjective; we know what we are talking about when we speak of them, but there is a lack of testable evidence in their support. Accordingly, consciousness has always been chiefly a subject for religion and philosophy. Science is probing it, however, and biologists and neurological scientists are seeking to find out if there is any 'neural correlate of consciousness'. Essentially, this means that they are trying to find out, via scans of the living brain, whether there is any specific difference discernible in its activity between people who are conscious and those who are unconscious. The break-through will come when a scientist can look at a brain-scan and know, instantly, if it was taken from a conscious or unconscious subject.

Perhaps this will be possible one day, but such scans are unlikely to reveal what the activity within the brain may be that actually *makes* us conscious. To date, no one has found a specific brain area which is active when we are conscious, but inactive when we are not. Because I subscribe to the currently unfashionable idea that mind and brain are separate, and must combine their roles for full consciousness to result, I do not expect this brain area to appear. In time I might be proved wrong, of course.

Problems would still remain. Why should brain activity *feel* like anything? Why do I see the grass as green? Why, if I drop a brick on my toe, does the resulting sensation feel like pain? This type of question relates to what is known as the Hard Problem of Consciousness. One school of thought seeks to explain it as being the result of the interactions between neurones, but not found in the neurones themselves – i.e. what happens when neurones *do* things, but is not a property of them. I am not convinced.

This so-called 'explanatory gap' has given rise to many strange ideas and oddball theories, my own among them, often involving quantum mechanics or complex mathematical ideas requiring synchronous oscillations of brainwaves. However, currently the hunt is still on.

Could the 'explanatory gap' be bridged at all? Are our brains even equipped to understand their own consciousness? Is consciousness an illusion in the scheme of things; i.e. who am I fooling when I say I am 'me'? It is, as I said, a minefield – and a wonderful old muddle at present.

I want also to tackle the concept of Mind, which I would roughly define as the *way* in which individuals use their brains, both consciously and unconsciously. I stress the roughness of my definition, for the concepts of both consciousness and mind are presently under scrutiny and adjustment by many branches of science. To which I will add that it is high time that such work should be done, for we know too little about ourselves and the way in which we perceive Creation.

'Mind' in the *Oxford English Dictionary* is pronounced; "**1** the faculty of consciousness and thought. **2** the source of a person's thoughts; the intellect. ➤ a person's memory. ➤ a person identified with their intellectual faculties; *he was one of the greatest minds of all time.* **3** a person's attention. ➤ a person's will or determination. …" and many shades of meaning, plus common uses with their examples.

What we have here is the basis upon which we can appreciate our personal, 'psychic', or 'mind-using' / intellectual selves, the *way* we are made – "the *way* in which individuals use their brains, consciously and unconsciously", to reiterate my own rule-of-thumb definition. Just as the physical appearance of our body identifies each of us materially, so our mind is our identity in mental terms. Of choice, we can adjust our mental identities, and we do so in ways which give us a moral quality. The world may know us as, 'High minded / Low minded', 'Open minded / Closed minded', 'Broad minded / Narrow minded', 'Pure minded / Dirty minded', and, indeed, a whole host more of such classifications which give our essential, personal characteristics as perceived by others. This is done automatically, and such descriptions are readily understood. Upon hearing one of them people will know broadly what to expect of any particular individual in their dealings with him.

Mind gives the individual his outlook on life. It is the *conscious* ('explicit', 'declarative', 'easily expressed in words' – to use the terms of current psychological thinking) and *unconscious* ('implicit', 'non-declarative', 'something you know without conscious thought – e.g. how to ride a bike') projection of his consciousness in his dealings with his fellow humans, and with Creation generally.

Let me repeat the definitions I am going to use as I proceed:

BRAIN – Not consciousness, but the machine which handles the data for consciousness.

MIND – The way in which individuals use their brains, consciously and unconsciously.

CONSCIOUSNESS – a sense of self and a feeling of embodiment… a history or narrative… how it feels to be you. This seems to me to be generated in the *interaction* of Mind and Brain.

I do not pretend that these definitions are all-embracing, full of insight, or even exact in terms of the esoterica of various scientific disciplines. They are rough and ready, but I am at home with them and I am going to use them.

12. The Independent Mind

I am taking time to try and show how we come to know the nature of Creation, the better to help get to grips with examining the non-material bits and pieces that are involved with it. These are both abstract concepts such as Love, and the downright spooky items – ghosts, reincarnation, telepathy, and various other 'anomalous phenomena', as we should correctly call them. All these are part of Creation, if only by cultural tradition, and since they are what people believe to have an existence in reality, their attributes are worthy of our consideration. God is in the same category, of course. To those who would state *a priori* that there are no such things as ghosts, God, – or even Love, beyond the stimulus to breed, pass on our selfish genes, and give them the best help we can to thrive – I would urge a little thoughtful examination of the material which refers to such concepts, and remind them that they are all products of consciousness, mind and brain. This is where our knowledge of them comes from, and to investigate the way in which the mechanism works is to arrive at a better idea of how we know about them.

We have skimmed quickly and superficially over the mechanics involved in the brain's processing of stimuli reaching it from the senses. The sort of stimulus we dealt with was from the material world, a noise in the jungle undergrowth, in fact. Noise, as we know, is composed of sound waves which are transmitted (in this example) through the air. These are external to our senses and have energy, generated by whatever activity in the environment produces them, (in our example, an animal stamping around). I want now to consider how we, having a sense of self and a feeling of embodiment, *consciously* use our brains to further our own purposes, not merely reacting to stimuli but using our free-will and making our choices in the process. This is indisputably the territory of the Mind – 'The way in which individuals use their brains, consciously and unconsciously', remember.

Although mind itself is an abstract concept it is readily detectable in matter, the physical substance of the brain. When the brain is given an electro-magnetic 'scan', what the mind is engaged in may be deduced from the various areas of the brain which the scan shows to be particularly active. I see this as the mind working through and with the brain, and not the brain's producing mind as a by-product of its own activity. People of other points of view would disagree with me, however. They might argue thus; Given that mind works with the brain, which is matter, mind itself can be influenced by matter acting upon the brain – e.g. drugs – and can behave in perfectly predictable ways as a result – e.g. drunkenness, hallucination. If a mind's disorder causes an individual to exhibit less predictable aberrations of behaviour, these are termed 'mental illness'. They may derive from chemical imbalances in the body's metabolism, and as such may subsequently be corrected by medicine. Psychotherapy may likewise induce a better balance in the secretions of glands producing mind-affecting chemicals and hormones, and so produce the desired cure. This is established medical practice, and relies upon the material intervention of the drugs in the mental processes. Therefore matter acts upon matter, and that is all there is to it.

Yet, to me, this still does not demonstrably make mind the brain's by-product. Mind is so very little understood that it may have an existence entirely separate from the brain and its functions. So whilst we know that we can influence it through chemistry acting upon the brain, what we may be doing with 'mind altering' drugs in reality is impeding the brain's ability to receive or act correctly upon requirements made of it by the mind, which remains unaffected but unable to do its job properly when the brain is incapacitated. Also mental illness may be an illustration of the mind's difficulties with its own identity which, in turn, affect the amount of information it is able to work with properly from the input that the brain is offering it.

Mind is elusive. As a subject, it inspires numerous 'Why?' questions which science is often not best equipped to investigate and answer. Why is consciousness, our sense of self, able to direct our brains in logical and structured thought according to our will? Why do we have will, anyway? Why does our mind make choices? Does our free-will shape our mind, or vice versa? Why are we purposeful? Are we as intellectually adept and logical as we like to think? Why do we like to think?

It is at this essentially basic level that we have to consider mind, our own minds, and what use we make of them. As far back as 1943, G.N.M. Tyrrell, a true Natural Philosopher, wrote upon the subject (*GNM Tyrrell, "Appartions". Published by the Society for Psychical Research, 1943*). Since then others have pressed consideration further, but have tended to deal with epistemological (the theory, application, and extent of knowledge) aspects of mind. I am more concerned with what mind allows us to do and, therefore, how it works. I appreciate Tyrrell's wisdom, which I quote here:

"For the present purpose the main thing to grasp is that, in certain important respects, material things are not what they seem. If we are looking at a common object, such as a brick, we *feel* that in the act of looking at it, we are being made directly aware of the existence of a brick and of some of its properties. *There is,* we say, a brick about such a distance away – an oblong shaped, solid object with square corners, reddish in colour and having a rough surface. We say this without any feeling of doubt. In fact, to the person who is entirely unacquainted with the philosophy of sense-perception, it probably seems absurd to suggest that there is anything in it to argue about. His view is that 'seeing is believing'. We feel that in this act of vision we *know* that the brick is there and what it is like. But, in fact, we do not *know* this. The feeling we have is not *knowledge* but only *belief.* We may, after all, be mistaken. The object may turn out not to be a brick at all but a very skilfully made cardboard imitation. And even if we are right about its being a real brick, reflection shows that we cannot be right in our conviction that we are *directly* aware of it *as it now is.* For time must have elapsed since the light left it which now reaches our eyes… The total time no doubt is very short in the case of a brick, or of any object near at hand; but if it is a star we are looking at, thousands of years may have elapsed since the light left it which now reaches us; and for all we know the star we think we are seeing *now* may no longer be in existence…

"Again, in looking at a brick, although we have the impression of being aware of the brick as a complete object, we are not, and never can be, simultaneously acquainted with the whole of its surface, or with the inside, although all these exist at the same time. ... Sensation is therefore fragmentary both in respect of space and time, whereas the brick is supposed to be a temporally continuous, three-dimensional whole. Vision does not, therefore, give us *direct acquaintance* with material things, as, in looking at them, we believe that it does. It only gives us indirect information about them, and this in a piecemeal manner. In perception we go ahead of our data...

"There is, however, one element of vision (and indeed of all sense-perception) about which no mistake is possible. When we look at a brick we are immediately aware of a coloured patch of a particular shape, size, and tint standing at a certain distance away from us in space. On this point there can be no delusion. Whether or not we mistakenly believe this patch to be part of the surface of something else, or of no object at all, we cannot be mistaken about being aware of the patch. Either it is present to our consciousness or it is not. We are here in the region of *knowledge* and not *belief*... The coloured patch is called a 'sense-datum'; and the act of being aware of it is called 'sensing'. With the other senses it is the same... All these sense-data are correlated with brain-states, on which, in normal perception, they appear to depend. None of the senses is therefore prehensive, [*OED; Prehension; an interaction of a subject with an event or entity which involves perception but not necessarily cognition*] whether it purports to be so or not.

"The distinction between 'sensing' and 'perceiving' is not one which we draw in ordinary life. *Sensing* gives indisputable knowledge, gained from sensation in the act of sensing a sense-datum. *Perception* is a mental act built on the foundation of direct acquaintance by sensing. It is an act which *takes for granted* the existence of a particular material thing forming part of our environment. In perception we *jump* from the *knowledge* that there is a coloured patch to the *belief* that there is a brick over there... On sensing the sense-datum we make the jump of uncritically taking for granted that a particular material thing is there. This uncritical taking-for-granted may turn out to be wrong: but awareness of a sense-datum can never be wrong or mistaken...

"It can only be stated dogmatically that the sense-data sensed by each percipient are *private to himself and originate in processes which take place in his own personality*... the material thing is in part the percipient's own construct on account of these sense-data which he supplies... *In perception we are never acquainted with anything but our own sense-data.* Never do we achieve direct acquaintance with the physical object itself, which we suppose to constitute the real brick. The 'material brick' is totally formed by the two factors, *the 'physical object' together with the sense-data which we provide.*

"One other point is worth mentioning. Where there arise doubts about the nature of the physical world which are due to the nature of sense-perception, it is no use turning to science for an answer or a decision. Whatever doubts infect sense-perception must also infect the whole body of experimental science, which ultimately rests on sense-perception. Scientists no doubt discover a great deal by the use of instruments; but it must be remembered that these are aids to the senses, not substitutes for them. In fact, epistemological questions (i.e. questions concerning the philosophy of the theory of knowledge) are of fundamental importance in any search for truth and take precedence of the appeal to experiment."

This is worth re-reading a time or two. The idea conveyed in it is essential to understanding how we come to build up the mental picture(s) of Creation which we use in living our lives from day to day. To assume that we are truly logical about anything, or *can* be truly logical about anything when we are simply using tried and tested assumptions, concepts, mental constructs, and 'imaginings' – in the sense of creating images in our minds – to get along by, is simply put out of court. We are in our lives what our minds make of us, and, awkwardly and conversely, what we make of our minds. The assumptions we make when we anchor the point of a figurative 'mental geometrical compass' to start fixing our individual places in Creation will make a deal of difference to what we subsequently sense / perceive around us, therefore.

One assumption, that Science and Religion are necessarily mutually exclusive, seems to cause unnecessary anguish in some quarters. I have on record a letter to a scientific publication in which the writer asserts that Believers profess to believe in at least one supernatural Being of omniscient intelligence, who knows them all individually, and commands them to conduct their lives in specific ways which may range from particular observances of dress and diet right up to a requirement to kill people of differing Faiths. This is a strange idea that the correspondent has picked up from somewhere and, as a humane and decent individual – as witnessed by his letter overall – he is clearly troubled by it. He is relieved that for such a God "there is no testable evidence whatsoever" – as am I, upon such terms! – and takes moral comfort in atheism. Leading a perfectly normal cultural life, he admits to being moved to tears by Bach's *St Matthew Passion*. And why not? It is part of the Christian heritage we both share.

To me it seems that the writer has snatched materialist 'Scientism' from the jaws of spiritual experience! Yet this is his choice; he has spiked his compass firmly to the board of 'Scientism', and then made the assumption that all that comes within the tracing of its circles is real and proven. As we with reference to Tyrrell have just suggested, one cannot honestly be that dogmatic. Yet his mind, at the time of writing, was expressing the perception of the individual who responded to choral evensong, usually from one or other of our great cathedrals or major centres of Christian worship, whilst blocking out any possibility of subjective spiritual justification for it. There is in fact no automatic 'God wavelength' in our brains which would have obliged him to do otherwise. In the context of any form of perception, psychological experiments have found that there is no automatic correspondence between a stimulus and the complete experience of something. It was discovered that when it became possible to cure congenital blindness by surgery, those whose sight was thus given to them when they were well advanced in life had to work hard at learning that circles were circular and rectangles had four corners, whilst triangles could boast only three. There was, in other words, no in-built notion of circularity, rectangularity, or triangularity in the brain. The properties of the whole environment had to be learned from scratch. This likewise applies to one's cultural environment.

Perhaps this is why infants of up to about 18 months old spend such long periods apparently just staring at the world around them, and then grasping and 'testing', to the limit of their senses, such bits and pieces of it as they can reach. Their brains at this stage of their development soak up all data available to them, indiscriminately and without critical structure, and undergo an increase in cortical cells to enable this to be done. The neural circuits receiving repeated information in this way develop ever stronger synaptic connections, whilst the brain parts which are not so stimulated atrophy. Therefore we may say that familiar and repeated inputs to the brain affect its structure in ways which are peculiar to the individual, and derive from – and ultimately contribute to – his environment. Experiments involving brain scans of licensed London taxi drivers who had 'done the knowledge' – of London, in order to qualify for their licences – showed that the brain areas associated with spatial memory in the rear of the hippocampus were, in fact, enlarged when compared with the population generally.

Such studies as this showed the established idea that our brains do not alter in structure or shape after about the age of 25 to be wrong. Even learning new skills later on in life altered the size of the relevant parts of the brain as more neurons were needed to handle and co-ordinate the new data. This was particularly clear in relation to some middle-aged subjects who took up juggling. The eye-hand co-ordination required to make progress had enlarged parts of the hippocampus after as little as three months' practice. As a result, therapies for people who have suffered brain damage – a stroke, for example – are being reassessed and redeveloped, the idea being that the undamaged parts of the brain might be able to take over the work of the parts which have become impaired, and allow a much higher degree of recovery than was previously thought possible. As an adjustment of medical practice to an increase in scientific knowledge this is commendable.

Intriguingly, it appears that to practise meditation regularly may also physically alter the brain. The evidence is less certain than the visible changes shown by the brain scans made of the newly competent jugglers, but there are indications that meditation alters chemical secretions, and thus the emotions and moods they cause or influence. Conditions such as asthma and some forms of indigestion can be relieved in this way without the clinical administration of drugs. We have noted that matter –

drugs – can influence matter – brain – and yet here is the brain apparently dosing itself as needed. Is it? I would say that the brain is neutral in the business, and what we are involved with is the mind, that 'sense of self' provided by consciousness, using the brain's in-built capacities – here its ordering the body to secrete drugs – for its overall benefit. The mind is exercising its will, to make time to meditate, to relax the body physically, to think in terms of calming or positive concepts, and to expect a beneficial outcome. It is the benefits of the meditation which the mind expects; the details of the chemical processes involved are probably unknown to it, and are in any case not its prime concern, – which is the well-being of itself, its identity, and its selfish genes. Therefore the mind will work with, upon, and through the brain to bring about this end. We are not observing mechanical and non-conscious matter – the brain – acting purposefully upon itself, but under the influence of the mind's acting upon it.

In the brain information becomes sorted out in the pre-frontal cortex. As this area develops, so does consciousness. The infant begins to distinguish between himself and what is around him. He comes to control his environment *at will*, e.g. he can pick things up and put them down, by *choice*. Thus he develops free-will, and can consciously use it to impose his own wishes upon what is around him. This is the stirring of mind. As he grows older his development will increasingly be influenced by the culture in which he is raised. This will provide, or limit, the stimuli and options open to him for obtaining the necessary information about his environment and its part in Creation overall. He will not somehow 'make up his own mind as he grows older', as some of the stranger ideas about bringing up a child might like to believe. Certainly he will individuate as he matures, but the patterns underpinning his culture will channel the course of his development, either as he conforms to them or reacts against them in his own environment and generation. His options for 'making up his own mind' will be predetermined to this extent as a result.

Throughout, though, it will be his mind which makes his choices and directs his course. He is not some sort of puppet dangling upon strings attached to God. He has free-will, and he exercises it, both consciously and unconsciously, via his brain (which I have defined as the machine which handles the data for consciousness). Mind, brain, and consciousness therefore are the main 'psychic attributes', to use a good old term, of that individual. Their exact form in his case is personal to him alone. Exactly how they contribute to any given situation will likewise be personal to him. So far, so adequate; but no one is yet sure in any definitive sense about which constituent of his psyche predominates in any part of his life. Time and research may render this statement obsolete, however. Meanwhile we must do what we can with what we have by way of such knowledge.

Therefore, in order to continue our examination of the human condition in relation to what we think we know of Creation overall, let us make a stab at showing mind and brain, as two separate entities, working together.

13. Consciousness – a Product

Mind and Brain tend to be viewed as one and the same thing. Certainly they interact very closely, and from this process probably comes our personal consciousness – our 'sense of self'. We are conscious because *we* know what we are doing, and why we – and not someone or something else – are doing it. "To me the evidence of a continuing self is not that it thinks, which it can do without massive assistance from the brain, but that it has feelings and experiences (termed 'quales' by philosophers). Thus, a rectified version of Descartes' statement might be: 'I'm nauseous, therefore I am.' (Douglas M Stokes; *Paranormal Review, Issue 50, April 2009*). Let us also recall our attempt at defining consciousness. It is entirely subjective. It is what we feel in ourselves about ourselves – and other people just have to take our word for it. Brain scans can show which parts of the brain are engaged in specific tasks, and these have revealed how consciousness sets the brain to work on its behalf. But there is no discrete brain area that is active when we are conscious and quiet when we are not. Which need not surprise us, for our brain's 'automatic nervous system' keeps our hearts beating, governs various secretions to allow digestion, infection-fighting, and so on, and does much other routine mechanical work within us besides, all without engaging our waking and conscious involvement in such processes. We would not last long if it did not. So our brains are working throughout our lives and, in addition, our consciousness employs them to do for us those things which are chosen and governed by our minds, which are – as I have ventured to define them – the *way* in which we use our brains, both consciously and unconsciously. It is important to remember that we have an *un*conscious aspect to our minds as well as our full waking consciousness. We shall refer to our unconscious minds again.

But there are still problems. Why should the activity of a mass of neurons feel like anything? Why does pricking a finger feel like pain? Why does grass appear green? This has been dubbed the 'hard problem' of consciousness, and some people have tried to explain it as an emergent property of active networks of neurons – in other words, something that arises from the interactions among neurons, but which is not found in the neurons themselves, as we have already noted. This 'explanatory gap' has given rise to many oddball theories, and will doubtless continue to do so.

To suggest that mind and brain may be separate entities is, of course, to waltz straight into this area. However, it seems to me that mind and brain are indeed separate entities in relation to the jobs they do. It may even be that mind is 'of no fixed address' in any part of the brain, and flits elusively around its neurons as it directs our consciousness in maintaining and adjusting its own 'self-image'. Probably my own 'self image' is so unique to me that my mind does not behave in exactly the same way as the minds of all other conscious beings upon Earth and, for that reason, will not be detectable in its activity by any brain scan. It will not 'show up' in the same brain area as anyone else's mind even if we are both engaged upon the same mental task, in other words.

A useful illustration of this view of the mind's working would be a piece of jazz improvisation. The brain would be the tune, the basic musical theme – the task upon which it is employed – and the improvisation would represent the mind as it works its individually chosen variations upon that theme. Because the music is improvised upon a unique occasion it takes on the features of that occasion – the emotions, the response to the setting, the acoustics of the venue, the feelings of the musicians, and the reactions of the audience. No other performance will ever be quite the same. Yet if the performance chances to be recorded, the recording, be it on disc, tape, or some other medium, will endure as a record of the performance as it was at the time. In this way it has recorded the – one off – spontaneous improvisation, and it is this which conveys what the improvising musicians were doing at the time of the recording. But exactly the same improvisation will not reappear in any other live performance of the main jazz theme. If in a brain scan we 'play' the main theme – the task – as it is performed by any number of jazz bands, the tune will show up as the areas of the brain engaged in the specific task of playing that particular piece of music, but the improvisation will simply be 'noise', a random flicker around the brain, and of no indication of anything but capricious synaptic activity. It is unlikely to be seen as the mind's willing and controlling the improvisation. Accordingly the mind may be pronounced undetectable, or be disregarded as an unimportant off-shoot result of the main task.

However, if a recording of the event suggests to some other mind the way in which the original mind had influenced the improvisation known from the recording, and if this second mind were then able to conceive in detail the circumstances of the whole performance whenever that particular recording came to its attention, what then? Would this be a possible mind-to-mind communication deriving from the physical recording, or even a sympathetic reaction by the second mind to the theme of the music? Could the second mind employ its own associated brain to recreate a good approximation of the performance? If so, is it perhaps possible that human experience, usually with an emotional charge, may in some unknown way be recorded and then subsequently reproduced by a sympathetic mind acting upon a different brain, perhaps at a very much later time?

This is my own preferred 'oddball theory' – more a useful working idea – on the subject, and I make no apology for it. I simply find it useful to view mind and brain as being separate, in order to highlight their individual functions. This helps to account for some phenomena which are definitely 'subjective' – and thus beyond the scope of narrowly preoccupied science – but none the less real to those who have encountered them.

So I will present the brain and the mind as being separate, but in close and constant communication with one another, producing consciousness in the process. (And if this is to let loose an oddball theory, then I have been accused of doing far worse things in my time!) Please imagine, by way of illustration, the 'How Richard Todd won the Second World War' type of film. Think of a portrayal of a Battle of Britain RAF control centre plotting room. This is centred upon a plotting table, which is a large map of some part of the United Kingdom upon which are placed cubes of wood painted with symbols; roundels for the RAF, swastikas for the enemy. Each block has also a card fixed to it to show which particular aircraft squadron it represents. The position it occupies upon the plotting table's map shows its latest reported position in the sky above. Thus the aerial battle is plotted, monitored, and directed as it takes place.

WAAFs using gadgets akin to croupiers' rakes push the blocks around the table in response to information reaching them via their earphones. This information, suitably channelled and directed to them, has its origins in all sorts of sources 'outside' – aerodromes, radar stations, Royal Observer Corps posts, Air Raid Precautions posts, and perhaps even a spy or so near an enemy airfield. In response to it they move their blocks to the correct positions upon the map. Around the walls of the room are status boards indicating which squadrons are engaged, when they need to refuel and rearm, weather conditions, and so forth, including 'kills' and casualties, all of which have a vital bearing on the battle in progress. Instructions to fighting units are passed via the 'off table' sections of the plotting room. I will liken the plotting room and all work connected with it to the brain.

Overlooking the plotting table is a gallery where sits the Top Brass, Group Captains and the like, who are actually fighting the battle, issuing the orders to the fighting units in the air and the back-up below. To do so the Top Brass must be able to see and understand all that is happening in the plotting room, and be in instant and reliable communication with those who are doing the fighting. They take and communicate decisions, they plan moves and have them executed. A constant stream of instructions based upon the gallery's decisions goes out to the active units and information sources, via the 'off-table' sections of the plotting room. Priorities will be modified, instructions brought up to date, mistakes corrected; and all of this will be communicated to the plotting table and status boards – along with information from the external sources – and shown upon them. The gallery will remember what has been done, and why. Notes will be made for future analysis, and for the information of the next watch to man the gallery. All of this will be available to the scrutiny of posterity, for training, development of better tactics, reports to Government and the Media, official histories, and the like. I will liken the gallery to the mind.

Crudely, what I am suggesting is that the brain processes information, shows things as they are known to be, as they are believed to be on the strength of present data, or as previous experience of them presents them *pro tem* to the senses whilst awaiting better information. It remembers basics, monitors actions, and keeps the mind informed. The mind, however, makes the decisions, keeps track of the overall environment, remembers, acts upon memory, and gets things done via communication with the parts of the brain that control actions. Its records are the memory, and its consciousness is of a more thematic, long-term nature than the frantic second-by-second adjustments made by the brain. I have seen the latter 'scored' at over one million synaptic events a second, even when the brain is not being worked particularly hard. I credit the mind with a broader view of what is happening in the world, and suggest it can judge current events with the benefits of hindsight and experience.

Thus the brain's job is to keep track of its environment, and tell the mind about what is happening around it. The mind needs to be aware of this in detail in order to proceed sensibly with whatever business it has in hand. However, most of what the brain is telling it will not be needed for anything immediate by way of reflection or action, so it all registers 'unconsciously' until something needing closer scrutiny or a decision prompts the mind to organise itself and its resources in concert with the brain, and become 'conscious' in order to do some work. It then communicates with the brain – and via the brain with the surrounding environment. The mind does the administrative business of life, and the brain is its five senses – plus computer, executive, and 'legs'.

The interaction of mind and brain within this system – the RAF in our example – its organisation and the various things it does, represent consciousness. It is this that mind and brain serve, whilst at the same time producing and sustaining it. Overall it is a complicated, though effective, business.

There is, at last, a little empirical evidence which backs this construction of consciousness' working. What it suggests is that we rely very much upon our *un*conscious for keeping track of Creation. This is an interesting suggestion. It makes very good logical sense that our brains should be receiving sense-data the whole time – awake and asleep – but only bring the important bits of it to our full consciousness when they rise above some sort of threshold of interest, related to our survival in the context of our lives at the time, perhaps. This gives substance to the 'There I was, wide awake, sitting up in bed and listening intently, although I haven't a clue what it was that woke me. But it's just as well that something did, because…' experience. The 'unconscious' – located in the brain? – monitors our environment, and engages our mind when circumstances appear to require our full consciousness in order for us to make urgent decisions about them. Work is being done on this idea at Seattle's University of Washington, where Dr M Shadlen neatly sums up the whole business as "…an unconscious decision to be conscious." In essence, he views the subconscious and conscious as being two parts of the same system, rather than two separate brain functions working independently. I agree entirely. Try this for proof; can you feel the shoes on your feet? You can now! But you could all along, *unconsciously.* My question came from the gallery.

It could be even subtler. At University College London, Peter Dayan, Nathaniel Draw, and Yael Niv, theoretical neuroscientists, depict the unconscious and conscious as having two parts apiece. Consciously we are good at rational decision making, especially when there is little information to go on, and we can come up with decisions that are complex, rational, and reached quickly (Episodic Controller, and Goal-Directed Controller). Unconsciously, we excel at everyday instincts and conditioned responses to given stimuli; also such learned behaviours – e.g. driving a car – that are so familiar that they become habits. Thus our attention is directed quickly, and our fast, effective responses are certainly a survival mechanism (Pavlovian Controller, and Habitual Controller).

Obviously a couple of sentences cannot do justice to the arguments for these ideas, but I see in them the 'Conscious' components corresponding quite well with the gallery, and the 'Unconscious' elements supporting the plotting table equally well. These ideas are quite new – circa 2007 – and have been arrived at experimentally, moreover. I reckon the researchers' 'Controller' terms I have included in brackets will become widely used in this context as these ideas are developed and extended. There is nothing aethereally theoretical about them. Conceivably Haynes and Libet are on the same trail. For simplicity's sake I am duly emboldened to continue referring to the plotting table and gallery for the respective work of brain and mind.

Further, work done at Oxford in 2008 by Dr Lorimer Moseley used as its basis an old 'party trick' known as the Rubber Hand Illusion whereby an artificial hand within view of the subject is stroked whilst, at the same time, his own hand – which is not within his field of view – is likewise stroked. The subject is then surprised to perceive the artificial hand as his own because he can both see and feel the consistent sensation of the stroking. Conversely, in cases where a limb has lost its sensation, as the result of a stroke for example, it may be 'disowned' by the patient although it is still visibly attached to him. Strangely, in such cases the temperature of the 'disowned' limb is always lower than in the rest of the body. Dr Moseley has found that the temperature of the subject's own limb also falls during the Rubber Hand Illusion. Since temperature is controlled in the brain via the thalamus, it accordingly appears as though the mind is telling the brain, "This rubber hand is not mine, despite an illusion to the contrary, so do not bother supplying it with blood." In terms of our plotting room, the gallery knows that there is something wrong with one of the markers upon the plotting table, and ceases to pay attention to it. Just as the Rubber Hand will not move if required to, a false marker on the plotting table is not communicating normally with the gallery. The implication that mind and brain are distinct from one another, although both are needed for normal consciousness, is again strongly suggested.

I appreciate that there will be howls of protest from neurologists and philosophers alike about this analogy of brain and mind. There are objections to it, I know, but it will serve well my purposes in considering phenomena which are in themselves subjective and not susceptible to being produced for examination on demand. I would add that each mind will have its own memories, culture, preferred modes of analysis, priorities, and so on. Therefore every mind will perceive and interpret the environment in which it finds itself slightly differently. This is what makes the mind personal to each individual. This is his subjective consciousness. It is an agent, along with genetic characteristics, in forming his personality. As it perceives Creation, so shall Creation appear to it, and be dealt with by it. It has been truly remarked in this sense that the whole universe is no larger than the space between any individual's ears. What he cannot / does not / will not sense, perceive, conceive, and construct does not exist for him.

I want to examine this by discussing anomalies to everyday experience. By these I mean the sort of experiences which are generally regarded as 'spooky', and classified as 'the paranormal'. On various grounds some people deny that these have any reality, subjectively or objectively. For my own part I suspect, based on my own accumulated experience, that somewhat over 30% of the population has had some sort of brush with the paranormal. In the UK that would mean above twenty million people. Even allowing for some bad observation of natural phenomena, and a spot of wishful thinking here and there, it seems that there is too much 'paranormality' around to disregard it blithely on the grounds that for its existence "there is no testable evidence whatever", to misquote the *St Matthew Passion* atheist, so therefore such a belief is irreconcilable with the standards of scientific investigation. Something anomalous is being experienced by numbers of quite normal and everyday human beings. Therefore, what are we to make of it as part of Creation?

This question causes more trouble to the 'Scientismist' frame of mind than to the average individual.

One quite common anomaly in the usual scheme of things involves receiving telephone calls. If one has a particularly emotionally-charged relationship with whoever is telephoning to make contact, it is often found that one knows who will speak even before one picks up the receiver. This might apply to the love of one's life, whom one will always be pleased to talk to, or to one's bitterest foe – e.g. the Bank Manager – whose calls one dreads. A strong emotional element would be associated with the process of telephoning by either of these individuals, however. In theory, when the phone rings there should be a 50–50 chance of the call's coming from any particular individual. Thus one has a 50–50 chance of predicting whom one will hear upon raising the receiver. Granted that particular types of phone call are more likely to come at certain times of day than at others; the Bank Manager will probably only phone during office hours, for example. Then the total number of calls one receives also needs to be considered. If the overall number is high, the chance element is accordingly greater and the anomaly more remarkable. However, once all such considerations have been given a statistical weighting of probability, if one still knows who is about to speak on above 50% of occasions one has an anomaly. Why is it so? Dr Rupert Sheldrake has addressed such questions boldly, and we will refer to his work on anomalies in due course. I have also known people who have experienced this telephone anomaly but later, in changed emotional circumstances and disregarding their carefully compiled evidence, denied that it had ever occurred. Such is human nature! But there was something odd happening in relation to them at the time, so what was it? We can learn more about Creation and ourselves by pursuing such anomalies. We ought to do more about it.

We are dealing with consciousness, mind, and brain. As I have already said, I view mind as being separate from brain, and I can support this somewhat by referring to a Near Death Experience (NDE) reported in the *Journal of the Society for Psychical Research, Number 865, October 2001*, and also *The Lancet*, vol. 358, p2039; "This case created much interest because the clinical features were closely monitored, the patient was clinically dead for most of the 45 minute operation, and yet an NDE was reported. This concerned a patient who was operated on for a brain aneurysm in the course of which the blood had to be diverted from the brain. For the major part of the operation, the procedure resulted in a totally flat EEG, and the cessation of auditory potentials indicating an absence of brain stem activity. (Brain cells were kept alive by cooling the body.) Despite all these monitored signs of clinical death, the patient reported a classic NDE with claims of being able to meet deceased relatives and observe details of the operation, which she correctly reported. Since there appeared to be no electrical activity in the brain, it is difficult to explain the NDE by temporal lobe seizure, and since hearing was blocked and the patient's eyes were taped shut, it is difficult to explain the ESP (Extra Sensory Perception) by residual sensory perception". Quite so. I shall deal with NDEs themselves later on.

What is reported in this case is that a 'dead' brain picked up correct sense-data (cf Tyrrell) about its owner's state and surroundings at the time, and also apparently perceived other sense-data in or from a different time, i.e. a meeting with dead relatives. What is going on, therefore? Do we cry 'Fraud!', or 'Fairies!'? And if we do, what grounds have we for doing so? Will it serve to state, "These things are anomalous to everyday experience. Therefore they have no validity. Therefore there is something dishonest about a report of them. Therefore it must follow that someone is seeking to deceive?" To take such a position, I suggest, is to demonstrate shocking prejudice. The details of the case are clear. The situation in which the experiences were obtained is as 'controlled' – i.e. an operating theatre – as any investigator could wish, and if one is to discount the experiences rather than accept their subjective validity and wonder how they came about, one cannot lay claim to an open and enquiring mind.

I cannot direct the reader to any source which states, "This is what occurred. It proceeded via steps 1, 2, 3, ... and so on". I wish I could. It would clear up a host of questions concerning consciousness for a start. That is why I keep an eye open for results from the mind / brain investigations being done currently at various universities around the world. A sudden leap in understanding the human condition could come about at any moment. But it has not occurred yet. I suggest all we can say about this case is that, with the brain apparently dead and out of action in its 'plotting room' capacity, the patient's mind communicated – in ways not known – with, presumably, the minds or brains of the medical personnel in the vicinity, and perhaps with other minds, even discarnate ones. Intriguingly, this latter possibility must be considered in view of the reported communication with the minds (or conjectural minds?) of certain relatives *enduring post-mortem.*

One might, of course, put the latter down to subjective hallucination on the patient's part. One must, however, demonstrate this possibility; it is not good enough merely to assert it. One should also consider what the patient was 'hallucinating' *with* at the material time. And what would have been the material time; during the operation, or at some later stage? Still, what remains is a strong suggestion that mind and brain are different entities which act independently, whilst normally in constant direct communication. Where might mind be found in everyday space and time, therefore? At present any suggested answer would probably fit the category of 'oddball theory'. Yet does this wreck science as an intellectual discipline and method of investigation? No – for if the answer were demonstrable it would be truth, and is not truth the goal of science? Never mind if ideas must change in arriving at the truth. That is all part of the process.

I have found another little piece of experimental evidence which could be suggestive of mind / brain separation. Professor Jerome Kagan of Harvard University has done experiments which show that our reaction to a sentence, spoken or read, which contains a 'semantic inconsistency' like "apples are cats", produces a specific brainwave pattern which is detectable in brain scans. This pattern does not occur for a grammatical error such as "apples is fruit". Therefore the brain is responding to meaning, not to the slip-shod presentation of information. Prof. Kagan suggests that this could imply a distinct separation of brain states and cognitive states. Words alone do not affect the brain's specific responses. Now, in justice to Prof. Kagan, he has *not* said that mind and brain are different. However, his 'brain state' seems to me a bit like the 'plotting room' whilst his 'cognitive state' suggests the gallery. If nonsense is presented to the mind, the mind apparently queries it with the brain; but if the presentation of reasonable or expected sense-data is merely a bit sloppy, the mind can take it in its stride. Perhaps if mind and brain were the same, the same standards would apply to both types of 'odd' (or even oddball) data, and there would be only a single brainwave reaction, or, indeed, no reaction at all. More work in this area is needed, I think. It is interesting as it stands, none the less.

Perhaps mind is the same as soul? I do not think it is, and I had better explain why.

14. The Mind at Work

Is mind the same as the soul? We have suggested that mind can continue, somehow, to function when the brain is dead. Therefore, is not mind effectively the same as the soul which, as we traditionally conceive it, endures *post mortem*?

I doubt it, and my reasons for doing so derive from an account of a case of reincarnation investigated by Erlendur Haraldsson (*Journal of the Society for Psychical Research, Number 859, April 2000*). It concerns a Sri Lankan soldier called Dayananda M. Pedidurayalage. The report states, "On the morning of 15 April 1986 Dayananda was in a group of 14 soldiers in two army trucks who had been ordered to proceed on a route-clearing patrol... On the way one of the trucks was caught in a massive landmine blast. The patrol commander reported that after the blast Dayananda was found unconscious near the vehicle, which had overturned and was completely wrecked. A few soldiers were killed and others were severely wounded. Dayananda was taken by helicopter to hospital... He never regained consciousness, and died on 18 April. From the report it can be inferred that there was no contact with enemy soldiers." Five or six years later a three-year-old, Chatura B Karunaratne, began to talk about his 'previous life', which had in it many specific features which related to Dayananda. Further investigation revealed that Chatura was also able to identify people and places associated with Dayananda. The report in *JSPR* gives all the essential details. There can, in my view, be no doubt that something of Dayananda's self-identity transferred, either *post mortem* or after his loss of consciousness following severe injury, to Chatura. Dayananda died 18.4.'86; Chatura was born 20.4.'89, incidentally.

So far this looks like a normal [Sic] instance of reincarnation. However, it is apparent from what Chatura – as the reincarnated personality of Dayananda – states that Dayananda *believed* himself to be dead when the landmine exploded, that is, about three days before he in fact died. His 'death', as referred to by Chatura, dates from his loss of consciousness, not the end of life in his body, which included his brain of course. We have suggested that mind is the way in which individuals use their brains – both consciously and unconsciously, remember. During the final three days of his life, Dayananda's conscious and unconscious mind-brain interactions were not functioning. Thus his mind, fixed at the point of his loss of normal consciousness, suggested to him that he was dead; its non-engagement in its normal two-way contact with his brain had ended his sense of 'me'. This prevented him from appreciating the truth of his situation; 'he' was no longer there.

In terms of our plotting room analogy we could put this way:

Injury produced shock / trauma (damage) to the nervous system, which caused an overloading of the brain, parts of which ceased to work normally. *Plotting table in chaos. Some personnel injured or absent from their posts. Thus signals not being received in the normal ways or in usual quantities. Only random and uncoordinated activity possible upon plotting table. Therefore signals not being processed properly, if at all. Situation shown upon the plotting table becoming increasingly out-of-date, inaccurate, irrelevant, and useless.*

The mind cannot make sense of the 'apples are cats' type of data presented to it. It cannot obtain any response to its queries about the data, because the brain is not working normally and responding to mind. The usual two-way perpetual contact is broken. This is loss of consciousness, the sense of self. *Gallery sees that plotting table is in chaos. Instructions to re-establish orderly working as per procedure not heeded. For the present, plotting table has ceased to function.*

In order to understand the situation which has arisen, the mind refers to the last data it registered. It registers shock / trauma. It then refers to the memory for the best probable context in which logically to set this data. This context was a military patrol with some possible expectation of small arms fire upon contact with the enemy. *Gallery refers to notes of latest situation. Finds reference to possibility of contact with enemy involving expected small arms action. Assumes this must have occurred.*

In the absence of any better data to work upon, the mind makes the logical assumption that there has been contact with the enemy, shooting, and that the result has been bodily injury which has resulted in loss of consciousness. It has no indication of whether this situation is temporary or permanent; for this it requires the restoration of normal brain activity. *Gallery evaluates its situation; lack of fresh data, no response to queries, no interaction with plotting table. On basis of last apparently reliable data, plus previous context of situation overall, concludes that it is incapable of functioning for the present.*

After a period of time the mind concludes that interaction with the brain is unlikely to resume. Thus it presumably regards the brain as absent. In this situation, mind is an entity existing by itself. *Gallery continues unable to make contact with plotting table. Concludes it is in isolation and no longer part of the overall operation – i.e. the functioning RAF. Concludes its operational purpose is past. Seeks another role.*

This analogy throws up parallels with a gramophone record; the mind, which is useless without a gramophone – the brain – or a tape without a tape-recorder / player, or any of a variety of discs without computers / players. We can go along with this illustration provided we make a point of remembering that an analogy is just that, and not the way in which the mind and brain *necessarily* work. But it is only a construction, and *one* possible construction at that, which we are putting upon what may be happening in this case. Also, let us recall that our brains constantly monitor our environment subconsciously, so that whenever the input becomes important enough, the subconscious decides to engage the conscious. The decision to engage at all is, in effect, an "unconscious decision to be conscious." Looked at in this light, it would seem that the conscious mind is switched off until the brain decides otherwise by providing sufficiently important stimuli for it to take notice once more – which reinforces the picture of the mind as the disc without the disc-player. We also need the mind to be equipped with a sense of its own identity, and a memory, too. Later we shall find that this often appears to be the case – anecdotally but frequently; almost 'normally' in fact. Which is intriguing. For the present, though, let us stay with the case of the unfortunate Dayananda.

Chatura reports that his previous life – i.e. Dayananda's – ended when he was **shot**. So far as can be determined, and infuriatingly the record is not clear beyond objection on this point, his death injuries were exclusively the result of the landmine blast. The remainder of the patrol made no contact with the enemy, nor are there reports of any shooting, both of which facts suggest that the idea of a fatal bullet is wrong. Therefore we may conjecture that, although Dayananda's *expectation* was that any incident which befell him that day would involve small arms fire, the landmine blast was what actually occurred. Accordingly when he sustained his fatal wounds, he thought, "I've been shot," his *expectation* of the worst danger that could befall him. If so, this would have been his last *conscious* thought. The truth was different, but not known to the then unconscious Dayananda.

So what about his soul?

My Christian cultural belief is that a personal totality, a soul, exists and endures throughout eternity. There is "no testable evidence whatever" for anything of the sort, of course, so my belief – or subjective prejudice, if you prefer – is simply an aspect of my Faith. And even the most dogmatic, atheistic scientismist has faith, be it purely in the power and objectivity of his own capacity for rational thought. Faith, therefore, is an aspect of consciousness. Humanity is equipped with it. My soul, to settle the matter here, I regard as existing in a parallel state of being, where it represents my 'virtuous' capital in God's bank – in the crudest of terms – to form the 'me' state in which I shall be incorporated after death has disposed of my Earthly body (Matthew 6. 19-20). This is essentially what I believe about my soul, and I try and conduct myself accordingly as part of my personal relationship with God. Atheistic scientism may just regard me as mentally deranged. I would expect Dayananda's soul to be similarly accommodated. So I do not view the soul as part of our present consideration of consciousness, mind and brain.

The mind makes plans in relation to the stimuli reaching it from the brain. We should view the 'Goal-directed Controller', and the other 'Controllers' we have noted, all as one indivisible package. Parts of Mind have specific functions, but it is not separable into independently functioning entities. Its role as a single administrator is likewise borne out in this case by some plans that Dayananda had had to use his army pay to buy his family a small tractor to improve their farm. Chatura states that this tractor is a fact. Dayananda's father confirms that it was discussed, but remained simply a plan which, had his son lived, would most probably have come to fruition. Therefore we may conjecture that the tractor was part of a mental construct which, bar the formality of actually purchasing the machine, was as good as real in Dayananda's mind. It also adds to the implication that mind has a memory. I have no difficulty in supporting this, because my memory of who I am and the steps through time by which I have become my present self, are an essential part of my being *me*.

I had better add a cynical note, here. Perhaps the tractor is a mistake on Chatura's part, but part of a hopeful ploy by a Sri Lankan small farmer to elicit sympathy from a – comparatively – rich Western psychical researcher, who might just find it in his generous heart to buy him one. I reckon this is a shocking suggestion, but it is the sort of 'explanation' which some dogmatic materialists tend to advance when faced with evidence of the anomalous. We may as well have the possibility of it out in the open as we proceed.

So where is the mind if it does not cease when the brain dies and decomposes? We shall look at a couple of 'oddball theories' later. The sort of questions we need to address are how mind achieves survival, for how long it may remain 'alive', in what state of worthwhile mental organisation it may 'live', and where it might be – as in the period between the Earthly lives in our Sri Lankan case. It would appear to dissociate itself, locally, from the body's continued functioning once consciousness has been lost, as we have seen, both in the NDE case already quoted and Dayananda's ultimately fatal wound. There are many other cases suggestive of the same 'behaviour'. Exactly what does it do when we sleep, I wonder? I have found no definitive answer to this question, either. Perhaps it is unfair to ask it at our present state of brain / mind knowledge, because any answer will bear directly upon one's perception of the brain's functions and all aspects of consciousness generally. These have yet to be fully examined and defined, as we have said.

In so far as it makes choices and regulates the conscious actions of the body, the mind ought to be credited with the capacity for morality. As mind is, so its possessor behaves, in effect. This seems instinctive to us, culturally, as we have noted; we talk of people as 'open minded' or 'closed minded', and so on.

The essential quality of particular individuals is given well enough by such descriptions. If mind can exist independently of brain, do such attributes form part of it in its disembodied state? I would suggest that they do; mind seems to be a package in this respect. We shall find this when we consider what are broadly viewed as *post mortem* communications 'from the beyond' by individual personalities. Exactly *what* is communicating is the key question here.

Could it be the soul? As I have already stated, I do not think that it is. I do not see my soul as attached to me and constantly interacting with my brain. I suspect it is, as I have said, in another state of being. There, in terms inseparable from my religious Faith, I regard it as a combination of chronicler and 'banker'. I base this upon Christian tradition, and also upon eschatological grounds (matters concerning death, judgement, fate of the soul and of the material universe itself). When I die my chronicle and bank account will show the full nature of the life I have lived, and I shall be judged and dealt with by God accordingly. This is purely a matter of belief, and has "no testable evidence whatever" in its support.

Now, if I die in a state of mental and moral degeneration due to illness in my advanced age, is it my condition at death which is liable to judgement, or is some consideration to be taken of the quality of the rest of my life? Here the chronicler may come to my aid. Similarly, had I been born mentally handicapped, and essentially incapable of moral understanding in consequence, should I face judgement upon death as though in possession of the normal human range of moral faculties? Probably not, I would suggest. Therefore I view my soul as a species of 'aetheric double', as a Spiritualist might term it. It is not available for day-to-day cerebral, mental, or psychic labour. Thus I doubt that anything to do with a soul transferred from Dayananda to Chatura.

So what did transfer in order to give Chatura memories (and characteristics) which should have been exclusive to Dayandanda? The late Prof. Ian Stevenson, who did an immense amount of research into cases of reincarnation, put forward the idea of the 'psychophore' ('soul-bearing') as the means of transmission between people in reincarnation cases. He saw it as carrying data from the 're-incarnating personality' to the child in the case. He credited it with a form of will-power in so far as the psychophore appeared on occasion to have the ability to get its own way and be reincarnated into a specific, pre-chosen child – on the sole evidence of that child's speaking of the 'interim' state of the reincarnated personality. It could also carry physical attributes, such as birthmarks or physical defects.

This last apparent property is particularly interesting in that, for it to be feasible, it would have to affect the DNA in the cells of the developing embryo. Heredity, through DNA, instructs cells how to divide and develop – to become an organ or a limb, for example. The DNA not only governs what the cells shall become in the developing body, but also regulates such matters as size, apparently by instructing the appropriate cells when to start and stop their dividing. Thus if the instruction to "stop dividing" is slow in coming, a particular organ might be extra large, or a certain limb unusually long. Stevenson's very careful research shows that such characteristics are often present in the case of the 'new' body of the reincarnating personality. It is legitimate to ask 'Why?' and 'How?' Dr Rupert Sheldrake has also investigated the same sort of anomalies that are implied by reincarnation. He has evolved the idea of the 'morphic field', which extends from one individual to another, and has an influence of much the same type as the psychophore. Both ideas support the concept of a transfer of information between one personality – *post mortem* – and another – i.e. the reincarnating personality, which is genetically independent and in most cases yet to be conceived. None of this ought to happen, according to material laws; but it apparently does, nonetheless. We shall look a little closer at reincarnation later.

If the mechanism is, somehow, 'all in the mind', what attributes of the mind might bring it about? I am viewing the mind as being independent of the physical, mortal brain, so I need to suggest where the mind may be, both when the brain is alive and when it is dead. This pitches me right into the area of 'oddball theories', which are quite likely wrong, but uninvestigated because so little work has been done upon mind and brain anomalies. In one sense this makes any speculation virtually worthless, because there is not much sound data to work upon in the first place. There are also many *a priori* utterances to the effect that there is nothing to investigate, so it must follow that to finance any work in this field is to waste resources. Obviously I do not agree with this line of thought, yet I cannot advance anything more respectable than an 'oddball theory' or two as alternatives to counter it. Hopefully, by setting them up for examination, I shall provide targets for those of differing points of view who must then either knock down what I present, offering better alternatives or, perhaps, develop it in more promising directions.

15. Mind – Synaptic Science

We have suggested that the mind works independently of the brain, and is capable of existing after the brain's death. Where might the mind be, therefore, especially *post mortem*?

Brain scans show the electrical output – or overflow – from our neurons' interaction via their synaptic gaps. Therefore we are accustomed to think of brain activity as being exclusively chemical / electrical by nature, and only detectable as such from beyond the bone-box of the skull. But, in addition, it is also true that magnetoencephalographic (MEG) images show brain activation, somehow, *outside* the skull. Prof. Peter Mansfield, 'founding father' of scanner technology at Nottingham University puts it this way, "MEG images can be a shocking mess. It's not good enough to see this cloud of activation outside someone's head and tell people simply not to pay any attention to it." (*Psi Researcher, Number 16, Spring 1995*). This suggestion of non-attention implies that there has been some *a priori* reasoning in progress somewhere.

It has also been demonstrated that two individual brains' electrical activities can 'harmonise' with one another; "Evidence obtained from over twenty studies using electroencephalographic (EEG) and / or functional magnetic resonance imaging (fMRI) indicates that direct brain to brain communication can occur between pairs of participants when completely isolated from each other but remaining in mutual rapport. According to orthodox neurophysiology, such communication is impossible because brains depend solely upon their outlying sensory systems for incoming information. These studies indicate otherwise, so something must be going on." (R Charman *Journal of the Society for Psychical Research, Number 885,* October 2006).

Is this 'telepathy', therefore? "Most *SPR* members would probably agree with Chamber's dictionary definition of telepathy as; 'Communication between mind and mind otherwise than through the senses'. This very reasonable definition is based upon thousands of anecdotal accounts each, therefore, a conscious experience, and is assumed by ganzfeld [an experimental procedure] and other studies where the 'sender' endeavours to 'send' conscious imagery to the 'receiver' who is verbalising their conscious impressions. Many may well extend this definition to include apparent mediumistic communication with brainless minds, implying survival of conscious self after brain death with the development of an advanced ability to communicate your thoughts through the brainmind of someone you never met until now. In this scenario each conscious mind possesses a deathless autonomy separate from its brain, with the latter relegated to the role of optional extra to be discarded without loss and, it would seem, positive gain… In contrast, EEG and fMRI 'sender/receiver' paired studies find only brain to brain communication with no conscious awareness that communication has occurred." (R Charman *Paranormal Review, Issue 45, January 2008*).

From the work Charman quotes it is obvious that "something must be going on", but electro-magnetic waves do not seem to be doing the job. In any case, there is an additional difficulty in that such waves do not travel very far at the low energy levels generated by the brain, so even if two 'brainminds' in a state of 'harmony' – i.e. their electrical activities showing the same things to the scanning apparatus – can achieve this harmony over short distances, their harmonious state will not be detectable beyond a few metres.

Is there anything else which may account for the "thousands of anecdotal accounts" of anomalous phenomena? Quantum Entanglement, the process by which any two atoms which have at some stage been associated with one another remain responsive to one another ever afterwards, is one 'catch all' which would be applicable to this problem. For its action in this context I know of "no testable evidence whatever", and I do not like to employ long words and complicated theories to dodge awkward questions which I cannot address in plain terms. I do not like Quantum matters, either; they offend common sense, even though the answers I seek may lie within their operations. We must touch upon them shortly, just in case.

However, perhaps what we are seeking is not electro-magnetic waves, but light. For good or ill, I have come across the following, which is possibly just another 'oddball theory'.

Writing of 'Free Radicals and the Wholeness of the Organism' (*Scientific and Medical Network Review*, Spring 2005) Roger Taylor sets out the following – which I have edited slightly:

"All biochemical processes are transactions of energy. So first we must remember that energy is packaged into precisely defined units called *quanta*. The energy content – or size – of a quantum is measured in electron volts, and depends upon the frequency: thus a quantum of light is bigger than one of infrared or microwave. A molecule which absorbs a quantum stores the energy as some kind of higher-energy state. In the case of infrared, there are a variety of states of molecular vibration. But a light quantum has sufficient energy to push an electron out of its stable ground (or *orbital*) into a higher energy orbit. The whole molecule is then said to be in an *electron-excited state* (EES). But all these energy stares are unstable and, after a while, the energy is released again as a quantum of the appropriate frequency. So in the case of EESs the electron jumps back again to its stable orbital, and a quantum of light is released. This quantum can then either be directly transferred to another molecule (where it may contribute to a chemical reaction) or it can be emitted as a photon of electromagnetic radiation. In turn this photon can either be absorbed by another molecule, or lost as heat.

"Most biochemical reactions as studied in the test-tube, involve transactions of infrared quanta rather than light. This is one reason why the importance of light in the living being is still not generally recognised in the West. It is a different story in Russia, where they have benefited from the work of Alexander Gurvich… As far back as the 1920s, he discovered that dividing cells produce an ultra-weak radiation (now termed biophotons) which could stimulate mitosis (i.e. the division of cells, each producing daughter cells with the same characteristics as the parent cells) in resting cells. Even then it was clear to Gurvich that this light constituted an information bearing signal. This finding lent support to his field theories of biological organisation…

"Since then scientists from many countries have contributed to the development of what we may call 'quantum biology'. Whilst it has not been entirely proved to the satisfaction of the mainstream (scientific Establishments) all this work is pointing to the conclusion that a living being is unified by a single quantum wave-function in the same way that an atom or molecule is. (For further reading see Mae-Wan Ho's book *The Rainbow and the Worm*.) In this conception Light plays a central role. And excited molecules are understood to be *de-localised* and shared at least over large molecular ensembles, and probably the whole organism. Moreover, as the EESs decay they are continually regenerated. Thus an organism normally stores a lot of light.

"How is this light generated? It is here that free radicals come on to the scene. Prof. Voeikov makes the critical point that none of the usual biochemical reactions is of sufficient energy to generate light. This can only be done by the reactions of free radicals. (Prominent among these are Reactive Oxygen Species – ROSs) ... the Brain uses some 20% of the oxygen we take in ... Oxygen used by the Brain must represent a different type of metabolic pathway (from the processes in the rest of the body).

"...The characteristic wholeness of an organism must have been present (in evolutionary / biochemical terms) from the beginning: that is, long before the molecular signals, such as hormones and neurotransmitters, were evolved. Such wholeness could not have been achieved by molecular signals alone, because these require time to diffuse towards their receptors. Instead it would seem to require an underlying network of instantaneous communication. This is now coming to be understood as a field of delocalised electrons excited by light energy – now often termed a *photon field*. Furthermore, as maintained by Mae-Wan Ho, for all life's processes to hang together, they must also cohere into a single complex rhythmic order, in which the fastest rhythms (and these are very fast: resonant energy transfer between molecules takes 10^{-14} sec) are nested into progressively slower ones, such as brain waves, heart beats, and hormonal cycles, ultimately to the slowest; the life cycle.

"The rhythmic release of this energy, which is capable of a wide range of frequencies, going up even to the megaherz region, is consistent with their role as pacemakers of metabolic process. Indeed Voeikov suggests that modulations of frequency rather than amplitude may be the most important informative factor in cellular regulation.

"All these complex temporal patterns… are also precisely localised in space. Thus we have a deep space-time structure, which is intensely dynamic in all its aspects…"

In short, there is an intriguing possibility that much of what goes on within our bodies, which of course includes our brains, would appear to generate minute quantities of light, albeit upon a sub-atomic level. Light, as energy, would therefore be present within us if this idea proves correct. Detecting and analysing it are different considerations entirely, of course! How might light tell the world outside us anything about our brains and/or minds, even if it is the communications' medium?

An answer might lie in a theoretical concept of Creation which has six-dimensions. Extra dimensions to our normal perceptions of 3D plus Time are perfectly respectable in physics, let it be remembered. Our 6D universe would need to include features – or concepts – dubbed 'Twistors':

According to Claude LeBrun of the State University of New York, twisters… "unlocked a huge reservoir of algebraic geometry that could be applied to physics." In layman's terms the essential idea of Twistor Theory is that our familiar world of three dimensions plus Time does not necessarily describe the whole of Creation. There could be deeper realities in its construction than we deal with as a matter of course. In this vein, the concept of space-time is a facet of a six-dimensional universe which we may refer to as 'twistor space'. The geometry we learn at school is founded on the propositions of Euclid, making a point in space the basic geometrical unit. In terms of twistor space, however, the fundamental unit is a twisting ray of light – apparently infinitely long and stretching back into the past as well as projecting into the future. At this stage we have to place our trust in the logic of mathematicians who are confident that any point in space-time which seems to us fundamental is, in fact, a derived quantity in twistor geometry. But this is what makes it interesting in terms of what it does to twisting light rays. They intersect at that same point.

Mathematically, twisters can be dealt with by the concept that every twistor can be represented with four complex numbers. (These take the form of 'a+b where i is the square root of − 1 and a and b are real numbers'. One of the complex numbers turns out to be redundant, and because each remaining co-ordinate depends on two real numbers, twistor space is six-dimensional.) This is not our everyday view of Creation, and that is why I am obliged to take the concept on trust. The idea of twistor space was well known in mathematical circles over a century ago, but physicists only became interested in its possibilities in the 1960s, thanks to the work of Roger Penrose at Oxford.

I venture to suggest that light may be the connection between EESs and Twistor-space. If a six dimensional Creation is, in fact, the reality, we are living upon only that portion of the material 'iceberg' which is visible to us above the water. The additional dimensions which are out of sight to us − in normal circumstances − could be the essential bulk of the universe which keeps it all in balance. Whilst I am not − I repeat, I am *not* − trying to suggest that the extra dimensions necessarily contain the 95% 'dark' matter and 'dark' energy which we cannot account for, it seems fair enough to state that if we can accept this unknown 95% of material, we should at least be prepared to countenance the extra dimensions suggested by Twistor Theory. Let us also recall that twisting ray of light − apparently infinitely long and stretching back into the past as well as projecting into the future.

If this ray of light stretches back into the past, it can be said to have a *history.* If it has been interrupted or refracted slightly at various times during this history, perhaps these characteristics will endure within it, rather like the light pulses travelling along a fibre-optic cable. So, if a point in space-time that seems to us to be fundamental is a derived quantity in twistor geometry, and if twisting light rays intersect at that point, might not some of these 'points' comprise the energy of photons deriving from synaptic activity in the brain but transferred to the extra dimensions of twistor geometry by light, which is a universal property of Creation? Could light therefore be a factor common to *all* dimensions? Could this light carry information from the brain into the dimensions of twistor geometry, and there retain it for as long as the twistor light rays endure? Could the result be an active and enduring part of mind? Such ideas must surely be worth informed consideration.

If so, is it not possible that information might remain in its twistor state after the death of the brain and, if accessible to people still living – I suggest a role for the mind here, perhaps itself located in twistor geometry – and perceptible by them, provide an explanation for many anomalies such as reincarnation and ghosts? If we can consider this as a possibility, can we not also investigate it by employing the normal physical sciences, since we are not dealing with anything that is anecdotal but with possibilities which can be expressed in terms of mathematics and physics?

A similar idea occurred to Prof. Ian Stevenson, to whom we have referred as a notable authority on reincarnation. In the *Paranormal Review, Issue 47, July 2008*, Donald J West recalls that Stevenson was amongst a group of investigators considering "…the work of the Polish clairvoyant Stefan Ossowiecki. [One of the other investigators] noted that many of the tests with Ossowiecki were designed to exclude telepathy, but even when it was not excluded he could only produce targets that had some personal significance to the agent [whose visual stimuli / memory he would have been required to view clairvoyantly]. She argued that if he was able to view the past independently of telepathic rapport, then the past must exist in some form open to viewing. Ian seemed to concur, since his last words in the [report] were; 'The phenomena of Ossowiecki and of some of the other gifted persons show that minds can function independently of brains. They show too that the past continues to exist. I doubt whether scientists can discover any more important facts than these.'" (cf *"A World in a Grain of Sand"; Ian Stevenson, Mary Rose Barrington, Zofia Weaver*)

In short, might not such indications and reasoning provide a useful link between hard science and the anecdotal type of evidence for all those sorts of things which 'Scientism' dismisses, or avoids, as being untestable and unrepeatable? Surely some serious investigation should be undertaken. Will Alexander Gurvich's work stand up to rigorous modern scrutiny, for example? If it does, will it produce a basis for reappraising ideas about all sorts of anomalies and the attitude of the sciences towards them? If it does not, then it will have been eliminated from these areas of research. Nothing is lost by considering it.

The mainstream search for consciousness tends to concentrate upon electro-magnetism. Prof. J McFadden of the University of Surrey reckons information is held in an electromagnetic field *surrounding* the brain (*Synchronous firing and its influence upon the brain*; Journal of Consciousness Studies, vol. 9, 2002). He cites cases of hyranencephaly – a condition in which as little as 5% of the 'normal' amount of brain tissue may be present within the skull, and yet the affected individual functions quite normally, suggesting perhaps that a great deal of the brain's function is taking place 'elsewhere'. We have noted above that MEG scans show something going on outside the skull. Is this a lead to follow?

A few easy charges of heresy might be levelled at anyone not taking it up and, instead, pursuing light quanta or 'biophotons', as I have seen them referred to. There does not appear to be a great deal of interest in anything associated with the bio-photon idea in 'respectable' or classical scientific circles, anyway. Which is a pity, because a certain amount of work along these lines has been done, if only by theorists, and there seems to be something here to consider. Probably the main difficulty is the practical one of actually observing bio-photons in action, in order that their properties may be tested under experimental conditions. It is all very well to say, in effect, 'Let's pretend…' as, effectively, I have done above, diving into extra dimensions for good measure. I can offer no observation or experiment to consider, I can cite no circumstances repeatable to order, and I have no conclusions which are based upon such foundations and are able to be tested by others. In short, what I have suggested lacks the basic disciplines of science. Yet I still view it as an intriguing possibility.

Electromagnetic waves associated with the brain do not seem powerful enough to travel very far from their source, and their decay does not make them promising candidates for causing *post mortem* phenomena, let alone supplying the medium for all that is often bundled up together in the term 'telepathy'. So, if we accept that such things exist, in so far as they are experienced and reported, it seems to me sensible to look at some other source of energy, or data-bearing medium, which might the better explain them. Bio-photons are at least available, and various researchers have reached conclusions about them. So rather than treat the biophotons and the researchers as something undesirable, why not start research from the knowledge-base which they have constructed to date? I do no doubt that there will initially be found to be more 'bathwater' than 'babies' in the case, my own suggestion very likely coming within that category. Accordingly, the thing to do is surely to strain off the bathwater and see what any emerging babies look like. I say again, nothing is lost by considering and testing a currently 'non-respectable' idea. It might suddenly produce a great "Eureka!" cry from someone, and a whole new branch of physics would then be the plaything of graduate students working upon their PhDs.

If this looks a little startling, any idea borne out by properly done research which suggests a means by which minds communicate, both when alive and *post mortem,* must be worth investigating. I am attracted to the possibility because it may provide a mechanism via hard physics to examine all manner of spooky things – or anomalous phenomena, if the term is preferred – which present means of investigation, often based upon psychology alone, have not delivered all that well.

If this is an 'oddball theory' par excellence, let us leave it there, but remember it in conjunction with Twistor Space as a possibility.

16. Out of Body Experiences

I have suggested that brain, mind, and soul are separate entities. The activities of brain and mind I have likened to the working of a World War II RAF plotting room. The soul I conceive as an entity apart, and exclusive to the individual's relationship with God. It is not involved in the mechanics of material life. Some means by which the mind might continue to exist *post mortem* have been outlined. None of them is necessarily correct but, given our present lack of knowledge concerning mind, brain, and consciousness, I consider all evidence-backed hints at possible means whereby the mind may endure, and thus account for reports of various anomalous experiences, to be worth noting. I want now to survey, as thoroughly as possible given the limits of a few pages, the broad field of just such anomalous experiences, and show that they are both surprisingly common and suggestive of the way our minds function.

We have noted a role for the mind in an Out of Body Experience – OBE – in a clinical context. By means that do not seem to have anything to do with the patient's brain, which was effectively dead at the material time, the patient was able later to report accurately upon her surroundings, and also told of meeting other identified personalities in a *post mortem* state. Intriguingly, some OBEs have been experienced by people who were born blind. An account of their experiences is given by Kenneth Ring and Sharon Cooper in their book *Mindsight* (William James Centre for Consciousness Studies). The blind had the same view – from near the ceiling – of the operating theatres that our quoted case reported, and some of them apparently ascended through floors and roof to obtain, and accurately report, panoramic views of the surrounding area. One woman described the view of her body on the lower bed of a two-tier bunk, from a position where it should have been denied to her. Some found their first experience of seeing "not a big deal", whilst others described it as unsettling in various ways.

Experimentally it appears that when the visual areas of the brain are impeded for a long time, e.g. in experiments where a blindfold has been worn for a week or more, these areas have been shown by brain scans to have started processing stimuli for other parts of the brain. This may have some bearing upon the 'just know' element of 'mindsight'. More work needs to be done to clarify exactly what may be happening in such cases. One possibility has to be that the blind person's mind, in its OBE state, is somehow picking up stimuli from the brains – or minds – of the sighted, and using them to inform itself of its status and surroundings. This could explain the 'local' information, e.g. the reports of what was taking place within the operating theatre, but it does not seem to account for the ascents to the roof plus the descriptions of the view obtained from it. If there actually was someone else upon the roof at the time, was it that person's visual stimuli that were 'tapped' by the experient's mind? We have no information from which to follow up this possibility, unfortunately. Could it have been that the mind of the caretaker, or one of the builders of the roof, perhaps, was somehow available to provide the necessary visual information? And if this was the mechanism, was the mind still living, or enduring *post mortem*? Too many questions are left unanswered for the reports to be dismissed blandly as, for example, hallucinations. There are any number of *What?* and *How?* questions which suggest themselves here, and which science is best equipped to answer.

Some scientific interest is in fact being taken. There is, apparently, an experiment already running at a prominent teaching hospital in which a lap-top computer with a programme comprising strong shapes and bright colours changing in a predetermined sequence, is fixed near the operating theatre's ceiling. Anyone reporting an OBE whilst undergoing surgery is to be asked, "What did you see on the computer screen?" But to me this seems to be perhaps the wrong question.

Logically the first question should be, "Did you notice a lap-top computer in an odd place?" and the second, "Were you able to see the screen?" If both answers were "Yes" and a clear narrative followed, the experimenters would have the beginning of a case to pursue. I would suggest that a better idea might be to have someone located in a room near the operating theatre with a pile of magazines (titles and contents unknown to the operating theatre personnel) and under instructions to read several, chosen at random, for the duration of the operation. If the patient, perhaps even briefed in advance, to "Go exploring with your mind, if you get the opportunity" can subsequently describe the reader, the contents of the magazines, and even the reader's reaction to them, then there would be a definite mind-to-mind contact possibility to follow up. This approach seems to me better than the hopeful discovery and viewing of a lap-top screen. No doubt the results of the experiment as presently constructed will be published one day, and we shall then see what has occurred.

I wonder why OBEs tend to be experienced from up in the air. We are used to living in three dimensions, to-and-fro, side-to-side, and up-and-down. However humans are restricted in the vertical dimension to what we can see and reach, and the 'down' effectively means the ground we stand upon. This is not the common experience of fish and birds, however. Perhaps in our hunter-gatherer evolutionary past the 'best-fitted' of the age were those who were good at climbing trees, and who could accordingly obtain a much better view of the land around them than those who had to labour away scouting out the possibilities entirely at ground level. Thus a gene which encouraged a 'take to the trees and get a good view of the land before setting off to hunt and gather' approach to life would have given those possessing it a useful advantage in the battle to eat, and possibly to mate, too. Perhaps, therefore, a mind under stress automatically seeks to go upwards and scan the terrain for opportunities and dangers. This is nice and plausible until we ask ourselves what is providing it with visual stimuli in the circumstances of OBEs in an operating theatre. Do we tap into what the decorator who painted the theatre's ceiling saw and remembered? And how about the caretaker, or one-time builder upon the hospital roof? Do they offer a way out of the stress of contemplating the operation? At present we can only ask such questions.

OBEs can occur spontaneously in daily life, and I can offer an example at second hand. A lady I know well once cheerily told me that, a few days earlier, she had been driving her car when she suddenly 'found herself' sitting in mid air about six feet above it, and slightly to the right – effectively in the middle of the road. She proceeded thus for some hundreds of yards before 'returning' to her driving seat. What had happened, did I think? I explained about OBEs and asked if she was under any stress at the time, had slept badly, had taken medication, or was in any other way not feeling 100% well. No – she was her usual robust self, she assured me. She is, for the record, a singularly stalwart, perpetually busy woman, who leads an active outdoor life, usually gardening, and who walks dogs for an elderly neighbour whilst exercising her own horse. Her attitude to life is uncomplicated, and markedly no-nonsense. "If it happens again, for goodness sake pull in and stop," I urged her. "It might be the start of a stroke, or something, and I might be driving along the same road at the time!"

She laughed heartily at this, but a couple of weeks later had to go and see her doctor about digestive troubles. It transpired that that she had suddenly developed an allergic reaction to certain types of food. Since she was in her mid-sixties at the time, this occasioned quite an upheaval in her diet and life generally. Possibly in its early stages her trouble had something to do with her OBE. Experimental work by neuro-scientist Dr Olaf Blanke has suggested that trouble in the brain's temporal junction, which is known to produce what are, broadly speaking, termed 'location displacement sensations', may have had a hand in the matter. It is located at the far end of a tree of blood vessels. If blood pressure drops, this area will accordingly be affected before those enjoying a better supply. This could be one reason, in purely clinical terms, for OBEs.

There are also reports of an OBE state in which the experient can travel, at will, apparently in real space and time, obtain verifiable information about locations, people, and events near and distant, and also become acquainted with *post mortem* personalities. At such times the normal bodily processes of the experient are under stress – e.g. during an operation – and consciousness, in its plotting table brain-input portion, is disrupted. However, whatever it is that does the perceiving during an OBE is still active, perceptive, and functioning – driving a car, for example. Certainly in my friend's case it could be argued that the first stirrings of her allergic troubles might have caused her metabolism to disrupt the normal working of her brain, so that its spatial perceptions of a familiar landscape went askew and she hallucinated that she was outside her car and 'airborne' for while whilst still in control of the vehicle. This seems a sensible idea, although there is "no testable evidence whatever" for it after the spontaneous event. Laboratory work involving drug-induced states in volunteers might provide some, one day.

The accounts of the 'Travelling consciousness', both blind and sighted, from patients upon operating tables are not as straightforward. They are, by their own validated reports, experiences *out of* the body. The centre of consciousness has migrated, somehow, to a different location. Whilst my friend driving along a familiar road might have had no difficulty in unconsciously imagining (but why?) how the scenery would appear from a different viewpoint, it is not commonly the case that patients in hospital for brain surgery wander around upon the roof before undergoing the operation, especially if they are blind. Therefore we have to account for their accurate reports which suggest that this is precisely what their minds, at least, were doing independently of their brains. The use of visual input from other brains, obtained in ways not known, is perhaps the simplest explanation in these – and similar – cases on record, but we really do not know what we are dealing with. By the same token, we do not know what we are looking for. Every suggestion will need to be followed up if we are, eventually, to hit upon the truth, I think.

Science can probably come up with the answers by established means, but may have to extend its present acceptable boundaries somewhat in order to do so. Prof. John Poynton writing in the *Journal of the Society for Psychical Research, Number 864, July, 2001* puts it this way; "As suggested at the beginning of this paper, OBE tends to challenge prevailing ideas of what is 'normal' and 'real'. These ideas are largely carried over from the nineteenth century, and even in parapsychology have tended to remain untouched by radical advances in twentieth-century physics and philosophy. The view developed in this paper is that as long as psi [anomalous / psychic] phenomena are expected to be "Explicable within the framework of accepted principles of mainstream science" (Irwin, 1999. p2) as seen from the perspective of psychology, the phenomena will remain inexplicable." He argues, in detail too great to be reproduced here, for greater and more broadly based scientific involvement in investigating OBEs.

However, for science to provide answers, or at least suggest lines of logical, evidence-based enquiry, it will first have to take the usually anecdotal evidence – such as my driving friend's report of her OBE – seriously. If it will do so, it can then proceed from the point of view that there really is something to be investigated. OBEs are part of the phenomena of Creation. People experience them, but we do not know how or why. For a fuller and more truthful understanding of ourselves we surely ought to be taking steps to try and find out. Science has a role to play in the investigation. It is the truth of the matter which we seek, and all means at our disposal should be employed. Is such an approach too 'oddball' to justify?

17. Near Death Experiences

OBEs are in many ways closely akin to NDEs – Near Death Experiences – investigation of which is often shunned by scientists of the atheistic-scientismist school because it can be too suggestive of an afterlife. Since all good scientismists know, *a priori* that there is no *post mortem* consciousness, let alone existence, it follows that reports deriving from NDEs of another 'world' are all hallucination or falsehood, and simply not worth bothering about. But there is too much anecdotal evidence simply to dismiss what is reported, be it hallucination pure and simple, or the experience of some other state – physical or of consciousness – which could be defined and investigated if only it could be pinned own in the first place.

Let us look at an NDE. We could do worse than refer to a case from the early eighth century, recorded by the Venerable Bede, no less. He had his information from a monk named Haemgils, who had befriended the individual who had had the experience, a certain Drycthelm (Penguin translation; *A History of the English Church and People,* book 5, chapter 12). Drycthelm "...died in the early hours of the night. But at daybreak he returned to life and suddenly sat up to the great consternation of those weeping around the body, who ran away... He described what he had seen as follows; 'A handsome man in a shining robe was my guide, and we walked in silence in what appeared to be an easterly direction. As we travelled onwards we came to a very broad deep valley of infinite length. The side to our left was dreadful with burning flames, whilst the opposite side was equally horrible, with raging hail and bitter snow blowing and driving in all directions. Both sides were filled with men's souls, which seemed to be hurled from one side to the other by the fury of the tempest... I began to think that this was Hell... But as if in response to my thoughts, the guide who preceded me said; "Do not think this, for this is not Hell as you imagine.'

"When he led me gradually to the further end, much alarmed by the terrible scene, I saw the place suddenly begin to grow dim, and the darkness concealed everything. As we entered it, this darkness gradually grew so obscure that I could see nothing except it, and the outline and robes of my guide... When my guide had brought me to this place, he suddenly disappeared and left me alone in the midst of the darkness... whilst I was thus beset about by... black darkness... there appeared behind me on the road by which I had come what appeared to be a bright star shining in the gloom, which grew in size and came swiftly towards me. As it approached ...it was clear that it was my former guide, who took a road to the right and began to lead me towards the south-east. He soon brought me out of darkness into an atmosphere of clear light, and as he led me forwards in the bright light, I saw before us a tremendous wall which seemed to be of infinite length and height in all directions. As I could see no gate, window, or entrance in it, I began to wonder why we went up to the wall. But all at once... we were on top of it. Within lay a very broad and pleasant meadow, filled with the scent of flowers... In this meadow were innumerable companies of men in white robes, and many parties of happy people were sitting together. And as my guide led me through these crowds of happy citizens... he said, "No, this is not the Kingdom of Heaven as you imagine."

"...I saw ahead of us a much more lovely light than before, and heard a sweet sound of people singing, whilst a scent of such surpassing fragrance emanated from the place that the earlier scent I had thought so wonderful now seemed quite indifferent... As I was hoping that we should enter this delightful place, my guide suddenly halted, and without stopping, retraced his steps and led me back along the road by which we had come... "For when I left you for a while, I did so in order to discover what your future would be." When he told me this, I was most reluctant to return to my body, for I was entranced by the pleasantness and beauty of the place I could see and of the company I saw there. But I did not dare to question my guide, and meanwhile I suddenly found myself alive amongst men once more."

The experience had such a profound effect upon Drycthelm that he put his worldly affairs in order and became a monk. I have edited the account rather, in the interests of brevity. I also suspect

Brother Haemgils of having altered it here and there to give it an orthodox contemporary Christian slant. It has, though, all the features of a 'classic' NDE, even though it dates from about AD 710. But why should that make it unreliable? The Scriptures of all religions are ancient, as are the foundations of our historical and philosophical knowledge. We are happy enough to build upon them. Yet because of their age and subjective origin, records like this NDE for which there is "no testable evidence whatsoever" are all too often rejected automatically. Which is a pity.

In his book *The Paranormal – A Bishop Investigates*, Bishop Hugh Montefiore sets out a dozen features generally agreed to be common to NDEs. See how closely the report of Drycthelm's experience coincides with them:

1. A pervasive feeling of peace, joy, and bliss, essentially inexpressible beyond metaphor.
2. Leaving the physical body. Quite often the body is then perceived as though from some location above it.
3. Entering a 'tunnel', or an enclosing blackness, usually with a pinpoint of light at the other end.
   "We came to a very broad and deep valley of infinite length… A bright star, shining in the gloom, which grew in size and came swiftly towards me."
   (The features of a tunnel were possibly beyond Drycthelm's cultural experience. The present-day fame of Hezekiah's tunnel at Jerusalem (2 Kings, 20.20*)* was not a feature of the Latin Bible available to Bede, where it would have been rendered *rivus* or *aquae ductus* – channel or conduit – as opposed to *cuniculus* the Roman engineers' term for a tunnel.)
4. A sensation of movement and of approaching / being approached by a brilliant, but not dazzling, white or golden light.
5. Meeting a 'Being of Light'.
   "A handsome man in a shining robe was my guide."
   Explanations are given in response to thoughts.

(This is the first Being of Light who seems to take the role of a guide, as opposed to the second Being of Light who generally has more to say by way of explanation.)

6. Coming upon a barrier, seen as physical or assumed as part of the new location, that marks a point of no return.
"I saw before us a tremendous wall which seemed to be of infinite length and infinite height in all directions."

7. Arriving at another location, often a pastoral scene as it would be known to the NDE experient.
"Within lay a very broad and pleasant meadow ...scent of flowers... Light greater than the brightness of daylight."

8. Meeting deceased relatives and other loved ones, and perhaps conversing with them.
"In this meadow were innumerable companies of men in white robes, and many parties of happy people were sitting together."

9. Experiencing some form of a life review, occasionally there is given what seems to be some intimation of the future life the NDE experient will live upon return to earth.

10. Reaching a decision to return to earthly life. There is often a marked reluctance to leave the blissful state for the known hum-drum of the experient's normal daily life.
"I saw ahead of us a much more lovely light than before, and heard in it a sweet sound of people singing, while a scent of such surpassing fragrance emanated from the place that the earlier scent I had thought so wonderful now grew quite indifferent... My guide suddenly halted and retraced his steps. I was most reluctant to return to my body."

11. Rapid return to the physical body, often with a thump.
"I suddenly found myself alive amongst men once more."

12. Aftermath – in which all fear of death is removed and the experience regarded as the most vivid and profound of a lifetime.

Is it not interesting to note that Drycthelm's account from another age, another culture, different material parameters, and transmitted to us via the filter of an ecclesiastical background, accords so well with Bishop Montefiore's dozen features common to NDEs, which are derived from very many of the cases on record? Could those people whose NDEs comprise these cases all have had a working knowledge of the works of the Venerable Bede in order to account for their essential confirmation of the features of Drycthelm's experience? Some sceptics might wish to have it that way. In addition, the dozen or so features which we have suggested typify a NDE are given independently in various forms of words by other researchers (cf K. Ring *Life at Death, 1980;* Ian Currie *You Cannot Die*, BCA), and are also common to all cultures.

At the risk of becoming boring let me give another NDE account, this time from October 1979, (Please see *Driven by Eternity,* John Bevere, *Warner / Hachette.* for the full text). It concerns the ten-year-old son of an American Evangelical Minister. This lad had placed a small television set upon the edge of his bath in order to watch a football match, and had somehow knocked it into the water. Upon recovering, apparently against medical expectation, he recounted a present-day NDE which I shall give here in summary:

The boy viewed the experience in terms of a visit to Heaven. The electric shock caused him no pain, and he was grabbed by an Angel – the first Being of Light – who held him by the right arm and flew with him through a tunnel. After a short journey made at inexpressible speed, they landed together on a street in Heaven, which was evidently conceived by the lad very much in terms of the New Testament *Revelation of St John,* 21.18. The streets, as in the Biblical text, were made of transparent gold. He was greeted by various deceased relations, some of whom, interestingly, he had never met whilst they were alive on Earth and whose names he had not heard prior to this NDE. Whether, of course, their names had been mentioned in the course of family conversations which he had overheard and remembered sub-consciously, we shall never know. For such a supposition there is "no testable evidence whatever". A neighbour, who had died only a few weeks earlier, was also in this group, which would suggest that there is little scope here to explain her presence by some sort of inherited family genetic memory.

There then occurred a rustling sound, and the group stood back to reveal Jesus – arguably the second Being of Light in this NDE. With him the lad toured Heaven, and confirmed it to be a New

Jerusalem style of city. There was music, too, for flowers, grass, and even the stones sang in harmony in constant praise of God. The vegetation was indestructible; flowers crushed in the process of their walking around resuming their shape once the boy's weight was removed. It is noteworthy that flowers do not feature in *Revelation*. Also, to his evident pleasure, he found that he had become a fully grown man. Perhaps this suggests some quality of Mind as opposed to material Brain? His senses were enhanced, particularly to visual stimuli, beyond anything he had ever known on Earth, enabling him to enjoy a new and wonderful experience of colours, some hitherto unknown to him. Rather than sitting in Drycthelm's Elysian Fields people occupied 'mansions', and he was shown those of some deceased members of his family.

Jesus at last brought him to a 'veil' – the barrier – which, once pulled aside, revealed the boy's father calling him back, in frantic prayer, even as the ambulance crew was working on him. Perhaps the 'calling back' suggests that the boy's brain was still receptive to auditory stimuli at some level, and that therefore he could hear his father. Alternatively, the father's mind, in stress, could have been in contact with his son's mind. Equally the Divine element may be the correct one. For all these possibilities there is again "no testable evidence whatever". We make our own choice in relation to the evidence, a process perfectly consistent with Creation's working. At this point in the narrative Jesus quietly but firmly told the boy that his father had the authority to call him back home, and that he must accordingly resume his Earthly life. The lad regained consciousness in hospital. So pleasant was this NDE, however, that later he told his father not to interfere should he die again in an accident.

As I have noted, the imagery of this account is influenced by *Revelation*, as we might expect from a member of an Evangelical Minister's household. Making due allowance for this, it has many features which are in Bishop Montefiore's list, and also identifiable in Bede's account. We can accordingly suggest that there are features of NDEs which appear to be universal.

We are, I think, quite safe in saying that when the brain starts to shut down as if in death, the associated mind finds the customary interaction with the brain disrupted, and the resulting altered consciousness produces the experiences reported. But why these particular experiences? Between our two examples here some 1200 years have passed, yet they are very similar. Perhaps the Christian assumptions in the minds of both experients have some bearing on the matter, but non-Christians tell of the same things, too. It seems that the whole human race is inclined to find these features in NDEs, and I cannot convincingly suggest why this should be so. Also, as I have mentioned above, there is no tunnel that I can find in Biblical scripture. The 'valley of the shadow of death' (Psalm 23) is as near as we come to it. The old Testament Jews had little idea of an afterlife, anyway, beyond a kind of dug-out they termed *Sheol* where the spirits of the dead wore feathers and sat in gloomy silence. This concept has origins in ancient Sumeria. It was Jewish contact with the Greeks which cheered things up and gave the cultural background for Jesus to speak of Paradise.

But the tunnel, the intense darkness, the two Beings of Light, the barrier, the rural landscape, are all part of the same story. Who, or what, is telling it? The information is possibly coming in terms of simile and metaphor. That the reported barriers and rural landscapes actually have a physical existence in another, parallel, physical universe is always a possibility, of course, but our minds are accustomed to dealing with the Creation we know. To roam too far from it without very good evidence and cause is to entertain too many oddball theories to help our understanding, I suspect.

We may conjecture that in the NDE the mind is incapable of receiving data from the brain whilst the stress which induces the experience persists. If so the experient is unconscious and the mind has to use its own resources – memory. The Second Being of Light is often perceived as Jesus by Christians; an angel, by Jews and Moslems; and one of the Hindu pantheon by Hindus. Thus cultural expectation governs the nature of the result, it seems, as is evident from Rev'd. Bevere's account. Apparently, and perhaps to their embarrassment, atheists may see Jesus, too. So we may conjecture a fail-safe, or fall-back, cultural factor in our minds, An 'archetype' image reinterpreted by the subject's mind in the stress of a crisis. At any rate, it seems obvious that our minds know that we – but how much of us? – are supposed to be dead, or as good as dead, when they present us with an NDE.

This bears out what can be conjectured from 'shot' Dayananda's assumption upon losing consciousness in the landmine blast.

Nor are all NDEs benign in content. It is thought that 10–15% involve frightening or 'hellish' experiences. There is a suspicion amongst researchers that these tend not always to be reported, or at least not reported fully and accurately, for reasons of the individual's self-esteem. We have already conjectured that the state of mind – e.g. 'high minded', 'low minded', and so on – bears directly upon the individual's decisions and, so, upon the type of person he is and the life he leads. Perhaps here is the confirmation of this idea, in that certain individuals are ashamed of themselves in relation to what the NDE reveals to them. This could also imply that the mind definitely has is own memory and capacity for moral judgement, even if it is no longer able to interact with the brain. If so, is this the mind being thrown back upon itself – and conscious only of itself – without recourse to the data and computing capacity of the brain? Might a 'nasty' mind in this situation be able to conceive nothing but its own attitudes to Creation – personal relationships in particular – throughout eternity, and be overwhelmed by the unrelenting 'nasty' intensity of them in the absence of other stimuli and much of the ability to rationalise? Is this, perhaps, what scares people when they come to face it? This is simply an idea, but one which could account for the distress of some individuals who have experienced a NDE.

Only about 10% of those who experience a NDE apparently report doing the 'grand tour' of the other 'places' before returning to their bodies. Some 60% merely report floating peacefully, and the remaining portion have experiences somewhere in between, but still consistent with some of the dozen features we have noted (cf Adrian Parker, *Journal of the Society for Psychical Research, Number 865, October, 2001*).

The core of the problem of understanding both NDEs and OBEs is that virtually no research into them has been done. Adrian Parker reviews these phenomena and such work upon them as is recorded and concludes, "…little progress has been made in understanding the exact nature of the NDE. Several neurobiological theories are advanced as, or greeted as, 'facts', but are often at best acts of faith seeking to persuade others by ignoring inconvenient findings. Nevertheless, given the contemporary research ideology, if NDEs are more than neurochemically or psychologically derived illusions, then it is likely that this can be clearly shown only when there is a renewed interest in parapsychological research in this area." Meanwhile the reports do not go away, and a dualist mind / brain interpretation of them fits the anecdotal evidence pretty well,

We must also look at what the dying themselves tell us. Dr Peter Fenwick (*Paranormal Review, Issue 46, April 2008*) has co-ordinated the production of nearly 1,000 reports of what he terms End of Life Experiences – ELEs. They are important because "the dying are embedded in the death experience", as he expresses it. The most commonly recurring themes of these reports were of the dying having sudden experiences of joy and love, and of deathbed visions just prior to death. Some 40% of the visions involved someone coming to take away the dying individual. The main categories were: (deceased) parents – 24%; other relatives – 14%; friends – 3%; angels – 3%. The dying speak of the vision as reassuring them, confirming that it is time for them to leave this life, and to be taken upon a journey. Occasionally the vision can be negotiated with as to the time of death, in order to await the arrival of someone at the bedside, or to settle some piece of business. A delay of death may thus be negotiated for a few hours or even a day or so. Very rarely, but most importantly for proper investigation of the phenomenon, the relatives of the dying person may also see the vision.

Dr Fenwick rejects drugs as the cause of these experiences, because drugs do not typically cause such visions. Likewise he rules out the 'dying collapse' of consciousness, for this typically causes confusion, not coherent experience. Both believers and atheists have such experiences, so cultural expectation – beyond a 'failsafe' mode – does not seem a likely cause, and the idea of a comforting delusion was also rejected by Dr Fenwick on the grounds that there is no adequate mechanism in this idea to account for specific and identifiable visions.

He supports claims that, sometimes, a mist, haze, or smoke-like disturbance appears to leave the body at the moment of death, and likewise accepts reports of the appearance of a light or a snatch of music. All these would accord with Eastern traditions, but to come across them in Great Britain is a little singular; there is no hint that they are only reported in contexts where the dying are of Eastern faith or origin. He confirms reports that there can occur an 'apparitional co-incidence' which tells those at a distance of the death, and are best received by those asleep or in a drowsy state at the time. Those who are wide awake generally experience a 'sense of presence' or hear a voice telling of the death in some way. These anomalies fall squarely into the category of Crisis Apparitions, which we shall look at later. It also appears that the old song about Grandfather's Clock "…which stopped / Stopped, never to go again / When the old man died…" has a grain of truth in it, various pieces of apparatus associated with the dying person being reported as having broken down in some way at the moment of death. One case in this category was 'TIM' the old Post Office speaking clock, which seized up completely and auto-switched to a back-up machine at the time of the death of the lady whose recorded voice was on its glass discs. All the very sensible people who took note of this occurrence dismissed it as coincidence, but such phenomena taken as a whole are sufficiently frequent to suggest that some sort of psychokinetic element could sometimes be involved in the process of dying.

Unfortunately the curse of scientism hangs over ELEs. Which junior doctor would care to report someone exhaling 'smoke' at the moment of death, if he hoped for professional esteem and a normal medical career? And who, alas, shall blame him in his reticence? He has to make his way in the world, after all. And 'the right sort of scientific people' know *a priori* that there is nothing to existence but the material body. Let no one dispute that dogma, therefore. It is settled – just like the Sun's revolving round the Earth in the Vatican of Galileo's day. Heretics shall be penalised.

Many medical people will speak in confidence of what they have witnessed at death beds, and it has been part of my ministry (as an Anglican Lay Reader) to hear, comfort, and reassure some of them as best I have been able. Let no one wonder that even the most professional and long-serving nurse can be upset by the death of a patient whom she or he has cared about. But few want to go on record for fear of what may happen to them in career terms if they are labelled 'abnormal' in a variety of subtle and insidious ways.

Which means that the truth, however subjectively or emotionally experienced, is denied and suppressed. What a state to be in!

18. Reincarnation

In arguing for the mind's ability to exist independently of the brain, both in different states of consciousness and *post mortem*, I keep returning to the case of Dayananda. He, of course, came to my notice because he was apparently reincarnated as Chatura, and his case was properly investigated. It was the circumstance of the gap between his loss of consciousness and his death that set me wondering about what his mind was up to in this period, and what it was capable of doing both at that stage and in its normal state. All of which is relevant to the traditional view of reincarnation. So let us have a look at what this is held to involve.

Reincarnation is essentially the belief that, following death, some aspect of the self or soul comes to be reborn in a new body. This new body may be human or animal. There is a progression from good to worse reincarnations – e.g. from king to rat – for souls which have behaved badly in their latest life, or from bad to better for souls which have learned their lessons in this world and are accordingly on their way upwards to a state of bliss, such as the Buddhist nirvana. To achieve this, reincarnations may need to occur many times in the course of any individual soul's spiritual career. The idea is mainly found in Eastern religions, but has a wide diffusion – and has always been lurking in the background of Western religion and philosophy. Pythagoras was inclined towards a variant of it, as were some early Christians, until the Conference of Constantinople in 553 decreed the idea unacceptable dogma. At its purest, it is a spiritually based system of *karma* – rewards and penalties – lived out in successive lives until reincarnation in a material body is dispensed with, and the enlightened soul reaches bliss in a purely spiritual state.

These days there is a 'New Age' variant around. A friend of mine puts it this way; "I do believe in reincarnation as it seems little use to come to Earth to learn only to be, for example, a Caucasian female of middle-class society. How then would I ever be able to understand a disabled Chinese man, for example?" She would have it that she has somehow chosen her present state – her current incarnation – having been something / someone else only one incarnation ago. But there is no particular moral rigour or *karma* to her view of reincarnation. It is to her a perpetual learning experience, which continues until one has achieved a sufficient enlightenment and no longer has to bother about this Earthly existence. One is left with the impression that nothing very taxing is supposed to happen in the process. "If in eastern thought *karma* tells us all is as it should be, then New Age puts a post-modern consumer twist on this by claiming all is as I have chosen it to be" (Steve Hollinghurst, *New Age Paganism and Christian Mission,* Grove Evangelism Series 64, www.grovebooks.co.uk). "The desire here, like much magical understanding, seems to be to eliminate chance as an explanation of events, to push back the chaos of the post-modern void by creating spiritual laws by which to live in replacement perhaps for apparently failed scientific ones."

I would add that to do science properly one has to learn quite a lot about Creation and scientific techniques, and then apply them rigorously. What has 'failed' in such cases, I suggest, is the individual who has not troubled to make the necessary effort.

Christianity does not nowadays countenance reincarnation among its beliefs, as we have noted. From a Christian point of view one would normally say that an individual is required to love God and one's neighbour as oneself, and seek to know God and his purposes better through prayer, Bible reading, and quiet reflection / meditation. If one has the opportunity to introduce one's neighbours to God, then one should do so. In this way my friend's 'disabled Chinese man' could come to hear the Christian point of view. He might already have heard about The One, and loving one's neighbour as oneself from the Buddha, of course. Thus I would argue that one does not actually have to become the Chinese man in order to have a deal of empathy with him. But if God requires it otherwise in some specific cases, then why should he not arrange for a reincarnation to occur to meet his purposes, as a 'one off'? I conceive God as being capable of arranging it. It is up to God. I am not fond of teaching God his business, and I set no limits to his abilities. He is Almighty.

The main investigative work into reincarnation has been meticulously undertaken by the late Prof. Ian Stevenson, whose book – one of many he wrote – *Children Who Remember Previous Lives*, (University Press of Virginia, Charlottesville. 1987) is an astonishing revelation to all who come new to the subject. In fact, I would say that Stevenson's work is essential reading. He has charted the basic characteristics of a large number of reincarnation cases as reported by young children that he and his associates have investigated to standards which in any other branch of science in the field would pass without challenge from those of differing viewpoints. Since reincarnation suggests survival *post mortem* of some part of the personality, however, the *a priori* scientismic detractors assail his, and allied work, vehemently and dogmatically. Which is unhelpful in the pursuit of truth.

His main findings are:

Pre-death predictions are often made by the 'reincarnating personality', which we shall abbreviate as 'RP', cf the-much-written-about procedures for finding the Dalai Lama, Panchen Lama, and others.

'Announcing Dreams' – as so interpreted by the potential mother, or other close relative, when a RP is about to be conceived. These will only be recalled as 'significant' in the event of an apparent reincarnation's having occurred, of course.

Birthmarks and birth defects – corresponding to wounds or other marks on the body of the RP. In Stevenson's survey these were confirmed in 30 cases by post-mortem or medical records, in addition to the anecdotal evidence of witnesses.

The child's own statements about a previous life proving correct upon investigation.

The RP's manner and apparent age as revealed in the child's speaking of the previous life.

The subject mentions RP's name in 86% of the cases recorded. Oddly, the names of other people formerly associated with the RP are sometimes confused, as though there is difficulty in recognition via the child's senses.

The mode of death is mentioned in 76% of the sample. Where mention is made, it is more likely to be mentioned – 94% – if violent (murder, accident, snake-bite) than if non-violent – 52%. Is this a further hint of emotion / stress in relation to the mind's being part of the mechanism involved?

The RP makes itself known as soon as the child can speak.

Usually the child gradually ceases to speak as / about the RP by the age of six or seven. It would appear that the child by then is sufficiently individuated to know that its own 'persona' and the RP's are different, and that the RP is not an integrated part of the child's world. This may suggest that the RP is 'static' and does not develop, as does the child. It could also be evidence in support of the idea of the mind's having its own memory file which does not increase once the brain's input has gone – unsurprisingly.

The child has phobias related to the RP's claimed mode of death in 45% of the sample.

In Sri Lanka there was relationship, or acquaintance, between the child's family and that of the RP in 68% of the sample.

The median interval between death of RP and birth of the child was 14.5 months.

The median distance between the child's home and that of the RP was 6.5 miles. In mediaeval England it was reckoned that a fair distance between markets was 15 miles, i.e. an average 7.5 miles from most points in between, there and back. This may perhaps shed some light upon the 'mental geography' limits of people in a little-motorised social setting, at the dates of some of Stevenson's examples.

RPs' principal memories, and themes – e.g. daily habits, basic assumptions about domestic arrangements – tend to cluster around the circumstances current during the last year or so of life; cf Dayananda's proposed purchase of a tractor.

RPs have a strong desire to go and visit their past environment.

The child's behaviour strongly reflects the RP's own previous habits. In cases where RP claims to have been a priest or teacher, for example, the role is adopted in play, expertly performed, and fully accepted by other children.

The child may display untaught skills to high degree of proficiency, e.g. sewing, performing priestly ritual.

The child may exhibit atypical appetites, addictions or cravings. There may be 'sexual precocity'.

Sometimes the RP has switched genders – to general confusion.

There may be aggressive tendencies which are fully appropriate to RP's former existence, but illogical in the child's own circumstances.

Left-handedness or speech peculiarities known in RP when living may be claimed as incarnation evidence.

There are instances on record where the RP appears to have 'fitted' the natural personality of the child to such an extent that the child has never ceased to speak about the time 'when I was big', and in adult life has taken up the RP's claimed role, e.g. as a priest. Implications of parental encouragement, social status, and family advantage might make us a little wary of such cases, however. The cultural expectations of societies where reincarnation is accepted as normal are rather different from Western scientism! This said, there are well-researched cases of apparent reincarnation in European and American contexts. These latter have tended to be 'hushed up' by the families concerned as being abnormal and therefore socially unacceptable. Which attitude and action, however reassuring to those families, hinder research (cf *Six Cases of the Reincarnation Type from the Netherlands*; Titus Rivas, *'Paranormal Review'*, Issue 29, January, 2004).

Everything listed by Stevenson will fit the concept of a discarnate mind perfectly well. As we have mentioned, he himself has proposed the concept of the 'psychophore' (soul-bearing) 'something' which:

Carries memories from the RP to the consciousness of the child.

Is credited with its own will-power and ability to get its own way with respect to reincarnating in specific and pre-chosen circumstances.

Carries the RP's physical attributes – birthmarks, physical defects – to the child. The implication is that the 'psychophore' must adopt a new mother at, or very soon after, a successful conception.

What do the RPs, through the children 'inheriting' them, have to say about all this? Strangely, perhaps, there are only a few features of the NDE reported by RPs. Perhaps NDEs are more N than DE; 'One cannot extrapolate from what is here and now.'

(Hume). A typical report is that of Purnima Ekenyake (Erlendur Haraldsson; *Journal of the Society for Psychical Research, Number 858, January 2000*) – "She told her mother how she closed her eyes after the [road] accident and then she came 'here'. Her mother asked if she had been taken to a hospital. 'No,' she replied. She added: 'A heap of iron was on my body'. Purnima related that after the accident she floated in the air in semi-darkness for a few days. She saw people mourning for her and crying, and saw her body up to and including the funeral. There were many people like her floating around. Then she saw some light, went 'there', and came 'here' [to her present home]." This account is pretty typical for the Sri Lankan cases of Stevenson, with whom Haraldsson has worked. I recall another RP, reported in one of Stevenson's books, who stated that he had drifted around in a sort of half-light in familiar places between local paddy fields and the forest. He then saw his 'new' mother as she came to a river jetty to wash some clothes, and decided he would like to be born to her, which in due course he achieved.

Jenny Cockell in her book *Yesterday's Children* (BCA. See also Mary Rose Barrington's investigation, *Journal of the Society for Psychical Research, Number 867, April 2002*) describes her pre-reincarnation life in terms of drifting in a sort of transparent sack through subdued light, seeing many other 'souls' in such sacks, and being able to communicate with them in terms of a kind of empathy. She was then born again as Jenny Cockell. Read her book; incidents she describes in her previous life were confirmed and explained in context by her 'previous' children, by that time Old Age Pensioners. Some psychophore type of collected recollection remained in suspension after her death as 'Mary' – the previous incarnation, who died in 1932 and is confirmed as genuine by the OAP children and the appropriate civil records – and then reappeared in the mind of Jenny herself. The evidence for the survival of these memories from Mary's life, and known in RP form to Jenny, is good. Jenny had to seek out the children *after* recording the memories of her previous life, so it does not seem likely that she had somehow 'telepathically' been told of a 'previous life' by them, and then fitted herself into the picture emerging.

The only reservation I have in her case is the role of a hypnotist in 'recovering' the memories. In various other cases I have read about where hypnotic 'regressions' have been undertaken to supposed previous lives, the preferences and presuppositions of the hypnotist in the case have suggested themselves. The message has been, I suspect, somewhat rephrased here and there, just as I think Drycthelm has been edited a bit by Heimgils before the latter passed his story to Bede. This does not necessarily detract from the essential genuineness of the material, but it must leave open a few questions as to its worth in establishing a mechanism for its retention *post mortem* and its reappearance as another person's conscious identity.

So what are we to make of reincarnation as a mind transferred rather than a soul reincarnated? The case can be argued either way, given the very small amount of evidence which can be produced. Everything which I have come across in the context of reincarnation can be explained [Sic!] in terms of a disembodied mind (plotting room gallery) attaching itself to a new plotting table area. The mind comes with its store of life experiences, its preferences, its assumptions, and its memories. The memories are good for the recent past, but tend to tail off for earlier incidents in life, just as one's memory does. A certain amount of will, intention, and moral judgement seem to be present, but when the developing conscious mind of the child finds that the RP does not develop and adapt to the child's circumstances, the child's own mind / consciousness seems to assert itself and say, "Hey! I'm actual me, not when-I-was-big me. Interloper, get out!" And bang goes the evidence we might collect from a child more mature than about six years old! This is the way I see it. My 'New Age' reincarnated friend, on the other hand, appreciates what I am arguing, but is more at ease with the idea that she is developing spiritually, and by her own choice, in a new set of circumstances. I shall not discuss the evidence for her own previous life as she has described it to me, for I do not have her permission to do so. I can say that it is good, but still within the compass of what I attribute to the mind. Happily we can agree to differ, and concentrate on probing what can be stated with some degree of certainty. Which is not a lot.

So if we put mind at the centre of anomalous conscious experiences, let us see what it can suggest.

19. Hypnotism

Stevenson's work has shown that birthmarks and birth defects can seemingly be transmitted to a child by the supposed RP. Purnima, of the road accident, had discoloured skin around the area of her RP's fatal injuries. Dayananda, likewise, took some discolouration in the area of his throat on his 'new' body as evidence of the fatal 'bullet', in reality the debris of the landmine blast. This throat wound was borne out by photographs of his corpse. The frustrating factor in his case is that his medical notes had been lost by the Sri Lankan Army's Medical Corps by the time of the investigation; in fairness to those involved, Dayananda was dead, and the army had no logical need to file them away carefully. In many other cases blemishes of various sorts appear to confirm the RP's version of events, as Stevenson has again noted.

It is likewise thought that some terrible shock suffered by a pregnant woman may result in blemishes which correspond to her fears appearing upon the child she bears. Perhaps 'chicken and egg' type questions are in order here, though. Folklore has it so, at any rate, and it is not at all clever to dismiss traditional beliefs without close examination of how they arose in the first place. The mind is clearly able, in some cases, to produce alarming 'psychosomatic' results. In one of Stevenson's books he prints horrific photographs of a torture victim's limbs deforming, years later, at the recollection of their one-time abuse. Stigmata appearances seem to be a similar case, although such wounds generally manifest to match the traditional depiction of Christ's crucifixion. This is markedly at variance with the anatomical mechanics of this mode of execution. Therefore the mind must be imposing its own version of events upon the physical body. Exactly how this occurs we do not know. Neither does the question seem to inspire much scientific research, which leaves us in ignorance of this phenomenon and many more which are probably allied with it.

An obvious parallel is hypnotism in its use as a method of inducing anaesthesia. The popular perception of hypnosis is that it is a method of putting an individual's behaviour under the control of someone else. It seems to be accomplished by inducing an exaggerated degree of suggestibility in the hypnotised subject, but even this much is open to argument. We know what its results can look like, we know how hypnotists apply the technique and, equally, how certain personality types respond to it better than others. But why it is effective currently eludes us. Hypnotism is still largely in the province of the sea-side variety show on the end of the pier.

Yet note the *What?* *How?* and *Why?* questions which arise quite naturally once more. They suggest that hypnosis is not some physical attribute of the brain, but is definitely in the sphere of the mind's working. Nor need it be a sinister process. It is possible for a hypnotist to anaesthetise one part of a person's anatomy, whilst keeping that person fully conscious in all other respects. So a dentist might 'forbid' pain in his patient's lower jaw, whilst enabling the patient to 'open wider, please' or turn his head in co-operation with the dentistry in progress. Yet it is noteworthy that there is no area of the brain which corresponds exclusively to the pain-sensing susceptibility of the lower jaw. The 'stocking' or 'glove' effect, whereby a hypnotist can arbitrarily prevent sensation in a leg or a hand, is the same sort of phenomenon. It is demonstrable but not understood. The nerves of these limbs do not correspond exclusively with any particular area of the brain. Thus the hypnotist is effectively – very effectively! – suggesting to the patient that it is perfectly valid not to feel pain in some particular part of the body. The effect follows no known physical law, but we may suspect the mind to be at work and giving orders to the brain.

The patient's own mind is necessarily doing all the work in such contexts, and I would suggest that the unconscious facet of the mind we mentioned in passing as the Habitual Controller may have something to do with this. Its characteristics are given as 'learned behaviours – e.g. typing', and it is held to be fast, flexible, and 'allows attention to be directed elsewhere'. In this last attribute we may have a hint to help us. It has been shown experimentally that consciousness can *deny* the stimuli of something painful if led to expect that pain will not be felt. The faith of legitimate expectation allows the consciousness' attention to pass over the pain, in other words. The experiment involved subjects having a dab of an irritant solution applied to their shins. All agreed that it hurt. Some were then treated with a smear of cold cream, and told that this was an analgesic which would prevent the solution from affecting them. There was in fact nothing in the chemistry of this cream which could have had any effect upon the operation of the irritant, yet without exception those who were given the smear of cream reported that pain ceased after it had been applied. This result is physically irrational, and for the means of its working there is "no testable evidence whatever". Which is as far as the physical science has got, beyond referring to it as 'the placebo effect'. The OED defines 'placebo' as "a medicine or regime prescribed for the psychological benefit to the patient rather than for any physiological effect, ➤ a substance which has no therapeutic value…" and 'placebo effect' as "a beneficial effect produced by a placebo drug treatment, due to the patient's belief in that treatment." It has long been known that we can be fooled into fooling ourselves, as many a wise old doctor knows!

To digress a little in support of this concept; there are a couple of famous historical precedents for it. Oljeitu, one of the Great Khans, needed to undergo an operation upon his left arm. His doctor erected a short but strong stake in the palace, and attached firmly to the top of it a large metal ring. Oljeitu, standing, had his left arm passed through this ring, and then bound vertically to the stake. A table with a chess board upon it was placed to his right side, away from the sight of the operation. A 'grand master' rank chess player summoned for the purpose was then required to engage the Khan in a complicated game, which took place whilst the operation was in progress. Oljeitu never so much as flinched; his concentration upon the chess game was so intense that he was not the least troubled by the operation, which was a complete success. Although a degree of folk-story has doubtless coloured the history, this report is credible in the context.

A better documented case from November 1686 concerns an operation upon Louis XIV for an anal fistula. His surgeon, Felix, was given royal dispensation to try out his techniques upon sundry prisoners who were under sentence of death in any case, and enough of them survived for the king to have confidence in what his medical man proposed to do to him. Accordingly, the royal britches were dropped, His Majesty knelt upon cushions piled upon the seat of an armchair in such a way as to allow him to lean over the back of it and, in mitigation of the demands of the occasion, he removed his hat – although he scrupulously retained his wig. The courtiers of La Chambre du Roi waited beyond the door, but within earshot of the proceedings, to be attentive and ensure fair play as two lancings and eight incisions were made. This was undoubtedly the critical factor. As a man of courage and immense self-control, it did not become Le Grand Louis to show fear, especially with churchmen and ambassadors present. It is reported that the regularity of his breathing remained unaltered throughout the procedure. Incredibly, he was able to appear at a Royal Council meeting later that day, although "…his face was bathed in sweat and his countenance was livid…", as report has it. He made a full recovery, to the continued discomfort of Europe and fatal injury of the French monarchy.

The very imagination of such surgery makes me shudder, yet these operations were performed successfully. It seems to me that it was the mind's preoccupation with concentrating upon other matters which prevented the brain from registering the pain which the neural network must surely have been referring to it. This effect may derive from something we have evolved to do anyway. It is noteworthy that in cases where our selfish genes' survival is under threat and we must take drastic action to get away from the danger, we can sustain quite serious non-incapacitating injuries in the course of our fighting or fleeing, but only notice them later when the main danger to us is over. Our selfish genes are initially preoccupied with their own capacity to survive the danger; a fuller evaluation of their condition comes later. Other species have also evolved in this way. In 'management speak' the basis of this ability is clearly 'goal oriented'. We are required by our selfish genes to live to fight / breed another day; so long as we can achieve this much, lesser injuries are of no account in the process. Therefore in the crisis of a life-or-death emergency, our mind frees us from having to heed them, I suggest.

I have tried this conjecture upon myself when visiting my dentist, who plays a 'musical wallpaper' upon the radio in his surgery for his own distraction [Sic!] he tells me. I find, though, that by concentrating upon one instrumental part and teasing its notes out of the general racket, I can be largely unconscious of what he is doing inside my mouth. His requests to "Turn your head away from me a little, please," and the inevitable "Open a bit wider, please," sometimes have to be repeated a couple of times. Which is embarrassing for me because he is such a nice chap, doing his job well, and it is obviously to my benefit to co-operate all I can to help him.

But I have achieved my goal of a comfortable time whilst in his tilted chair, and this is welcome to me, even though dentistry these days is not a jot as unpleasant as it was when I was young. So, might we look upon the placebo effect simply as evidence of a 'goal achieved'? When the volunteer in the experiment has obtained his smear of what he believes is analgesic cream, he considers that the danger is past. He has no more need to worry about a smarting shin; that is now taken care of. Therefore he can forget it – and does. More consciously, both Khan and King had greater matters at stake than the normal reaction to pain, so they therefore concentrated upon their chess and status and, by preoccupying themselves by such means, achieved the goal of a lessened or discounted degree of pain. They had faith in the demonstration of their own might, just as the volunteer had faith in the smear of allegedly analgesic cream.

It would be interesting to re-run the 'shin' experiment using volunteers who did not understand the term 'analgesic', or who were told that the cream was simply a precautionary antiseptic. How might they have fared then, I wonder? It is a pity no one thought along these lines and tried this version of the original experiment.

How does the process of hypnotism help in this elimination or reduction of pain? If the 'goal' of the selfish genes is not to suffer and be distracted by pain from the need to survive in order to breed, it could follow that simple belief in the efficacy of hypnotism achieves it for them. Hypnosis is the process which works; QED. Someone who has been convinced of as much will have faith in its effectiveness in his own case. He is told that the 'cream' of hypnotism is an analgesic, he believes what he is told, and therefore his plotting room gallery can discount reports of pain by the plotting table as being entirely false. The plotting table reports them, but he has already achieved his goal of a pain-free shin, he believes, so he knows that the reports are untrue. He has permission, on the authority of the hypnotist, to ignore them and concentrate upon something else instead. His mind directs him to behave accordingly.

I have seen a filmed demonstration of analgesic hypnotism. It showed a successful operation done under hypnosis to remove two upper incisor teeth, and replace them with implants. This was the patient's 'goal', allied with the fame of having the procedure filmed as a demonstration of the effectiveness of hypnosis. An anaesthetist armed with a syringe of a fast-acting drug stood by the while, no doubt to everyone's reassurance. The patient had had a five-hour session with the hypnotist to gain faith in the efficacy of hypnotism and be able to relax – and keep her thoughts from the work to be done – to order, as it were. She was given a pen and pad of paper with which to communicate with the operating staff whilst the procedure was underway. This undeniably put her in control of the situation – another important point, I would suggest. It must have enhanced her confidence. She was deeply relaxed, and was told to report any discomfort – the word 'pain' was scrupulously avoided – upon a scale 0–9 by writing on the pad. Her instructions were mentally to 'turn down' the pain as though turning down the volume knob of a radio, and hold it upon 0. Once or twice she later reported 1, despite her best 'turning down' efforts, yet she was still in control of the discomfort and, accordingly, of the procedure overall. In this context she was the star of the show, which may likewise be significant; undenied self-importance equates with that reassuring sense of effective power, as with the Khan and King.

She then went, in the preoccupation of her imagination (if I rightly assume this to be the state of the mind under hypnosis), on a walk along the sea-shore with her hypnotist, being encouraged to feel the warm sun, warm sand, warm sea, nice dry feeling of the warm sand between her toes, and so forth. The idea seemed to be to suggest as many warm sensations as possible. Was this a fundamental human archetype of a memory of the safety and comfort of the womb? Is this comforting state a standard distracting technique in clinical hypnosis? This was not commented upon by the film makers. Neither was any question of the patient's faith in the competence of the hypnotist to do his stuff conclusively pursued.

So, what was the subject's perception of the process? Had she viewed the hypnotist as an authority whom she could follow in faith, or more as a guide to help her in her own endeavours to ignore pain? Was it faith, ritual, expectation, 'word of power', or something else which allowed her to undergo this surgery with minimal discomfort? These questions were not pursued; perhaps they could not usefully have been, for all answers would have been entirely subjective, or 'anecdotal', and have needed a mass of psychological testing for character-type and so forth to get anywhere near an objective assessment of this particular case, let alone some firm general principles governing whatever was taking place in the patient's mind.

Hypnosis was working successfully nonetheless. How was this echoed, if at all, by secretions of pain-reducing chemicals – endorphins – in the patient's blood stream, for example? On the film, at least, no samples were taken; perhaps this happened off-camera and the results will be published... wherever they may be. What was shown was obviously not faked, but what did it actually tell us about consciousness, and mind in relation to brain? Most importantly, in view of what we are trying to examine in the context of psychic anomalies, what does the mind achieve under hypnosis, how do the resulting effects come about, and why does it all work? These are our three good old categories of question, again, and we are not equipped to give sensible answers beyond describing what we have seen.

Clearly there is no 'fluence' passed from hypnotist to subject. Even in his own day Mesmer, who brought 'animal magnetism' as he termed it to public attention, was shown to be wrong about this idea. The work is done in the subject's own mind. Therefore, some inherent characteristic of the subject is able to rise above the discomforts of the occasion and do the job. This ability may just lie in the subject's sense of identity, as with Khan and King in full pride of their status. And a young lady whose appearance will be enhanced by two new and undecayable incisors may walk in a changed state of consciousness along a sunlit beach – with theatre staff, academics, the all-important reserve anaesthetist, film crew, and admiring friends, family and, by extension, film-viewers in attendance. Her five minutes of fame are assured, and her ambition ('goal') to flash a dazzling new smile once the blood has stopped oozing is guaranteed likewise. There is a high degree of self-esteem at stake in all three cases, it seems to me. Could this 'goal' be sufficient motivation to 'ignore' pain by assuming an altered state of consciousness, self-generated, but achieved by faith in the hypnotist and the, in this case, 'glamour' of the procedure's capture on film?

In my dentist's surgery, my own conscious decision not to be driven mad by his awful taste in music makes this music the main threat to my own selfish genes, I suggest. The mere jabs and vibrations of his instruments within my mouth become the secondary consideration accordingly. My selfish genes' preoccupation is to retain my sanity – not to mention the obvious superiority of my utterly exquisite musical taste, and the enhanced status I award myself on account of it! What he does to me by way of keeping my teeth in order is incidental by comparison. In this way I seem to be able to fool myself into discomfort-free treatment. Which pleases me greatly; long may he remain a pop music addict!

But what is doing the job is my mind. I have given myself permission to consider it acceptable to ignore everything but teasing out one instrumental line from the cacophony blaring in the surgery. To preoccupy myself with concentrating upon it and deriving from it musical figures of my own invention, is my selfish genes' 'goal'. Any hypnotist whose help I might seek to prepare me against an assault by musical mayhem, would no doubt reassure me that I had a perfect right to preserve my wits by descrying and rephrasing the sounds annoying me, and the result would be the same. "Concentrate upon your preoccupation with the well-being of your own sensibilities to the exclusion of all else," would be his brief to me, I think.

I am sure it would work – faith! – at any rate. I have proved it to my own satisfaction, and the result / 'goal' is personal to me as the most important person my selfish genes know. My self-esteem and integrity guarantee it. Now, if this really is the mechanism at work, it would explain very adequately why, under experimental conditions, hypnotism is said not to persuade the bearer of secret information to divulge it, nor direct the desirable young lady to allow the hypnotist his wicked will with her. Neither course would be a legitimate goal to the subject, and 'permission' to indulge it would be refused. Of course, if these subjects were feeling treacherous or lecherous to start with, or could be persuaded whilst under hypnosis that they could legitimately consider themselves to be in such frames of mind, who knows…? Our selfish genes are very selfish indeed, let there be no doubt of that.

Popularly we speak of a 'hypnotic trance'. We really mean 'an altered state of consciousness' in which *part* of our consciousness has ceased to function because the mind (gallery) is ignoring *specific* stimuli from the brain (plotting table) in pursuit of a 'goal'. So I might be persuaded by a hypnotist that I was a hippopotamus, or that I could dispense with the number 4 when counting. In both cases I would very likely remain mobile, and capable of co-ordinated actions and speech, because my brain would still be working normally. Only part of my consciousness – which is the interaction between mind and brain, remember – is not functioning; for the rest it is business-as-usual. However, what might happen if the hypnotist gave me 'permission' to have as my 'goal' a complete switching off of my conscious brain, so that my mind could associate with brains in use by other people and come to know their thoughts and emotions? If my mind were not busy with my own brain, could it latch on to someone else's instead? Could it even meet other minds, and swap information and ideas with them, chatting away in some other physical dimension until it re-associated with my own brain, carrying with it memories of the encounters? Would it even be necessary for the other minds to be attached to living brains, in fact? There is enough anecdotal evidence for such possibilities to be suspected. We shall consider matters like 'distance viewing' shortly.

No investigations into hypnotism have so far explained it in terms of hard and fast answers to the sort of questions it suggests. However, hypnotism and mind are closely associated, and until the mind is better understood in relation to consciousness, I do not foresee any fuller understanding of hypnotism arising. And it is science must grapple with such phenomena as hypnosis. I do not see progress resulting from any sudden revelation, or insights following the re-reading of ancient literature.

20. 'Telepathy'

We have just stated, again, that science has a major part to play in revealing what constitutes the mind. I have suggested that it may be in the province of physics, rather than neuro-science or psychology, to reveal its location. I seriously wonder whether the mind exists, wholly or in part, in another physical dimension from the brain. This could be a wonderful 'oddball theory', and we have already mentioned 'twistor space' as a possible area in which to track it down. Science and its methods, properly applied, are best capable of shedding light upon such ideas. Once we know what we are looking for, we stand a chance of seeing it. It is possible that a major paradigm change for physics may be necessary, the 'new' physics incorporating a link with 'mind', however established or defined. Prof. Bernard Carr (Worlds Apart? Can Physical Research Bridge the Gulf Between Matter and Mind?' *Proceedings of the Society for Psychical Research, Vol. 59. Part 221. June 2008*) of The School of Mathematical Sciences, university of London, summarises the idea thus, "The new paradigm must assign a central role to consciousness and there are already indications that this is a fundamental rather than an incidental feature of the Universe. I will present my own view as to what form the new paradigm might take. This involves a higher-dimensional 'reality structure' which is reminiscent of ideas invoked by modern physics." His arguments are scarcely light reading, but are certainly plausible and, above all, profoundly interesting. It is cheering to see science engaged in this way.

We have wondered in passing how a committed scientismist might react if he found that he could predict, better than 50% of the time, who was telephoning him before answering the phone. A fair number of people seem to experience this type of phenomenon, in fact. We noted also that it appears to involve some close emotional link between the telephoner and the recipient of the phone call. Vague utterances about 'telepathy' and 'curious coincidence' tend to result from casual consideration of it. And once the mathematics of probability have been duly exercised upon this anomaly, by Dr Rupert Sheldrake's research, for example, it still remains to perplex us (*Experimental Tests for Telephone Telepathy*, R Sheldrake and P Smart *Journal of the Society for Psychical Research, Number 872,* July 2003, and *A Filmed Experiment on Telephone Telepathy with the Nolan Sisters*, *Journal for the Society for Psychical Research, Number 876,* July 2004). It is real, in other words.

The same kind of effect is recorded as occurring between identical twins – e.g. one of the pair suffers an injury to a hand, say, and the corresponding hand of the other twin immediately swells and causes pain, even though the twins may be many miles apart at the time. A careful study has been made by Guy Lyon Playfair (*Twin Telepathy: The Psychic Connection. The History Press* 2008). No definitive mechanism for such phenomena is proposed, but the evidence suggests that there is a permanent unconscious link between the twins which makes itself known when one of them is under stress or otherwise emotionally aroused. It seems odd that such a promising subject for laboratory research is not assiduously pursued.

Even more remarkable is the anomaly of Crisis Apparitions, whereby two minds with strong emotional links to one another are instantly in contact, without any apparent constraints of time or inverse square laws, if one of them is 'in crisis'. The reports of this experience go broadly as follows:

"I was asleep / going about my usual occupation, when suddenly I 'saw' Joe Bloggs, my husband / very dearest friend, within a short distance of me. This shook me considerably, because at the time I thought he was flying off way up north to Alaska. He simply smiled and said, 'Don't worry. I'm quite OK.' And then he wasn't there any more. I had the presence of mind to note that the time was … such a time. Later on, whilst watching the TV news bulletin at … such a later time, I saw that there had been an accident at Seattle airport, where a large aeroplane had crashed on take-off. Mercifully, there were very few casualties. Joe Bloggs would have been on that plane, and I was anxious for his safety until he phoned me at … such an even later time, and told me that he had indeed been on the crashed plane and thought that he was likely to die. However, he had escaped, a bit singed and with a few cuts and bruises. The plane crashed at ... the local time, which, allowing for time zones around the globe is the equivalent of the time when I unexpectedly saw him close to me. I felt sure that he had thought of me in the stress of the crash, and he later confirmed as much."

Two minds have, on the initiative of the one under stress, been in contact with one another. The common factor in such cases is that the minds' owners are emotionally linked, and therefore in strong sympathy with one another. And that, for the time being, is that. We know no more, other than that these things happen. Any consideration of brain and mind needs to include the Crisis Apparition class of anomalous experience, therefore. It is too common in its various forms to ignore. A good read around one aspect of the subject is *'Dogs who know when their owners are returning home'* by Dr Rupert Sheldrake, who is not afraid to use science to probe what is not regarded as scientismically 'respectable'. (See also E Haraldsson *Journal for the Society for Psychical Research, Number 806,* January 1987; GL Playfair *Journal for the Society for Psychical Research, Number 854,* January 1999; Sylvia Hart Wright *Journal for the Society for Psychical Research, Number 857* October 1999.)

For a Crisis Apparition to occur, not only do two minds have to be in communication, but the gist of information input, as though it is the gallery's *interpretation* of data from the plotting table, has to be produced in the recipient's mind. By this I mean that the recipient obtains the message, 'Don't worry. I'm quite OK,' rather than a detailed report about the experient's current circumstances and the events leading up to them. The most obvious source of this information is the consciousness – mind and brain in interaction – of the experient under stress. Additionally, an image of the experient has to be invoked by the mind of the recipient – otherwise the apparition itself could not 'appear'. The apparition is presumably an image which we might reasonably allow to be held in the recipient's memory. Therefore it would seem that we have one consciousness – the recipient's mind and brain in interaction – actively responding at a distance to information which it has not received as stimuli provided by its own senses. This point could be important.

It is very tempting to see, once again, the mind – gallery – creating the grand concept, the thing which has to be done, and the brain – plotting table – filling in the detail, making sense of the gallery's instructions, and working things out on its own in relation to the stimuli it is receiving from all sources, memory included.

We have two minds, each still alive and with its own brain associated, which are in contact with one another. How? We do not know. Some reports, moreover, describe the Crisis Apparition as showing injuries or other indications of altered circumstances that its 'owner' has just acquired, and which very likely have contributed to the stimulus which has triggered the apparition in the first place – "I must let my wife know I'm OK despite my injuries, or else she'll worry once she hears of the plane crash – and that I love her anyway." If so, the brain-mind interaction, which I assume is the stuff of consciousness, updates the experient's mind in relation to its owner's current physical / mental state in the briefest 'real' time, before the recipient 'sees' the apparition in its latest physical condition. This could also be important if we are allowing for the involvement of two people's minds to account for the accuracy of the apparition's appearance at the time it communicates. It is also apparent that the experient remains conscious, or loses consciousness only for a time. Remember that Dayananda thought he had been shot. Perhaps if he had regained consciousness during the three days following his death injury, his consciousness – i.e. the restoration of his brain-with-mind interaction – could have informed his enduring mind correctly about his condition.

Occasionally Crisis Apparitions are only heard – "I heard Joe Bloggs' voice call my name. Then he said, 'Don't worry. I'm quite OK', and at the time I had no idea why." I assume the same essentials are still involved overall, however. Possibly the difference lies in the psychology of the imagery normally preferred by the recipient, i.e. some people argue, explain, or teach something, commencing, "Look..." whilst others begin "Listen..."

Are we looking at 'telepathy'? The word tends to be used very loosely. Even the OED merely states, "the supposed communication of thoughts or ideas by means other than the known senses". But, given our lack of knowledge, what better definition could it give? In the form of a crisis apparition I do not think we can claim any proof of telepathy in terms of ideas, although we can allow thoughts as the inspiration of the apparition. The gist of personal, emotion-based information is certainly conveyed, but there is no detailed message. Indeed, some crisis apparitions are reported as simply implying their circumstances – "Joe Bloggs was standing next to me, soaked to the skin. After a second or two, he just vanished." If it is later established that Joe Bloggs was 'Lost at sea; on such a date. Presumed drowned. No body recovered', and since the time of the report of his apparition coincides pretty well with the known particulars of his case, we have what may be the gist of his fate. We still lack the detailed circumstances, however.

But what if he only faked his disappearance, but had to swim rather harder than he had anticipated, his apparition commenting mutely that he feared he really was about to die – although in the end he did not? What arises must be akin to a NDE reported by a second party in the case – which becomes interesting, also! In all cases we have to judge, too, whether the source of the report, i.e. the recipient, is telling the truth. Perhaps the supposed recipient of the apparition of the 'drowned' Joe Bloggs is part of his conspiracy, for example. The whole business can easily become a mess, and very difficult to clarify.

In a law court anecdotal evidence is put to a jury, which makes a decision. In the investigation of psychic anomalies juries tend to be permanently 'out', usually hoping for better evidence. Like all scientific theories, any conclusions reached by psychical researchers should accordingly remain provisional.

Nevertheless, the literature of psychic anomalies contains many instances in which people in an altered state of consciousness, hypnotised subjects among them, have supposedly made 'journeys of the mind'. The hypnotised subjects have visited places where they were instructed to go, and have been able to look around them in detail whilst there. On their subsequent return to normal consciousness, they have reported with complete accuracy what they have seen in the course of their travels. (We have already come across something similar in the context of OBEs.)

Now, many highly reputable stage magicians base part of their acts upon producing information that they could not possibly have obtained by other than 'magical' means. Perplexing the audience is essential to the entertainment, of course, and there are well-established means of deciding in advance what information is to be revealed magically, and then setting up marvellous presentations to produce it from seemingly myriads of random or free-choice alternatives. This magic might be to reveal the fifth word on the eighteenth line of the umpteenth page of a thick book, newly purchased, selected at random from a number of books by a neutral party, and then 'memorised' by the magician in five seconds flat. Bearing this sort of effect in mind, reports of the achievements of some, but only some, nineteenth-century 'mental somnabulators' – as one of the terms then used describes them – suggest moderately clever conjuring rather than anomalous ability.

It is easy enough to speak of a visit to the house of someone in the audience, and then reveal what is in the third drawer down in the left-hand pedestal of his desk, if he is an accomplice, or if someone associated with the act has been able to brief the 'somnambulator' about the house and the desk's contents. The whole show is better still, of course, if one can first gain secret access to a house and desk, and plant some strange object in the desk drawer entirely without the householder's knowledge. One can then make him the victim of a 'forced choice', whilst apparently randomising the selection of his house from amongst the houses of all those who are present for the house to be honoured by a somnambulatorial visit – and Robert is your father's brother, as they say! Just send round a committee to scrutinise the desk and report marvels. Beyond doubt this sort of thing was done, servants being bribable, visiting tradesmen not being what they seemed to be, and so on. We know about such things; they are still done by private detectives and the like, and perhaps even by magicians upon televised occasion.

There remains, however, a body of reports about 'journeys of the mind' which cannot be dismissed. In certain states of consciousness it appears that some people have the ability to make them. Anyone can imagine moving through familiar surroundings. Possibly my lady driver friend's OBE had something of this in its make-up. It is also possible, of course, to move around in an entirely imaginary landscape. Over the decades I have evolved a 'dream land' of my own, where I am as likely as not to find myself mentally wandering around when in REM [rapid eye movement, dreaming] sleep. Its features do not change much between my 'visits'. I know where everything is in relation to everything else, and I meet the most unlikely people there, too. They are usually folk I have had dealings with long ago but have, for all intents and purposes, forgotten. Having carefully reflected upon the components of my 'mental construct', – for such it seems to me to be – I can identify many real places I have known during my life which have transported themselves there, and which appear in caricatured form, certain aspects of them highlighted to emphasise particular features of the originals. The overriding common factor in them all is that they are locations where I have had to take especial care – an old and ill-lit staircase, a tricky road junction, a very narrow path by a river, a cramped and noisy cafe full of people in a hurry, and others evoking similar emotions. The people, too, are not the outright heroes or villains of my life to date, but folk about whom I have entertained some unspecific doubts, of whose capacities and motives I have not been entirely sure, or who have inspired in me an 'I do not like thee, Dr Fell...' feeling. The dream 'construct' seems designed to remind me not to let my guard down too readily, although nothing alarming ever happens in the course of my very purposeful activities in this 'place'. Perhaps it simply hosts some sort of mild anxiety complex.

    The point I am suggesting is that my mind contains this mental baggage in its unconscious state, but that this only presents itself to me, openly, in my dreams. It may also influence my waking self, unknown to me, of course. Therefore, if I were to be hypnotised into becoming a 'mental somnambulator' I would take this baggage with me on my wanderings. At the very least, I suggest, it would colour where I wandered and what I interested myself in, in the course of my travels. If I 'saw' things, it would necessarily be through the eyes of other people, for my mind does not have eyes; my body, which includes my brain, is necessarily left behind in these circumstances. Thus I would have nothing with which to peer inside a lap-top computer attached close to the ceiling of a neurosurgical operating theatre, for example. I might be able to gain access to the consciousness, i.e. mind and brain, of whoever had programmed it, though. In fact, the programmer's brain would be enough, if I could influence it to set up its 'plotting table' to show my travelling mind-gallery the shapes and colours in the programme. I suspect also that I would have a better chance of finding the plotting table I desired if it had been set up by someone who, like me, dislikes dark and ill-lit stairs, semi-obscured road junctions, and all the rest of it. I would seek out a consciousness with which I was in empathy because it carried baggage similar to my own, in other words. That consciousness' gallery would be more likely to provide a plotting table my mind could understand at a glance and use easily for my purposes.

Could I do this at will, I wonder? Perhaps under hypnosis I might manage it; I have already described how the 'goal' of some nice new upper incisors enabled some dire dentistry to be done, with the help of hypnosis. The Khan and the King managed something similar on their own. So can people auto-hypnotise into states of consciousness in which they can do extraordinary things?

There are rumours, and they will undoubtedly remain as such for many years, that during the Cold War both NATO and USSR had programmes of 'psychic spying' on the go. The academic term is 'remote viewing'. To what extent these rumours were concocted in order to cover up the activities of more conventional spying methods, and thus to try and throw the enemy off the scent, I cannot say. It does seem very likely, however, that some serious attempts at psychic spying were made. The idea was that a gallery that was full of military baggage, as opposed to my own dark staircase sort, would seek out plotting tables on the other side of the Iron Curtain, and see what could be deduced from the markers upon them. These efforts, or bluffs to fool the enemy, certainly started off in the 1970s, but seem not to have endured much beyond the collapse of the Berlin Wall. Their final days had become a bit OTT in any case. I have heard of incense, candles by the ton, mood music, and orgiastic sex to 'stimulate the vibes'. Whilst no doubt such fun and games were all very enjoyable for those concerned, it is scarcely surprising that a fierce, focussed, no-nonsense, umpteen-starred US General with an operational background decreed that it should cease. Or did it? Provide your own conspiracy theory!

Laboratory work shows that remote viewing undoubtedly can be done. 'Different' states of consciousness play a part in it. Work is in progress at Northampton University to clarify the picture. In 2006/7 a series of experiments gave a success rate of broadly 85%. "...so something must be going on," in Rob Charman's down-to-earth phrase. (Chris A. Roe and Stuart Flint, *JSPR* October 2007).

21. Poltergeists

If the mind can 'somnambulate' under its own steam, has it some form of physical energy that it can employ when it wants to do so, or must it hitch lifts upon the brains of other consciousnesses heading in the right direction for its purposes? For example, if it wants to visit a particular house, does it leave its 'owner's' consciousness at home, and somehow move through the streets in our normal 3-D plus Time universe to the house in question? Does it then look out for that house's owner, and wait until he goes indoors before associating with his brain in 3-D plus Time, to prompt him to do whatever it wants him to do next for its information-gathering benefit? Or does the mind settle itself in some dimension extra to 3-D plus Time and, in effect, call out to other minds in that same state, "Please will any mind which knows the interior lay-out of number 4 Specific Street come and have a word with me. There are things I would like to know about that house"? Can one mind, dissociated from 3-D plus Time, 'talk' in some way like this to another mind in the same state, and so pass on information known to it? If it can, then Distance Viewing – as claimed – along with a whole host of other phenomena begin to make a little more sense. As we have noted, it appears that the mind can be elsewhere than in its owner's body / brain the whole time, and *post mortem* too. The question is rather, 'What can the mind – gallery – do on its own account when it does not have to concern itself with interacting with its own brain – plotting table – constantly?'

So does the mind somehow have its own source of energy, as a physicist would understand the term? I am not interested in 'vibes', 'occult power', and the rest of the pseudo-psychic mumbled jumble. I am considering energy because I want to look, as briefly as possible, at the phenomenon of poltergeists. They seem to me to branch off a bit from the main highway we have viewed so far of sense-data, perception, concepts built upon perceptions by the brain acting upon the stimuli it receives, and the mind's direction of the brain to carry out its wishes in relation to what the brain is showing it. Poltergeist phenomena, by contrast, make themselves known externally, and usually noisily, to the consciousness. Their behaviour has a chaotic quality which suggests the mind is directing operations in a rather dream-like way, divorced from the normal logic of mind-brain generated consciousness. But where is the energy for the creation of noise, or movement of objects, coming from? Physics, rather than neuro-biology or psychology, might be able to crack the puzzle, and so open the way to other means of investigation. Certainly neuro-biology and psychology ought to have a legitimate interest in poltergeists, but they probably will not make much progress separately towards our understanding them. This is ground where the Natural Philosopher might tread, to co-ordinate any number of separate disciplines.

Poltergeist translates roughly as 'blustering ghost'. I would rather term it 'psychic bully'. The precondition of an 'outbreak' of poltergeist activity seems to be some living person's distress, or suppressed longing – which could amount to the same thing, of course. The poltergeist latches on to this and makes it horrific. It is as if the worst fears of those involved are arising to persecute them and hurt them in their essential self-esteem. The world, via the poltergeist, has visibly and audibly got it in for them. We have noted that NDEs sometimes involve unpleasant scenes for those of a nasty turn of mind. The poltergeist outbreak goes a stage further, finds out such material, and announces to the world, "Do you want to see someone in a mess? Come and get a load of this, then!" The mind which is in trouble, I suggest, then somehow produces the alarming bumps, bangs, and other awkward manifestations that have the neighbours speculating, "I wonder what *they* can have been doing, then? We always knew that things weren't right in that household..."

Mercifully the trouble usually fades out after a few months, if only from the sheer exhaustion of all parties involved. I have, though, known very mild cases recur. These have struck me as involving some unfulfilled, and quite likely never articulated or even fully conscious, wishes of some of the people on the scene. I am pretty sure that one such case was of the "Oh dear; I do wish that we had decided to have another child..." type, a wistful regret, which made itself known whenever young children were staying at that particular house. The poltergeist just bumped a bit at bedtime, and was treated as a sort of family pet – i.e. part of the normal *emotional* make-up of that household. I have heard it myself several times. The lady of the house had her personal strong regrets though, I suspect; she was a very motherly individual indeed.

The only 'classic' poltergeist experience I have been associated with involved a rough-diamond character, H, who had once been Her Majesty's guest for a short spell, chiefly because his less than law-abiding family had set him up to carry the can when the Tax authorities became unhappy with their book-keeping. He had determined thenceforth to lead an honest life, had married, and was succeeding well in business on his own account. His parental family and siblings then tried, as he told it to me, to rob, compromise, and blackmail him horrifically in order to profit from his legitimate efforts. He fought them off, with some unpleasantness enduring. A death in the family, a dispute over a will, the embarrassment of several bad customers' debts, and then his wife's, W, diagnosis as suffering from a serious illness added to the stresses of his life. There were also various other troubles plaguing them. For her part, W had been married before, unhappily, and had a teenage daughter from that marriage. W had born H a toddler T and babe who was almost a year old at the time I met them. I came to know H because in desperation he had poured out his heart to a vicar, V, he had chanced to meet, and who happened to be a friend of mine. "What do I do now?" wondered Vicar, who was quite shaken by H's circumstances, as well as being expected to confront the poltergeist.

H, W, and their family lived some distance from the nearest town and in another diocese, to the potential professional embarrassment of V. In the event, since H was not exactly a church-goer at the time, the local parson was quite happy to leave him to V, rather than get involved with the following:

An unspecific feeling that all was not as it should be around the house.

Bumps and bangs which shook the house.

Furniture moving around by itself.

Sudden temperature changes. Because their youngest child had been born prematurely, there happened to be an electrical clinical thermometer in the house, and this registered drops of up to $7°C$ which occurred within seconds when the poltergeist was going to make itself known. I suspect that the 'missing' ambient heat may have, somehow, supplied the energy to bring about the moving of the furniture.

One very bad night when the household dogs had slept through the 'trashing' of a room, the supposed noise of it had woken H at 2.00 AM and brought him downstairs to investigate. Many items of furniture had been moved around or overturned, and a vacuum cleaner had come from its cupboard across the hall and entered the room, negotiating, somehow, two closed doors in the process. H and W had been in the room earlier in the evening; there was definitely no vacuum cleaner there with them then. The dogs were normally excellent guard dogs, and would 'go ballistic' at any unusual noise. So, was the noise of the 'trashing' real and audible to them, or auditory stimuli perceptible only to H? If so, how does a room become 'trashed' without disturbing the dogs? Were the noise and 'trashing' simultaneous, or even linked, in fact? We lack definitive answers, alas.

Toddler, T, suddenly objected to going to bed in a certain room, unless one or other parent slept there with her. It was in this room that the temperature drops were always noted.

H, having been woken one night by the sensation of taps upon his shoulder, saw a 'form' which beckoned to him and drifted away. He rushed to check on T in the 'cold' room, where he found her sitting up and pointing to the 'form'. H subsequently identified this form as his late grandmother as she had looked before the debilitation of her terminal illness.

Lack of sleep due to the disturbances affected H and W alike. As part of her medical treatment, W was occasionally required to take prescribed drugs to induce deep sleep − a profoundly altered state of consciousness. It was on one such occasion that the 'trashing' of the room occurred. In her drug-induced state she remained asleep and heard nothing. But was her mind organising the physical events, with the vacuum cleaner as a 'tidying up' afterthought? H is sure she did not move physically from their bed.

The electrical power supply to the neighbourhood came via a small transformer upon a pole. At the height of the trouble this burned out and had to be replaced. Whilst this could have been pure coincidence, poltergeists and electrical anomalies have often been linked, the best observed and documented case having occurred in 1967 at Rosenheim in Germany (H Bender, 'New Developments in Poltergeist Research' *Proceedings of the Parapsychological Association* 6, 1969). I did not try to follow up this incident with the electricity supplier because the poltergeist had responded to the steps V and I took, and I considered H and W had enough to contend with without being given a possible 'barmy crank' label – plus local gossip – by the electricity company, as a result of ghost-hunting enquiries by me.

There are sound, but confidential, reasons for not associating the teenage daughter with these disturbances.

What did V and I do? Very little, in fact, bar taking H and W seriously ourselves, and having them talk freely together about the various personal matters troubling them. From this emerged a much stronger relationship, and a determination to put a lot of nasty past experiences and their attendant emotional baggage behind them, and commit their joint forces to making an excellent marriage, plus building a prosperous business. V prayed with them quietly. I spoke of poltergeists as emotional safety valves, which blew off surplus emotional steam / energy when pressures and stresses became past bearing, but when love for one's nearest and dearest was an overriding concern amidst the mayhem. I stressed love amongst those affected as *the* important factor in the case, plus God's love for his Creation – i.e. all of us. In God's love, backed by honesty, truth and a life lived accordingly, there was no hold left for the poltergeist to batten on to. It would vanish – quite quickly, too. As it did; through God's Grace, basic psychology, the natural course of events, or a mixture of all these and possibly more. I cannot demonstrate a mechanism. Make your own choice.

For simplicity's sake I spoke throughout of the poltergeist as an entity of 'unknown energy' in its own right; which I reckon is near enough for practical purposes. The change to a positive psychological outlook replaced in H and W various horrific fears, – such as the possibility of an 'alien entity's' swooping down the chimney and physically carrying off the children. And this amongst quite sophisticated people in the twenty-first century! There is something amiss both with our educational system and popular culture. That said, even entertaining such an idea shows the mental state to which these events had reduced H and W. Poltergeists are self-generated bullies, pure and simple.

I still come across H and W from time to time. They are happy, prospering, bringing up a perfectly normal family, and have a quiet Christian faith which, I suspect, keeps their lives steady. They are, quite simply, good people.

So why, I have been asked, did I "drag your [Sic!] God into the mess?" For a start I believe in God; one God, one Creation, one human race, and one set of factors underpinning poltergeist cases. I can speak with conviction about what I know. Also, H had approached my friend the Vicar. His essential reasoning was that there was something spooky plaguing him and his family. Science had not come up with something in an aerosol can to get rid of a poltergeist 'fluence' permeating his house. Therefore he sought, in effect, a magician to cast a counter-spell to un-spook the place. That was about the extent of God in his reasoning. It is possibly to his advantage that he found V, with me in reserve, and not some earnest, newly graduated product of theological college who might not have had a clue, theologically, psychologically, psychically, or common-sensically. For one such to have gone charging in with a dramatic attempt at exorcism might well have made matters worse, if only by passing over the likely root causes.

The Anglican church does indeed have a 'Deliverance Ministry', as it is known. I know a senior cleric who has been involved in it, but it cannot be deployed like a pest control specialist called in to put paid to a wasps' nest. To deal with people in emotional / spiritual difficulty requires love. And I would define love, too, as ranging from a spot of opportunist after-hours unchastity in a pub car park right up to God's unconditional love for his Creation. It is of the higher end of the scale that I would speak to such as H and W. It is termed *agape* in New Testament Greek, and means essentially 'unconquerable good-will'. I shall touch upon it again in due course. I know of no greater love than God's, and that is why I 'dragged him into the mess'.

I have said that the poltergeist is a psychic bully. Let me illustrate this a little more by referring to a case reported in the *Journal of the Society for Psychical Research, Number 864, July 2001*; 'Report on Psychokinetic Activity Surrounding a Seven-Year-Old Boy, Maurice Grosse and Mary Rose Barrington'. "The boy is the son of …Jane Darcy, who is living with [his] father. Both parents have had two previous marriages. The father is Fred Finch, aged 62; Jane is 42. They have a two bedroom flat… The father has two children, now adults, from previous marriages. He is a salesman. The mother is of rather a nervous disposition, and has been on anti-depressants. Unfortunately she also has a drink problem, which she is endeavouring to overcome…" In short, both adults in the case had by then contrived to acquire for themselves more than a normal ration of life's problems. The psychological history and current relationships existing in this family would make a case study in their own right. It is no surprise that the 'safety valve' of a poltergeist outbreak occurred. But the psychic bullying, I would suggest, is being done inadvertently by the victims upon themselves, an awkward circumstance for all concerned. The disturbances in this case were confined to banging, which emanated from various items of furniture. The boy gave as good as he got, as he saw it, and banged back, which hampered investigation a little. However, events were recorded upon a camcorder; Panasonic NV-VX9B Standard Illumination 1, 400Lx Maximum 0.5x Long Play mode (2 hrs) using LED colour facility. Their genuineness is irrefutable. The banging, which was possibly being 'generated' somehow by the mother, was focussed upon the boy, and followed him to other places, e.g. school and his grandmother's home. Events ran their course between December and the following May. The SPR investigation was made in February, and after this the incidents slowly tailed off.

The following, from the same *Journal of the Society for Psychical Research* as a footnote, is worth mentioning; "The other case (Barrington, 1976) involving an anxious mother was reported in three instalments at five-year intervals in the *Journal of the Society for Psychical Research, Number 48* as the 'case of the flying thermometer', the final report appearing in June 1976. There the mother of a seven-year-old girl, a child who was originally presumed to be the focus of the incidents, disclosed five years later that at the time of the outbreak she had been in an acute state of emotional disturbance over the realisation that her husband, on medical advice, would not agree to her having another child.

"Five years later there were still more dramatic manifestations when he proposed that they should get rid of the pram in the attic and all the other 'baby things' still hopefully retained by her. These two cases involving a mother desperate to give birth suggest the possibility that the creative urge, frustrated of a biological outcome, may generate a paranormal force that appears to centre on the child who actually came to fruition."

It seems, therefore, that whilst the effects may 'focus' upon a child, or young and immature person, they could be generated by an adult whose love for / anxiety about that child has overflowed in circumstances where the adult is also having severe emotional difficulties in his or her own life. In some way, it seems, an overprotective obsession with the child's wellbeing results in some sort of unintended energy manifesting itself in the context of our normal experience of 3-D plus Time, cause, and effect. The plotting room gallery has called in allied forces for a special and specific strike operation, as it were, which ends in doing unwished-for damage to civilians in the vicinity, including the occupants of the gallery itself. It would be useful to know what this particular energy is, and where it comes from. It possibly upsets our customary electrical power arrangements, as we have suggested. Also, analyses of the banging sounds recorded in various cases show a vibration which is different from normal 'percussive' banging.

Dr Barrie Colvin (*Paranormal Review, Issue 46, April 2008 and Journal for the Society for Psychical Research, Number 899, April 2010*) set out his conclusions about such banging. In a case from Andover, "...Rappings were heard and communication [whatever this means in the context; someone was playing at 'spiritualism', it appears], via questions and rapped answers, was established with an entity named Eric... The vibrations caused by the rapping could be felt in downstairs walls [below the centre of activity in a bedroom] and heard up to sixty metres away... A question of particular interest to Dr Colvin related to whether the rapping sounds were different from raps produced normally. By analysing the sounds, he found that normal raps show a pattern of sudden maximum amplitude with a slow decay, whereas the Andover raps show a slower build-up towards maximum amplitude – the loudest point of the rap." He compared this with recordings of other poltergeist raps, which all showed the same characteristic. "To date Dr Colvin has not been able to replicate the wave form of the ostensibly paranormal rap by normal means, but he observed that it appeared to be generated by a non-percussive force – i.e. it was not knocking... His view was that rapping sounds of this type fell within a branch of physics yet to be understood, which involves the interaction of material objects and mental processes." This would account for the questions and answers with 'Eric', who might very well be an extension of a living personality in the case. And that, for now, is that.

But is the mind capable of generating its own energy, for travelling to do some Distance Viewing, for letting loose a poltergeist, for rapping, or for any other purpose we may think of? In various laboratory experiments with random number generators, or random event generators – REGs – it has been shown that subjects told to 'will' the REG to produce numbers in the 1 to 5 range rather than the 6 to 10 range can do so with statistically significant – i.e. strongly noticeable – results. This ability lasts only until they become bored, however! Feedback, to show how the experiment is progressing, helps hugely to keep something or other about consciousness focussed upon the task in hand. I suppose it is more reassuringly satisfying at 'caveman' level to pursue one's next meal if one can see it and so judge realistically the prospects of catching it, rather than just to run around hopefully in the jungle. If I am right in this supposition, here is a perfectly sound Darwinian reason for giving feedback upon the effectiveness of one's efforts in relation to providing one with encouragement to persevere. One will work if cheered by the prospect of success.

To pursue one's lunch cheerfully, or in a state of committed, high adrenaline fury, is the best way to catch it, therefore. Experimental work at 'micro – PK level' [PK – psychokinesis, movement thought to be caused by the activity of the mind] supports this idea, (*Journal of the Society for Psychical Research, Number 880, July 2005*; *Affect and Random Number Events; Examining the Effects of Induced Emotion Upon Mind-Matter Interactions,* James Lumsden-Cook). "Since emotion is often integral to orthodox human functioning, it seems reasonable to propose that it can impact upon psi functioning, particularly under more spontaneous conditions. Indeed parts of RSPK [remotely sensed PK] literature contain the suggestion that poltergeist effects are due to emotional suppression in living agents who live in difficult environmental conditions; and that may be the guiding emotion. On a smaller scale emotion may also prove relevant during micro-PK moments." Which bears out the cases quoted above. He subsequently shows that anger and happiness induction were significant in demonstrating mind acting positively upon matter. The whole article is twelve pages long, and has 48 additional references. I am not going to attempt to summarise it here. For future experiments, "...the role of feedback should be considered, and techniques could be utilised encouraging participants to become more and more emotional, via onscreen or verbal instructions, or through the presentation of graphic imagery such as archetypal facial expressions."

Somehow, then, it seems that mind can in fact produce, induce, or control some form of energy for its own exclusive use. The source of that energy remains to be identified, and how the mind uses it is still to be determined. We can but note what the mind can apparently do along these lines, however, and proceed as best we may from there.

22. Apparitions

I have deliberately avoided mentioning ghosts until now. By ghost I mean an apparition, the formless white-coloured entity which traditionally jumps up from behind a tombstone in a lonely churchyard at midnight and wails, "Whooo-oo!". They occur in all cultures, and have been known throughout recorded history. Therefore we can say with certainty that they are part of our normal human experience of Creation. Not everyone sees a ghost, of course, but neither does everyone break a leg during the course of their life. Both are part of life's lottery. Psychological studies suggest that people of a certain temperament are more likely than others to encounter a ghost, but not exclusively so. Potentially we could all come across one.

An apparition, in lonely churchyard or elsewhere, is simply something we 'see', 'hear' or otherwise sense – rarely taste! – when common sense suggests that there is something not quite right about it. It is anomalous to the prevailing circumstances, in other words. It is out of context. It ought not to be there. The reaction of whoever sees it may range from rapturous joy to sheer terror, depending upon that individual's predisposition. If someone expects a ghost to be terrifying, the expectation will surely be fulfilled. Certainly to come upon something unexpectedly can give one a start. Many a time I have nearly fallen off my bike when cycling in the twilight along country lanes and finding, at the last moment, that the nerves of a cock pheasant hiding in the ditch beside the road are not strong enough to let me pass by without his taking evasive action. Inevitably when I am nearly upon him, he has flown up with loud cry and clatter, swirling up the dust, and momentarily frightening me half out of my wits. A ghost may have a similar effect upon someone. But why should it intend to cause any more harm than my succession of nervy cock pheasants? Is a ghost even a conscious entity? If it is not, why be alarmed by it? Fear of ghosts is a cultural business, I think, probably connected with fear of death or the dead.

The apparition seems to me to be the product of two minds affected by some common stimulus, which may well have an emotional charge associated with it. There are instances on record of apparitional animals, buildings, landscapes and even whole events – e.g. the Battle of Edgehill – (*Apparitions* GNM Tyrrell), but usually ghosts are perceived singly and as people. They may be indistinct forms or anonymous figures, perhaps dressed in dated attire. Indeed, a naked ghost is definitely a rarity (cf Shane McCorristine *'The Clothes of Ghosts'; Paranormal Review, Issue 44, October 2007*). On occasion, though, when an apparition is described in detail, someone recognises 'Grandpa' from the description given, and then produces photographs, film, videotape or DVD of him when alive which clearly support the recognition. If the person who saw the apparition has never known Grandpa, or anyone connected with him, the mystery becomes more intriguing still.

Yet this is possibly the same basic process by which Tyrrell saw his brick. From somewhere, and I suggest it is the surviving *post mortem* mind of someone, let us say that it is Grannie, come something of her memory and emotions. These happen to coincide with what at the time is in the present percipient's mind, which is responding to something in his vicinity in the selfsame way that Grannnie used to do when she was alive. For example, Grannnie might have thought, 'How lovely the apple tree looks now that it is in blossom!' The current owner of the apple tree, chancing to view it from the same angle as Grannnie used to do, may have this same thought. This may be, I suggest, enough for his mind to 'contact' Grannie's mind, in which there is in addition a memory of Grandpa standing by the tree. The current owner then 'sees' Grandpa, from Grannie's memory, filed in the long filing cabinet drawer of Grannie's mind under 'Beauty of Apple Blossom, plus Grandpa'. Where Grannie's mind is at the time I do not know; we have already mentioned twistor space, but this is simply a guess.

In gallery and plotting table terms, the plotting table NOW shows the apple tree in blossom. In Grannie's mind / filed-memory there is the recollection of a plotting table THEN which showed the same apple tree in blossom and also had Grandpa standing by it. The NOW and THEN plotting tables coincide well enough in the view of the percipient's gallery, but Grandpa is an odd piece upon the plotting table. That is why he may look indistinct, transparent, only 'sort of' there. A second look at the table as it is NOW may banish him altogether as a reality – just as the gallery could, at will, banish pain stimuli in a particular sector whilst under hypnosis. The gallery is then saying, "There is no real Grandpa there. Ignore all memory of the THEN plotting table, therefore, and concentrate upon the NOW." So he duly vanishes, or fades out as NOW in the gallery's attention takes over completely from THEN, and contact with Grannie's mind is abandoned in the continuing context of NOW. In this way I consider ghosts as a mind-to-mind business. There is emotion involved somewhere, too; "How *lovely* the apple tree looks..." We are subjectively feeling something about that apple tree, not undertaking an objective analysis of its appearance.

The emotional impetus, for want of a better expression, seems to be important in the mechanics of psychic anomalies. We have noted *crisis* apparitions, *near death* experiences, OBEs during the stress of surgical procedures, and the over-strong love / anxiety in poltergeist outbreaks, "so something must be going on" for which there is "no testable evidence whatever" at present. Nonetheless, emotion seems to be important, and I note it as such. The wearing of clothes by ghosts is also perfectly logical if we are to take seriously the mind-to-mind idea of their origin. We do not often stroll around naked. Therefore, memories of us in locations where someone in the future may conceive the same emotion about that place as we ourselves – or someone emotionally linked to us – once felt, are going to be of us as we were then dressed. It is the context, the specific place and its features, which will inspire or provoke the emotion, too.

So, logically, a house which has been the family home to several generations is more likely to evoke emotions – e.g. 'This is a *nasty* dark staircase', 'What a *lovely* view of sunrise over the estuary we get from this window!' – that will cause much the same response over the years from subsequent members of the family – more settled and repeated than people might get from a new house which was first occupied last week. In this way an old building can build up 'atmosphere', as it is usually expressed, regardless of whether or not any ghosts have actually been seen there. Each generation shares something of the family's outlook / culture, and so reacts to certain stimuli in much the same way as its ancestors did, causing 'files' of very similar emotion-laden memories to build up and, I suggest, be available to the 'gallery' of every subsequent individual – family member or not – who senses the stimulus of staircase, estuary, or whatever it might be.

I have often heard it suggested that ghosts are 'in the woodwork', by which people usually mean that the ghosts are attached to the place as a sort wood-cell-based video recording which is played when someone 'psychic' comes along and sets the playing mechanism in motion. This is not a bad idea. It accounts for the preference ghosts seem to have for old buildings, and for the fact that not everyone who visits them actually sees a ghost as opposed to sensing an 'atmosphere'. However, it does not suggest how the ghost, or ghostly stimulus, gets into the woodwork in the first place. To view the matter in terms of mind-to-mind, though, accounts for both atmosphere and ghost. One might see, for example, a beautiful Elizabethan staircase and mentally exclaim, "Wow! What wonderful craftsmanship!", and then down it glides the Elizabethan lady of the house… But to think, "Grief! Look at all that carving! I'm glad I don't have to dust that every day!" might both affront the ghost and kill the atmosphere, because such an emotional response to the staircase is wrong in terms of previous generations' responses to it.

Why? Because the purpose of an Elizabethan staircase that had been made by the best wood carver that money could engage, was to demonstrate the wealth and status of the house's owner. He was showing off to all visitors who might come there – then and subsequently. So an appropriate, and usually normal, response would THEN have been, "I' faith! What a piece of work is this! Truly I stand now in the house of one of great wealth and lands!" The original owner's contemporaries would have viewed it in such terms, and if NOW one sees the lady of the house descending to welcome one, it is through their minds / memories evoked by one's own admiring reaction to the staircase that one does so. This possibility would account for the apparent fading-out of ghosts from very long ago, too. I can think like a Victorian; I just need to echo the attitudes of my grandparents. But to view an old castle with quite the emotions with which a returning Crusader might have beheld it is another business entirely. We shall look at the limitations of *post mortem* minds / memory files later.

So a personal emotional reaction to the stimuli provided by one's surroundings is necessary if one is to sense an atmosphere and perhaps glimpse a ghost. Imagination and expectation can also play their parts here to produce what might well be termed 'a ghost of the over-active imagination'. But if the experience of this ghost is frequent, consistent in detail, and widely reported, there might be more to it than merely imagination. A case I know involves a concrete trackway, laid down strongly and durably during World War II. It takes its course across a sandy heathland and then runs through a small wood. As it enters the wood from this direction, a footpath branches off from it to the left. There is nothing exceptional about it during daylight hours, but at night an area a few yards into the wood, and between fork of the track and path, takes on an appallingly frightening 'atmosphere'. I have known strong men fall silent and increase the length of their stride as they pass the affected place. I don't like it myself, and I am used to it. What can be stated for certain is that the contrast between the open heathland and the dark wood, especially given the light-reflecting concrete trackway, is greater than would be the case for a non-concreted track with, perhaps, hedges on either side to lessen the contrast still further. Thus the wood appears particularly dark. This is the situation shown by the plotting table.

However, the sensation of fright which rises in me, and in others who have admitted it to me unprompted, seems to be more than the primaeval part of my consciousness suggesting, "There might be a tiger in the darkness. Don't linger!" For a few yards around the fork between track and path there is something 'nasty' which is more than a straightforward reaction to a dark place, I contend. My researches have come up with no known reason for psychic alarm there. No ghastly 'orrible murder, or anything equally dramatic, is part of the local folklore. But I suspect, and I can do no more, that someone has experienced a particularly unpleasant emotion in that place, and such has been the effect upon that person's mind that it has associated the fork between path and track with horror ever since.

Accordingly, all other minds as they enter the 'tiger-potential' darkness of the wood at night receive, in addition, the alarm from the shaken mind – which may even still be in use by a living person, as opposed to a mind in its *post mortem* state. This, in plotting-room terms, would be in the notes passed on by a previous watch in the gallery, the alarmed mind's memory left for future reference. The darkness stimulates the alarm, which is then supplemented by someone's unpleasant experience. The combined effect is particularly disturbing. The first few yards along this trackway as it goes through the wood are known locally as 'the haunted bit', and constitute what a spooky place is supposed to feel like. Thus there is an element of expectation to admit to. The effect is just as apparent when one approaches the area from the opposite direction, too. So that bit of the wood enters the local folklore with a bad reputation. I feel so sorry for whoever was horribly scared – or whatever happened there in the first place – which means that I subscribe to my own assumption.

Let me now suggest something else which struck me years ago when I pondered how it might be that the ghost of Anne Boleyn was accredited with squatters' rights in so many different places. The vague explanations that 'she might once have been happy there' did not strike me as satisfying, for if dear Anne did not consider herself happy other people suffered until she was gladdened once more. So the idea of a rather sad ghost romantically revisiting scenes of supposed happiness was not convincing. Unlike her wise and wonderful daughter, Good Queen Bess, Anne made something of a profession of being a right obnoxious individual who inspired little love or loyalty. Yet she definitely gave rise to strong, if unflattering, emotions in those who knew her. So, after the sword of the specially provided French executioner had swept, did her disembodied mind go a-visiting, 'somnambulator' style, or did various servants mentally and emotionally jump to attention, just as they had done when she lived, every time a door creaked as though she were passing through it?

Is it Anne's mind which provides her apparition, or is it the minds of the servants recounting their own Anne Boleyn experiences – of anxiety and alarm, mostly – which provide the lady's reported manifestations all over the land? If we see Anne, is it just what the servants dreaded encountering which we ourselves perceive sympathetically? And do we perceive her, perhaps, because we are half-fearfully wondering if we shall see a – Ooh er! – ghost reputed by the guide book to walk through a particular door? Do we thus put ourselves in sympathy with the long-dead servants often enough for Anne Boleyn to 'walk' now and then, and by doing so keep a legend going? I suspect we do. We see, now, the same doors, windows, gardens, and other structures that Anne would have seen. Most of them have scarcely altered, and some may even be in a better state of repair than in the days when she knew them. Thanks to the emotions she inspired, she is still 'in the woodwork', I reckon.

I can claim my own experience of 'the woodwork', too. I worship in a church which is mostly of thirteenth-century construction, but is reckoned to be the fourth building upon that site. God has been worshipped in this place for 1,400 years and more. In the visitors' book there are many remarks about the 'lovely feeling' of the place; 'so warm', 'happy', 'beautifully peaceful', 'friendly', 'quietly inspiring' are typical comments. It would be, I grant, a touch uncouth to write rude remarks, but what goes into the visitors' book is spontaneous comment. I can endorse a pleasant emotion 'in the woodwork'. Throughout centuries people have seen this church's ancient stones whilst deriving spiritual comfort and direction for their lives from their worship there. Quietly musing in the place surely engages the mind with centuries of spiritual calm and hope derived from other minds, and this results in the comments in the book.

But what of funerals; are they not occasions of sadness, and sometimes bitterness and anger? Certainly, but they also mark faith and hope, and the service honours the life of the deceased. They are a 'closure', as the very useful modern term puts it, committing the dead to God's care, judgement, and righteous love expressed throughout eternity. The emotions of the moment are of the moment, and generally adjust to a future on this Earth as it needs must be for the bereaved. Life goes on. Our church has witnessed 1,400 years of people's lives, and their minds / memories still endure in it.

Do we have a ghost in our church? Sort of, is the best I can do by way of an answer. Sometimes when we are working in the building, or taking a break in our bell ringing, we hear inexplicable sounds which we blithely attribute to Philip the Monk – our first recorded priest – getting frisky. "Shut up, Phil!" we cry, and the noises cease. Why, I don't know, but 'he' does our bidding. We have, obviously, checked for mice, heating pipe movements, and all possible physical causes for the noises, let me add. We are left with only Old Phil to blame, however. He is, I suppose, a sort of poltergeist in so far as he makes a noise. I suggest that he may be the product of our frustration at not knowing much about our church's early history. He, as the 'oldest incumbent', fills a certain totemic role in this respect. "If only Old Phil were here to tell us what he had heard…" we sometimes say. The emotion works its way out in footsteps, rustlings and minor bumps, but we have never seen Old Phil. So long as 'he' does as 'he' is told, we are quite happy to have 'him' around.

In popular lore the appearance of a ghost is sometimes regarded as a portent or a warning. The ghost may even be expected to try to communicate in some way, and any odd occurrence which comes to notice after its appearance is invested with terrible significance accordingly. The idea is well portrayed by Hamlet's father in the play. Indeed, the strolling players of a couple of centuries ago seem to have been judged upon their ability to provide a really scary ghost for whatever cut-down version of *Hamlet* they were producing, if reports in provincial newspapers are anything to go by. Probably some particularly outrageous portrayals of his father became the standards by which all ghosts have been judged, then and since. Present day film and special effects ghosts are judged on their technical merits, though the scripts that support them can colour popular culture, as we have noted in the idea that 'alien entities' can come down chimneys to carry off children as part of a poltergeist case. Where there is neither Faith nor knowledge, both of which I suggest are necessary as a 'religata' package for well-adjusted humans, people are going to be the prey to such fancies indefinitely, I fear.

Do ghosts bring messages? We have noted crisis apparitions. Do ghosts attack people? We have looked at a couple of poltergeist cases, and found a deal of noise and mayhem but no breakages, let alone physical assault or abduction – via the chimney or otherwise. Is there something 'wrong' with a house, or its inhabitants, where there are ghostly goings-on? We have noted that emotion / stress has some sort of essential role in the psychic anomalies we have considered, including the seeing of ghosts which might become apparent through a simple emotional sympathy combined with a view of some feature of the building or vicinity, or perhaps from other stimuli such as sound or scent. Thus haunted houses are not necessarily 'bad' houses or the houses where 'bad' people live. This is sometimes difficult to explain in the face of popular prejudice to the contrary.

The most awkward things that ghosts do are to get themselves recorded, filmed, and photographed occasionally. I think psychic phenomena are just that, phenomena of the mind. So when I am shown a photograph of a ghost I have no ready explanation for its production. Supposedly mind and matter have somehow affected a film – or an array of pixels – in a way which is normally only achieved by light under well-defined physical and chemical conditions. What I see ought not to have been possible. It is therefore anomalous, but it has nonetheless occurred, "...so something must be going on". Which is why it is in need of investigation. The mind – matter implications here are great, obviously. Unfortunately photographic fraud is so easy to undertake, especially in this 'digital' age, that the sorting of the putative anomalous pictures from the fraudulent ones to the satisfaction of all informed and reasonable parties – to blazes with the bigots – is a nightmare. Quite possibly no definite judgements about 'ghosts' captured on photographs or films are possible at present, or in the foreseeable future, given the limits of our current knowledge and technology. This is a pity, but I think I am being realistic about it.

For the sceptical scientismist arguing *a priori* there is no problem, of course. He will maintain that since there are no such things as ghosts, photographs of them are obviously fakes and he can write 'QED' under that assertion with his scientismic integrity intact. There is nothing to investigate. Therefore waste no time or resources upon it. Which is his point of view. I could respect it more if he demonstrated how the 'faking' had been done, under the same conditions as those in which the photographic – or similar – evidence had been produced. This, however, is usually beneath this character's dignity, and very likely beyond his ability, too. He will insist that I myself must show what caused the image upon the film before he will even discuss possibilities, reserving the right to appeal to unknown scientific discoveries of the future to justify his attitude in the present. I, too, would like science to help, now and in the future, in clarifying psychic phenomena. But since ghosts are not clamouring to give interviews, all with yet more photographs, I cannot do much about this impasse.

In the 1990s a serious attempt was made by spiritualists and the SPR to overcome scientismic objections to the very idea of psychic anomalies. Its results will be argued over for all time, it seems, because a definitive breakthrough acceptable to all parties – assuming any psychic anomaly is admissible in any circumstances to an *a priori* sceptical scientismist – and the drawing together of the psychic and the sceptical to pursue a common purpose of investigation simply did not happen.

To review this attempt, I must venture into the territory of spiritualism.

23. Spiritualism

A fundamental question which arises when dealing with anything 'ghostly' is, "What happens when we die?" The Society for Psychical Research was founded in an attempt to provide answers to this question in definitive and scientifically demonstrable terms. At the time it was thought that they would be fairly straightforward to discover, but the SPR is wiser now. A huge amount of information relating to subjective experiences of the anomalous and to beliefs about them has been placed on record. Many experiments have been done and their results published. Certain patterns within the various categories of experience have been discerned; we have considered what constitutes a 'classic' NDE, for example. But a signposted road from here to eternity has not been mapped out. Given the progress in developing the material sciences which has marked the past century or so, it is unsettling to admit that advances in understanding the psyche of *Homo Sapiens* have been nothing like so great.

All religions have in common the view that some part of us survives death and continues in a different sort of existence – or state of consciousness – for eternity. The nature of that existence varies considerably, and seems to me to derive from the experiences or features of the culture which expounds it. For example, the Moslem paradise is well provided with water and leafy shade, both arguably scarce in the original Islamic heartlands. *Post mortem,* all the souls of the righteous are rewarded by living their future in the ideal state so conceived, whilst the souls of the wicked suffer torment in punishment for their indifference to God's will, or their wilful rejection of it, in this mortal life. Religions have their own traditions of belief about mankind's status in the afterlife, as well as its conduct in the here and now. They are part of the structure of faith which sustains believers, and I prefer to tolerate them as such.

So I question the justification for this sort of thing; "(Religion) encourages a kind of childlike slavish obedience (and this is) very negative. It teaches people to be satisfied with inadequate answers to profound questions… If you're told from your cradle that it's a virtue to believe in something in spite of the lack of evidence, that leaves you with nothing but faith. So there is nothing that people of opposing faiths can do but disagree. That is bound to cause confrontation… What hope is there when children are segregated and taught their own version of history with the other people as the bad guys? You're bound to get tribal wars… If your only reason to be good is that you're frightened of a great CCTV in the sky watching your every move, it doesn't say much for you as a person. There is something ancient about the impulse to morality, a strong empathetic tendency in the human mind, with clear Darwinian roots. This genetic empathy came first – religion climbed on the back of it." This is taken from a necessarily brief and selective interview by Prof. Richard Dawkins, given for *Radio Times* w/c 7th January, 2006. I could argue at length against what he states, both here and in his several books. Whilst I respect him as a biologist, it is clear that he is ignorant about religion and spirituality, and has not given these subjects much open-minded thought.

The same point is made, with greater authority than my own, by Alister McGrath (*The Dawkins Delusion.* Alister McGrath, with Joanna Collicutt McGrath, *SPCK Publishing & Sheldon Press*) Professor of Historical Theology at Oxford University. Referring to another piece of Dawkins' immoderate anti-Faith assertion he writes, "Many Christian readers of this will be astonished at this bizarre misrepresentation of things being presented as if it were gospel truth. Yet, I regret to say, it is representative of Dawkins' method: ridicule, distort, belittle, and demonize. Still, at least it will give Christian readers an idea of the lack of any scholarly objectivity or basic human sense of fairness which now pervades atheistic fundamentalism.

"There is little point in arguing with such fundamentalist nonsense. It's about as worthwhile as trying to persuade a flat-earther that the world is actually round. Dawkins seems to be so deeply trapped within his world view that he cannot assess alternatives…"

A true Natural Philosopher would calm the brawl with careful and co-ordinated research. His absence, as we have already noted, hinders the revelation of God's truths about his Creation, and our understanding of them. Prof. McGrath's little book (78 pages, including references) certainly puts Prof. Dawkins' outpourings in perspective – to the general good, too, if it ever receives the publicity and attention that Dawkins' rants can generate.

My theme here is to try and do justice to different points of view when considering the question, "What happens to 'us' when we die?" For Prof. Dawkins the answer is, presumably, nice and simple; death – end of brain's function – that's it.

But we have spent quite a while going over strong suggestions that something of us endures when the brain dies, decays, and turns to dust. What is this 'something'? I have suggested that the mind, as a separate entity from the mortal brain, endures in, perhaps, a physical dimension following the brain's death. I believe that what is universally known as the soul also endures. By contrast, however, I personally conceive the soul as being separate from the mind, having as part of its 'components' all of the mind's attributes with regard to perception, decision making, and so on. But I view it as having, crucially and in addition, what I have referred to as a chronicler and moral banker of the totality of the mortal life which was associated with it. This may be an over-complicated way of accounting for the evidence of survival of the total personality as is indicated by, I freely admit, little more than faith and revelation. It does not seem to be to be unreasonable, however, as I have already sought to explain.

I have heard views like my own lauded by some non-believers, scientists among them, as being belief and faith of the purest sort. Also I have known such faith and belief excoriated and vilified as the worst sort of superstition, devoid of any underlying benefit save as, perhaps, a dishonest method of fooling the gullible for personal gain. This latter reaction also discounted faith even as a symptom of psychiatric illness. It was scientismist materialism at its most bigoted and dogmatic. Once again, I stress that each of us has a free-will choice in the matter of belief. We must cherish this choice and make it honestly. It is truth we should seek, not fads, expedients, or merely an untroubled life.

Spiritualists essentially believe that the spirit / soul endures *post mortem.* They also believe that the soul may, *post mortem* communicate with the living, offering help, encouragement and solace. I respect such beliefs, but I do not share them any more than I can subscribe to the traditional understanding of, for example, reincarnation as I have all too briefly outlined it.

For me, the soul, the totality of all an individual ever was throughout his Earthly life, is in the care of the Total, Absolute and Ultimate that comprise God. Its own condition in the context of its relationship with God that it has, by God's grace, conceived and established – and therefore likewise responded to God's teaching when dealing with its Earthly neighbours – decides how close to God's perfection it may approach *post mortem*. This is generally conceived as Judgement. Traditionally the 'good' souls are then admitted to Heaven, and the 'bad' souls are consigned to Hell. I suggest that the concepts of both Heaven and Hell reflect the degree of closeness to God that the soul is permitted. Something akin to near union with God represents spiritual bliss. By contrast, the awareness of God, but with the soul's own sudden realisation – perhaps for the first time – of its own inadequacy in its self-centred, material thoughts and preoccupations, are its portion of hellish endurance, supposedly for eternity. In a purely spiritual existence material considerations are of no account. Relationships, of love, courtesy, and consideration are all.

There is some revelation that a self-improvement process – purgatory – may enhance and develop the soul's consciousness *post mortem* in this spiritual state and allow it to progress nearer to God. Since the soul would be fully conscious and purposeful, with its free-will intact, this seems perfectly logical to me. I do not, though, think that the soul returns to Earth in any form or by any means. The soul is beyond time and space as they are known to us.

By contrast the Spiritualist point of view would have the soul able to communicate with the living upon Earth. The soul is conceived, in various ways, as living a vastly enhanced life along the lines of its Earthly existence, on Higher Planes, or in Realms, or upon terrain rather like the classical Elysian Fields or Drycthelm's meadows. In special circumstances, e.g. as a *post mortem* Crisis Apparition or a more mundane 'ghost' apparition, it can return to Earth, usually with some specific purpose in view. Such anomalous phenomena are quite common, but I have already suggested other mechanisms which may account for them. I may be wrong, of course. Also certain individuals are believed to be able to contact the souls of the dead. I shall refer to them here as mediums, although other cultures provide them with different names and vary their job descriptions a little. Essentially, though, they are contacts with 'the beyond' and held to be able to communicate with discarnate human spirits and, occasionally, other entities of a more absolutely spiritual nature.

Let me state here that I believe that genuine mediums are as honest and as sincere in their beliefs as I am in mine. But there are, and always have been, false mediums whose practices are centred upon deception for the fulfilment of the usual range of human appetites. These people are wicked criminals, confidence tricksters of the worst and most damaging kind. There can be no accommodation with them.

Many people have received great psychological and spiritual comfort from the work of genuine mediums. Their belief systems are not my own, but to do good in the world is to walk with God. "By their fruits you shall know them…" as Jesus said of true and false prophets – that is, those who claim to speak of the ways of God (Matthew 7.15). The medium can speak for, or on behalf of, a discarnate personality – usually termed 'spirit' – which is able to produce recollections of events or personal tastes which are known by the living to be those of that particular individual when alive upon this Earth. These provide its *bona fides* by way of authentification. Some encouragement, advice, and helpful comment are usually delivered by the spirit, and the living are consoled and confirmed in their faith by the contact. But to me the spirit is a discarnate mind only, not a manifestation of the soul. I may be wrong, but this is the way I view the undoubted contact which occurs.

As we have seen, a mind can meet other minds in a variety of ways. The medium's particular ability is to be able to contact a discarnate mind which seems to want to communicate, although a medium will firmly point out that spirits seek out mediums and that mediums cannot 'conjure up' spirits. It is considered that the spirits know that the living who seek contact with them are taking steps to achieve it, and the spirits come to the physical proximity of those individuals accordingly. The medium then acts as a channel for communication across the gulf of death. Which process I regard as being fair enough, regardless of whether mind or spirit is actually involved. The materialist sceptic will have none of this, though, arguing that one cannot communicate with what does not exist. Therefore if the whole business is not fraud, it must be self-delusion, and the medium is accordingly talking to himself.

Committed sceptics advance a variety of explanations to account for the exactness, backed up by evidence, of many things told via the medium to people seeking to speak with the spirit. A 'catch-all' is to evoke Super-Extra Sensory Perception, a carefully non-defined process which somehow allows the medium to know that the lately departed Grandpa usually put a rubber band around the diary which he carried in his pocket, but just as usually forgot to tuck a pencil under it so that he could have it to hand in order to write notes. Such idiosyncratic information, which is true, convinces Grannie that she really is in touch with Grandpa, and that he is his usual absent-minded self even in the spirit world. The sceptic would have such knowledge come to the medium from Grannie's body language, perhaps. Or maybe telepathy – a concept that the sceptic would howl scorn against in any other circumstances – is what is doing the job; it is then Grannie's 'brain waves' that must be telling the medium all he needs to know about Grandpa.

In fact any old explanation will satisfy the sceptic, provided that the medium's ability to obtain truthful information about Grandpa by means which are at present unknown can be claimed to be deluded or, better still, criminally fraudulent. Quite possibly the medium has a band of 'private eyes' ferreting out information about Grandpa and reporting back to the medium in advance of Grannie's coming to see him. If she does so on impulse, at zero notice, then what the medium tells her shows just how extraordinarily easy it really is to find out about Grandpa and his diary. There is nothing spontaneous about it. Any fool could do it, – though but rarely is it even suggested how! Sceptics like to claim intellectual objectivity, and the discovery and demonstration of any mechanisms of trickery are below their dignity, because the sceptic is always a model of scientific purity and does not concern himself with such things. Which means that he simply does not need to replicate and demonstrate the 'conjuring tricks' to which he attributes the medium's abilities. There are ignorant bigots in every walk of life, of course.

I regard the idea of some form of 'telepathic' contact between medium and Grannie with much sympathy, although I would conjecture that it is a meeting of minds which cues the medium for contact with the surviving mind of Grandpa. What is presented to Grannie may just be a feedback of her own emotions concerning Grandpa, but I suspect that the better input from Grandpa comes from his enduring mind, to which the physical presence of Grannie has somehow given the medium access. It is in the same sort of category as someone's seeing the ghost of Grandpa by the apple tree, only here it is occurring to order, as it were. The sight of Grannie, as Grandpa knew and remembers her in his *post mortem* mind, might be the stimulus needed by the medium to gain access to Grandpa's mind and its contents. I can only conjecture this. Until research has shown clearly what mind is – and is not – I do not think that this line of conjecture can usefully be taken any further. It offers the approach I think most likely to bear fruit, at any rate. It does not need some pseudo-scientific Super ESP theory to do the job in the meantime.

Rather removed from the concept of a medium's work as normally understood was the series of sittings held in the 1990s at Scole in Norfolk. A 'team' of spirits spoke through two mediums to a large array of people, highly competent members of the SPR among them. In addition, various physical effects were produced at Scole, as well as in USA and in Ibiza, the changes of venue making the use of any van loads of the specialist apparatus which would have been necessary even to attempt to produce similar effects by normal means unlikely to say the least. In fact a professional magician, James Webster – Associate and Silver Medal Holder of the Inner Magic Circle – is on record as stating that the Scole phenomena could not be replicated by the skills of stage magic (*Paranormal Review, Issue 37, January 2006*). I regard the testimony of people who are highly skilled in the arts of deception as superior even to that of academics who, whilst specialist in their own fields, may have a knowledge of the techniques of conjuring which is no greater than my own – which is not too bad, may I add! I give Mr Webster's views great weight accordingly. The sittings have been reported in the *Proceedings of the Society for Psychical Research, Vol.58, part 220, November 1999*, Montague Keen,

Arthur Ellison, David Fontana, '*The Scole Report*'; and also in a book (*The Scole Experiment,* Grant and Jane Solomon, Piatkus).

Various spirits made themselves known regularly, as 'The Team'. They directed, from their own environment, a large array of physical effects. Amongst these were small lights which moved independently of the mediums and penetrated material objects, including the hands of the SPR investigators. Anomalous images were produced upon photographic film, Polaroid prints, and video tapes. Some 'apports' [physical objects e.g. coins, jewellery] were delivered to the sitters, and physical forms of hands appeared in the various rooms where they sat, occasionally touching the investigators. Of particular interest were attempts by the spirits to speak directly to the sitters via electronic apparatus such as a tape recorder without its microphone. In the presence of the SPR people only anomalous noises were achieved in this way, although in other sessions coherent speech apparently did occur. Whilst it was not possible to 'control' these events to standards of security more appropriate to a pathogenic laboratory, the scope for fraud was, in my own view, minimal. Something extraordinary was achieved at Scole. I support James Webster's judgement on the proceedings overall.

The whole exercise was predictably condemned as fraudulent by sceptics. A not very dignified verbal brawl resulted, and continues spasmodically. The Scole sittings ended for reasons we shall refer to later. In the SPR report we read:

"…it is relevant to add at this point that Prof. David Fontana is a psychologist who has not only specialised in the field of personality studies throughout his professional career but is also qualified in the field of psychological counselling. The career of Montague Keen was spent working with journalists, the media and politicians, whilst Prof. Arthur Ellison worked and liaised for many years with industrialists and businessmen. All have some experience of assessing the motives of others and in identifying their propensity for deception (including self-deception). …At no point in the experience of any one of us did we detect hidden motives or a hint of duplicity on the part of any member of the Group [of spiritualists]… As further evidence of the apparent probity of their motives, it is worth quoting their objectives as printed on the opening page of *A Basic Guide to the Development of Physical Psychic Phenomena Using Energy* [A book published by the Scole spiritualists];- '[The book] is offered to the public with our combined love for mankind and the spirit world, in an effort to help others to understand about their own spirituality within the greater scheme of the spiritual realms, and to experience for themselves the very special spirit-world phenomena in an atmosphere of love and harmony as we ourselves do at Scole on a regular basis.' Sceptics may scoff at such sentiments. Others may prefer to treat them with respect." Additionally the authors of the SPR report write; "There is a point beyond which honest doubt becomes obstinate rejection. We feel our critics may have passed it." In view of some of the implied accusations of dishonesty on the part of all concerned, investigators included, such moderate language is restrained indeed. Where are the cultured Natural Philosophers who can deal with matters like these in a rigorous but open-minded and gentlemanly way?

Nonetheless, the Scole sittings need setting in the wider context of what spirits seem capable of providing by way of evidence of some form of *post mortem* psychic existence. Let us proceed to this.

24. Post Mortem Minds – Evidence

Beyond dispute the Scole sittings are fascinating in their range and consistency. Equally there is nothing about them that will not fall within the scope of what we have already suggested mind is capable of doing, albeit at a staggeringly complex level in this case. No ordinary run-of-the-mill discarnate minds were involved in the Scole phenomena, it is clear. That said, a careful reading of the transcripts of the sittings is suggestive of almost a formal presentation on the spirits' part. For this reason I view the Scole spirits in terms of discarnate minds' memory files expressing themselves via the mediums' brains. There is an indefinable lack of something akin to normal conversational spontaneity. I cannot detect a fully functioning discarnate but yet independent *post mortem* consciousness involved in the proceedings, somehow. There is slightly disjointed information and explanation aplenty, and repartee also, but practically no rhythm of conversational to-and-fro. The effect is akin to a chattery and inquisitive child (the investigators) seeking the total attention of an elderly expert (the spirits) busy and engaged in work of his own, and not particularly good at dealing with children in any case. It reads as hard going for all parties, somehow.

In fact I would go further. In the course of the sittings the SPR investigators were asked by the spirits to make certain pieces of apparatus to help things along on the electromagnetic side of the proceedings – work with tape recorders and amplifiers in particular. What was asked made a certain sense to the experts on hand, but better and more up-to-date techniques would have produced superior results in accordance with what the sprits said they were trying to achieve. However, the experts' suggestions were either ignored or deftly turned aside. No particularly intelligent discussion of them was even attempted by the spirits.

Now, a cynic would say that this reflected the depth of knowledge, or lack of it, enjoyed by the mediums. One must simply acknowledge that the investigators were as alive to this possibility as any sceptic, and were prepared to address themselves to the spirits rather than to mediums who were not believed to be play-acting. Why, therefore, did the spirits not take up the improved technology which could have been made available to enhance their efforts at communication? They themselves gave no coherently satisfactory answer to such questions; they were more than a little evasive, in fact. The suggestion must therefore be made that they simply did not understand what the investigators were talking about. For all the intelligence they displayed, they were fixed mentally as they were at the point of their deaths – assuming as I do that discarnate minds were really the personae of the spirits – and could not in any way adapt to the progress which had been made in electronics since, at best, the mid 1950s. The spirits would appear on the strength of this quirk in their behaviour to be animated and ingenious memories, good at dealing with concepts, but not fully functioning and intelligent independent entities. They were less than the discarnate Self / soul / complete personality of any individual who had lived and become 'active' *post mortem* with all his earthly faculties intact. This aspect could benefit from further reflection by all involved, I think.

Then 'The Team' of spirits ended the experiments. They saw some sort of wickedness being undertaken by a living person in 'the future' who would try and use the communication techniques they were developing to gain Earthly power for himself. This looks to me like complete gibberish, a cop-out of low grade science fiction proportions when compared with the quality of some of the spirits' earlier utterances. What the spirits were in fact talking about I cannot fathom. Perhaps they are reflecting some unease in the mediums' own minds, and have switched from highly cultured superior intelligence to sci-fi cop-out as the best expression of it they can make. I cannot say. The plotting tables of the mediums' brains would show more markers relating to late twentieth-century contemporary attitudes to 'the beyond' than would have been present in the minds of, say, someone who died in the 1950s or earlier. Did these up-to-date ideas and possibilities alarm 'The Team', and the vaguely paranoid idea assert itself in modern TV sci-fi terms? Again, I cannot say.

I can, however, grasp at the spirits' expression of linear time. Is 'the future', to the spirits, what I call 'now'? Do their minds and memory files simply freeze time at the point of the loss of consciousness attending their deaths? If I am roughly right about the spirits at Scole being the discarnate minds of people who have been dead for some while by my own experience of time's passing, 'the future' to which they refer could well be my own present. Consider Dyananda's 'bullet' wound. We are as sure as we can reasonably be in the absence of his medical notes that he died of injuries sustained in a landmine blast. There was no bullet involved. Yet his surviving mind did not know this; it was fixed in the state of belief it held at the time of his loss of consciousness. It was fixed just as it was. It was pickled, fossilised. It could not develop. This seems true of the Scole spirits, too. They exist as they were at point of death, and nothing that has happened since on Earth has registered with them. Their brains and allied perceptive senses have died and vanished into dust.

Much the same sort of observation has been made about the mental condition of the spirits in various other cases. In *Proceedings of the Society for Psychical Research, Volume 58, part 218, October 1994, 'The Signatures on the Walls of Queen's House, Linton, Cambridgeshire, and Some of the Automatic Scripts and Drawings of Matthew Manning; An Appraisal'*, Vernon Harrison considers a certain Robert Webbe who made himself known by writing on walls about 240 years after his demise. A (then) young man called Matthew Manning provided the medium element needed to revive old Robert Webbe, and all sorts of strange occurrences resulted. I shall not recount them here. The interesting point is what Robert Webbe could and could not do to explain himself. He found great difficulty dealing with the idea that there was a future, and that that future included people he did not know who were living in what had been his house. The arguments around the details are complex, but Vernon Harrison puts his finger precisely upon the limitations of Robert Webbe:

"He dwells entirely in the past, apart from a limited awareness about what is going on at his house in 1971. He tells us nothing about his new mode of life and what new experiences he has gained since he died nearly 240 years back. The information he gives can turn out to be almost wholly unreliable. He cannot grasp anything that does not fall within the ambit of his earthly experience prior to 1736. All this suggests that we are not dealing here with a complete, developing human being. 'Robert Webbe' seems more like a temporarily reactivated part of the former Robert Webbe.

There can be a remarkable re-creation of the personality of the departed as far as memory of his former life, mannerisms, prejudices, and emotions are concerned.

The higher principles being absent, the communicator [spirit] shows no sign of creativity, adaptation to new surroundings, awareness of the new conditions, imagination, or capacity for making moral judgements. The result is ambivalence which is so characteristic of this type of communication."

This is the way I view the material from Scole. It is all there, but yet there is something human which is missing. On a personal note, ghosts I have seen have given no sign of being aware that I was present in their vicinity. They were only coincidentally in the time and space that I was experiencing; they were in my own mind, arguably. Whatever the ghosts' own state actually is, I perceived them as some sort of controlled hallucination on my own part which, of course, precludes any testing of their objective reality. I know I have seen ghosts, but who shall admit the truth of my reported experiences if he does not wish to do so? For it there is "no testable evidence whatever". This is a major obstacle to investigation.

Similar problems arise when hypnotists try and take their subjects back to 'former' lives. There are many questions begged by the very concept of former lives; who says we are supposed to have lived one, for a start? Leaving aside this rather important consideration, there is a fair selection of what various hypnotists have achieved by way of 'regressions' to what are presented as the previous lives of their subjects. My view is that these are not previous incarnations of the hypnotised subject, but simply other minds accessed by him or her in the altered state of consciousness induced by hypnotism. They are probably not anything to do with the hypnotised subject in any previous life, or in any other state. As hypnosis can dissociate the mind (gallery) from the brain's (plotting table) registering pain so, I suggest, it can just as readily separate a subject's mind from its interaction (consciousness) with its own brain, and allow a *post mortem* mind to use that brain's capacity for imaging and speech. Such minds are none the less real.

I am particularly impressed by one such case to which I have already referred. It is written up as the book *Yesterday's Children* by Jenny Cockell. Jenny had experience under hypnosis of having lived as Mary, a poor Irish woman who died in 1932. The records confirm the existence of Mary and, crucially, Jenny was able to meet some of Mary's children who confirmed and expanded trivial but precise and telling details of the life they had lived with Mary as their mother. I do not believe that such details could have been known about by any 'private eye' investigator researching Mary in any way and by any means which would satisfy both logic and common sense. It could, of course, be asserted that a small army of investigators had tracked down the former neighbours and friends of Mary – by then very old people indeed – without drawing any attention to themselves in the process, and had then extracted from them the most banal but accurate memories of Mary and her life. This done, they would next have needed to have conspired with Jenny Cockell and cross-checked all sorts of details to make a coherent picture with which to defraud a publisher for very modest gain. Indeed, I suggest that the cost of any such undertaking would easily outstrip the profits on the book! So why do it? There's nowt so queer as folk, of course, but the idea just does not make sense to me. Probably a certain type of sceptic would nevertheless prefer it to alternatives, such as the meeting of minds, or even re-incarnation itself.

I am satisfied that the *post mortem* mind of Mary somehow came into contact with Jenny's consciousness, Jenny being very much alive and, whilst under hypnosis, able to experience and recall much of the life led by Mary. Other hypnotised subjects have given astonishing and often contextually accurate accounts of past lives, too. In *More Lives than One?* Jeffrey Iverson worked with the late hypnotherapist Arnall Bloxham to record lives lived 'earlier' by various subjects. Peter Moss and Joe Keeton in *Encounters with the Past* also regressed their subjects to previous lives. Their conclusions provide much food for thought.

For a start, the hypnotised subject is not in a state which would commonly be termed 'unconscious'. Although the subject's eyes may be closed, he is mentally alert. He is aware of what is going on around him, and he can hear what he is saying as the apparent *post mortem* consciousness to which he has been 'regressed'. Yet he has no control over the thoughts which suggest themselves to him, nor the words in which he describes them and answers questions put to him. On his being restored to normal consciousness, however, he has a double set of memories – of everything that happened in his vicinity whilst he was in the hypnotic state, plus all that the *post mortem* consciousness did, said, and thought. From then on the memories of people, places and events he experienced as the other consciousness are, effectively, his own. Regardless of how they arrived in his memory, the very fact that they are established there for life should give one cause to have reservations about the reliability and veracity of 'memory retrieval' attempts by hypnosis, such as are sometimes used in the context of therapy or retrieval of witness' memories in crime investigation. In short, are such memories entirely real, or are they suggested, wholly or in part, to the hypnotised consciousness? In the latter case, who – or what – might be doing the suggesting?

It is apparently easier for the subject to speak about his 'regressed' experience once he has returned to normal consciousness and has at his disposal his full everyday vocabulary, present-day knowledge, habits of speech, and powers of verbal illustration. Subjects in the 'regressed' hypnotised state are found to labour for words in which to express themselves, and have terrible difficulties in dealing with any description or concept which is at all elaborate. Apparently the imagery available to the 'regressee' is strongly visual, and he may with equal likelihood find himself the central character in the drama, or merely be a spectator of the events he tries to describe. Yet when he is returned to normal consciousness, he can draw upon vivid memories to describe in his own words the details of the 'regressed' experience. This, I venture to suggest, may be a very clear indication that it is his mind which is altered or 'suspended' by the process of hypnotism, leaving the way clear for some other – or discarnate – mind to direct his brain for a while, but hesitatingly. By analogy, if I were suddenly called upon to drive a car very different from my own, and take it into dense traffic moving at speed and manoeuvring upon a town ring-road, crossed by many roundabouts and junctions, where I had never driven before, my own actions of driving would be decidedly cautious and stilted for quite a while until I got used to the different vehicle and its controls. So it appears to be with the 'regressed' subject's consciousness.

I see here a possible demonstration of the mind's providing overall concepts, and the brain filling in detail, including vocabulary and coherence. Since Moss and Keen were not looking for dualist brain-mind indications, however, they have reported the effects, and left the possible causes largely unexamined and without further comment. There is a possible line for future research to pursue here, I suggest.

I would like to pursue the difficulties with language a little further. The authors state, "...the spontaneous outpourings of fluent Sanskrit or Aramaic one reads about just do not seem to exist." I find this interesting. But perhaps it applies chiefly to volunteers for experiments in hypnotism, 'regression' included. *The Society for Psychical Research* has in its archives reliable reports of impeccably observed séances given by trance mediums at which the entranced medium has spoken in foreign languages of which he / she apparently had no knowledge, let alone fluency. The fluency and intelligibility of the speech so produced was vouched for on such occasions by those present who were at least competent in the languages spoken. It appears, in other words, that the mediums' utterances on these occasions were not just burblings enhanced by wishful thinking on the part of the auditors. Where this linguistic competence was coming from is another matter, of course, and I do not want to try and examine it here. What is pertinent is the presumed difference in the degree of altered consciousness between that of the volunteer and the practised trance medium. What may constitute the degree of alteration in demonstrable terms, and what may be implied by it, should prove another line of research well worth following.

There is material enough here to spark a terrific word-war between materialist sceptics and believers in spiritualism and reincarnation. Let me state again that my own view is that these phenomena can be accounted for by hypnosis allowing a *post mortem* mind to express itself via the subject's brain, but that this does not necessarily preclude other possibilities. I perceive in the context of regression hypnosis a number of points worth considering in relation to my own ideas, however.

Also, there are three minds involved in regression hypnosis; the subject's, the discarnate entity's, and the hypnotist's. Possibly others present at such sessions 'back-seat-drive' a bit, too. At any rate, I was struck by the fact that all Arnall Bloxham's 'regressees' published in his book shared the following features: names with a pronounced 'N' sound in them; the subjects were, on the whole, lonely or 'outsiders' with a mild chip on the shoulder; they were linked in some way to sea-faring; they suffered vomiting, or died deaths with stomach illness / cholera type symptoms. All of this applied to Bloxham himself, according to the potted biography at the front of the book. Perhaps the 'mental baggage' of his 'gallery' had those bits as the main elements that the minds he helped his 'regressees' produce for him needed to have in order to be sympathetic to the 'regressees'' minds, i.e. they were the 'givens' Bloxham had suggested – possibly quite unconsciously – to the 'regressees'' minds as they underwent hypnosis, and they produced other discarnate minds which most nearly empathised with them.

Messrs Moss and Keeton were preoccupied with warmth and fires in much the same way. I find this interesting. It implies, if my perception of the matter is broadly right, that the hypnotist is doing more about selecting minds for his 'regressees' than he might be aware of. He is functioning as a sort of searcher-out of what his mind finds interesting, and the minds in the nearest condition corresponding to his own mental baggage are somehow chosen to become the entities supposedly describing his hypnotised subjects' 'former lives'. Perhaps if I myself were able to 'regress' people, their 'former entities' would all report unease about dark staircases or obscured road junctions. This is not unlike Grannie somehow influencing the medium to speak of, or as, Grandpa. For what it may be worth, I suggest that the mind's memory appears to be formed of short incidents, perhaps each based on its emotional baggage. This might account for the 'personality' not knowing even its own name. If 'Joe Bloggs' – the 'personality' – had not been addressed as 'Joe', never mind the more formal 'Mr Bloggs' around the time of the incident the 'personality ' is recalling, the focus of the mind is upon the incident, and not upon incidentals such as his name, or what the government of the day has just unleashed upon him. If this is so, it could tell us something about mind and memory *post mortem.*

I have read elsewhere (*Reincarnation; True Stories*, Roy Stemman, BCA) that a couple of Bloxham's 'regressees' were providing details of works of historical fiction dealing with a thirteenth-century pogrom in York, and a Roman episode centred upon York and St Albans and featuring the usurping third-century Emperor Carausius. If true, some memory of the book could have existed in the minds which were undergoing or otherwise involved in the regression. But why not? Reading a book is just as valid a life experience as painting a door or going for a walk, I would argue. It does not of itself necessarily put the whole process of regression into the waste bin of fraud. And, to complicate the matter, might not the books' authors unconsciously have picked up something authentic from *post mortem* Jewish or Roman minds when in the creative state of writing their books? This will provoke the scientismists, but just try and discount it as a possibility!

It has already been mentioned that in the majority of reincarnation cases where the cause of death was known, the reincarnating personality had met a violent, sudden, or otherwise unexpected death. Similarly, the type of personality that experiences regression dreams, or regresses easily to 'previous lives' under hypnosis, tends to have had a rough time for a significant period of its own life – an unhappy and abused childhood, for example. Jenny Cockell is, on her own admission, in this category. In psychological terms the idea seems to be that in response to inescapable stress, part of the mind dissociates itself and goes day-dreaming in great complexity. It is even thought to produce an alternative personality, an alter-ego as a refuge for the essential self when real life gets too ghastly to be worthwhile. It is as if a child under stress wishes to be taken away by the fairies and live with them instead of with its own family, and later finds that it can do so by developing another personality to produce the desired result. Is this, in effect, something akin to a hypnotist producing a pain-indifferent jaw for dentistry, or the neurologically astonishing 'glove' or 'stocking' effect? It would serve the selfish genes' best interests, certainly. We are in deep and murky psychological waters here, but these phenomena, however anomalous to everyday experience, do occur, and they are not well understood. Perhaps a deal of human suffering could be alleviated if they were.

So are we to use the possibility of a secondary, or dual, personality to explain re-incarnation or hypnotic regression to 'previous lives'? A case can be made for it, certainly, but it seems to me that it all comes apart at the seams when the reincarnated or regressed personality starts speaking of details which are beyond the knowledge of other parties directly involved but are found, after much painstaking research, to be correct. Knowledge of this depth and accuracy should not be the product of day-dreaming and conjuring up a 'refuge' personality. However, who can give details of everything that they have ever heard on radio or television? Who can likewise recall everything they have ever read, or every conversation they have ever had or overheard? The very idea is ludicrous. But it is just possible that some of it lodges unconsciously in some part of our memories and is recalled in circumstances which make it seem miraculous in the new context. I am about as impressed by this sort of reasoning as I am by the suggestion that Grannie's body language could tell a medium about Grandpa's habits with his notebook and pencil, but I cannot, in fairness, reject it out of hand. It is just possible that enough information is absorbed by us all to create, unconsciously, a secondary personality which then emerges in circumstance such as hypnosis. I do not at all like the idea, but I have to allow it as a possibility.

Might anomalous knowledge come from 'the beyond', messages or inspirations from God, or his saints, or any allied source? To each of us God is a concept. We envisage him as we know him. This is our relationship with him. Upon the death of our brains there is no reason to think that this concept ceases to endure. We have argued that our minds, as they are at the time of death, survive in some form. So there is no reason why our concepts of God should not likewise endure. Given that this is so, and the evidence for the survival of the mind suggests as much, the *totality* of our non-physical being may likewise endure, especially if it is in some state of being entirely unconnected with our physical state to start with. This would be our soul, exceeding the mind by having within it the chronicler of all that we have been during our physical lives. Thus the soul should be equipped, as the *post mortem* mind evidently is not, to adjust to its new condition and develop further, becoming more identified with the Total, Ultimate and Absolute concepts which fuse together as God. For this there is "no testable evidence whatever", of course. This idea cannot be examined, dissected, or observed in action in the lab. Therefore it will not satisfy anyone who requires proof absolute, demonstrable and repeatable for every part of it. He will choose not consider the indications of what might be. At best, he will keep an open mind.

But his thoughts will be generated in the first place upon the plotting table of a physical brain that will die. By contrast, and by dint of 'unprovable' faith, the soul will endure and proceed towards God, "maker of all things, visible and invisible" as the Christian Nicene Creed puts it. The fact that the Nicene Creed dates from AD325 need not trouble us at all. God was as much a concept to believers in those days as he is now, and will be for ever and ever *in saeculum saeculi* …world without end. To any objection that *Homo Sapiens* may indeed be equipped with a mind that in some way survives death, but that a collective symposium of *post mortem* minds does not automatically equate with God, one might respond that if this is the way minds operate, then they were equipped to do so from the outset. This suggests that the concept of God was likewise present in the beginning, but before any human consciousness existed to begin to conceive him. Which line of thinking quickly becomes philosophically complicated…

And if there is no God, after all? To a believer this is unthinkable, but I could do worse than recount a tale told me by a teacher whose remit was to instil the national curriculum's depth of religious knowledge in pupils at a rather rough school in one the UK's principal cities. She had invited a wise old Imam to speak to a class of teenagers about God and Islam. He had spoken well and frankly of his beliefs, and had laid due stress upon good conduct and its rewards in the next life. At which point up spoke the typical fifteen-year-old male know-all of meagre intelligence and no particular accomplishment or ambition. "I don't believe in any God," stated this cultural phenomenon. "When I die, that's it, mate. So why shouldn't I enjoy myself and live a bit before then, eh? I've only got one life, and I don't want to be a dreary old loser sitting around hoping for something better that isn't there. Why don't you use your brains, man? You're wasting your time, and what's left of your own life." The Imam halted the teacher's, "Get outside and see me later!" in mid utterance. "You may be right, or you may be wrong," he said, directly and quite calmly to the boy. "It is a matter of faith, as I have told you. I am sure you heard me. But we shall both die, one day. If you are right, and there is no God, then I shall have no afterlife. But I shall have had the knowledge that I have lived all my life trying consciously to do so according to the very best guidance I can conceive that anyone should have, namely, the teachings contained in the Holy Koran. I hope I have been able to follow them closely enough to have helped many and given serious offence to none. But if I am right and you are wrong, think of your own case. Not only will you get an awful shock, but you will have to face the God you have denied and explain why you have ignored him. Are you up to that?" There was silence, broken by a little ripple of applause.

25. Cultural Ignorance – A Barrier to Progress

And it came to pass that on a day there went into a church a man who sat him in his chosen place. Next there came by a priest who cried with a loud voice, "Hast thou yet been washed in the Blood of the Paschal Lamb, thou sinner?" Whereat the man was much amazed, and ran forth from that church saying unto himself…

"Bloomin' heck! What was all that about? And where can I get this pass-as-cow lamb from, anyway? Do they have it in Sainsbury's? And I don't think my wife will want it if it's all bloody. She normally gets the oven-ready stuff. And why am I reckoned a sinner, then? I only went into the ruddy church to see whatever it is they do in there was all about. There's no harm in that, surely?"

And the Scribes, Pharisees, and Sadducees said unto one another, "He cannot have been a church person, and it is well that he hath gone his way into the wilderness and troubled us not." And they rejoiced, all, and sang Psalms unto the Lord.

There is indeed a problem with the specialist vocabulary of both science and religion, and with attitudes and associations allied to it. The basic trouble is that the fullness of our culture is not being transmitted adequately by our educators and institutions. There is no ready appreciation of history and the way in which we have developed socially, scientifically, and technically to arrive at our present state, and the vocabulary which ought to accompany this general knowledge is accordingly absent. Therefore people cannot express themselves easily in cultural terms, even when they want to do so. Also this is increasingly an age of specialists in small areas of competence. For example, the processes involved in manufacturing products which are either made of artificial materials or are built up from highly complex hi-tech components, demand knowledge beyond the average DIY range of competences. Which is well and good. But what is noticeably missing is the knowledge of the scientific principles underlying whatever makes any particular item work.

Overall, sets of skills and procedures have replaced it. Because of this, in subtle ways, we are no longer in control of our environment. And we should be. Our ignorance makes us uneasy.

There is also the cynical, political, materialist myth that all people are equal in each and every way. Abilities and weaknesses are somehow held to be the product of society, and nothing to do with genetic inheritance or personal effort. And since it is easier to discriminate against an ability in order to stifle it than it is to remedy a weakness to the advantage of the individual manifesting it, such a course of least effort has become normal. So, in pursuit of the 'equality' myth, standards in education and social requirements are lowered. One result is that allegedly 'difficult' areas of our culture, e.g. mathematics, the sciences, languages, music – in fact any area of human activity where effort, precision and discipline are needed in order to achieve a correct outcome – are neglected and denigrated. The term 'elitist' has been coined to suggest that, somehow, high standards, right answers and reliable data are socially unacceptable. Excellence in achievement has accordingly come to be viewed as anti-social behaviour, in some quarters. So our society produces fewer skilled and accomplished people – engineers and dentists, for example – than it needs. We all suffer as a result. Since, culturally, the 'elitist' ideals of achievement and excellence are taboo, a generation or so has matured which is unable to perceive that it has been denied the opportunities to aspire to them and, so, has been cheated of its heritage. It but weakly grasps that it could profitably know and do more which would enhance its personal satisfaction and practical dealings with life.

Yet there remain many competent folk who have a good grasp of their shared culture and civilisation, scientists and religious believers among them. Do these people talk to each other, and when they do can they all still understand the details of the conversation? It is natural that any group will have its own jargon and terminology. That said, if these prevent a ready and general understanding about what it is that a particular group is doing, the present cultural climate is unlikely to encourage many people to take much trouble to find out. A vague and inadequate folk mythology will suffice for them, with occasional outbursts of hysterical alarm born of ignorance – just mention anything relating to atomic energy, for example. In this way we find that all scientists are automatically deemed mad, and their work regarded as dangerous to ordinary folk. This is the ancient fear of the unknown surfacing in modern guise, to harass the very people who make known Creation and our condition in it. If they lack the skill to do their 'public relations' properly, there will now be few in the media with scientific knowledge enough to carry out the essential tasks of clear communication for them. Their work and the quality of our society will suffer, again, for they are interlinked. If what scientists do cannot be understood and applauded widely, there will be no pressing incentive for anyone, politicians in particular, to pay them to do it. We are too much beset by myth and 'spin' as it is.

Likewise, the Blood of the Paschal Lamb has a very specific meaning and significance in Christian theology, but is not widely understood or bothered about by people in general. It is akin to material for a degree course in Christianity. So why do Church leaders tend to refer to such matters when talking to people who are simply interested in finding out about Christian beliefs? Is it pure show-off? To deal with day-to-day life, what Jesus taught in the parables will be of far more use to people who want to know about Christianity and see if it can make sense of their own lives, giving meaning and purpose. And it is well to check that the meaning of the term 'parable' – an earthly story with a heavenly meaning / a story of commonplace matters which makes a spiritual point – is grasped and understood by everyone to start with. Otherwise one floggeth an horse whose breath hath departed him. And that looks better in everyday English, and all. The point is that knowledge and practice of the Christian principles which underpin our culture and civilisation are often absent, and labelled 'elitist' or 'indoctrination' by the very leaders of society who lament the social symptoms of their loss. Christians need to be more alert to such facts, and take the requisite PR steps to redress the position.

Neither can the scientist be sure that such terms as 'dimension', 'energy', 'field', 'acceleration', 'force', 'spectrum', 'inertia', 'species', 'bacterium', 'DNA', and – a beauty, this – 'mutation' mean to the layman what he himself understands perfectly by them. Can he therefore explain what he is engaged in to that eminently sensible man who rides upon the Clapham bus, in between his appearances in court? And can he do it without recourse to mathematics of a type which frightens the layman whose use of figures is mostly confined to keeping track of his bank account? If the scientist cannot do as much, then he must learn to speak in terms which most people will be able to understand. It is no good being an inspired genius if one sounds like an unworldly and out-of-touch idiot. For truth to be heard it needs to be readily understood.

The problem gets even worse when we enter territory where there is little intellectual work taking place and where each researcher has to coin his own terms in the absence of any that have been generally adopted and applied. I am referring here to life's spooky bits. Even those who are broadly of a particular academic or scientific discipline tend to come to grief linguistically when probing the frontiers of their own subjects. There is a desperate need for universally defined and employed terms in any field which involves biology, psychology, and the more obscure areas of physics.

For instance, does what I have termed 'mind' equate exactly with Prof. Ian Stevenson's 'psychophore'? I don't think it does, altogether; it is more on a par with what the Scole sitters termed 'spirit'. Tyrrell used the term 'mental constructs' to convey the idea of the pictures of our surroundings that we carry in our heads. Are these quite the same as Rupert Sheldrake's 'morphic fields', though? They seem to overlap a good deal, but I am not sure that Sheldrake and Tyrrell have exactly the same thing in mind. Does this hinder understanding and, so research? Probably there is too little research taking place for it to make much difference, but if a concept is being missed for want of a word to describe or illustrate it, someone coming fresh to the subject could innocently pass over much that might be highly relevant.

No one can explain and discuss what he cannot express.

Nor are things a lot better in psychology. Are we Super-self, Ego, and Id, or should we look only for our Conscious, Subconscious, and Unconscious? Religious people would also look for an eternal soul. But what is a soul, if it exists, and what use is it to them for getting by from day to day? Who says so, and why are his views reliable? What proofs does he give? As people kept saying to Jesus, "Give us a sign!" According to the Gospels he performed about three dozen miracles recorded in some sort of detail, apart from more generalised healings and 'driving out demons'. But we have only old reports of these matters. And there is a general assumption that people in past ages were fools – like those men who built the Pyramids or Stonehenge. Obviously such primitives could be duped by a little stage magic, just as we today can have our perceptions manipulated by those with the know-how. If we accept that much, then everything in the Bible can be dismissed as illusion and trickery, surely? In the shallow, 'quick fix', and instant opinion intellectual climate of our time, such a conclusion removes the need for serious, and difficult, consideration, and ditches Christian moral concepts at the same time. This approach makes life less demanding – and thus 'non-elitist', of course.

So, how about some proof that Jesus was not just a con-man? Well, the trail has gone cold, hasn't it? We don't know what really happened at all, now. So we are left with faith; faith that the Gospel writers were reporting what they, and others, saw, heard, and felt. Thank God for 'doubting' Thomas, who actually put his fingers in the nail wounds and spear-thrust injury of the Crucifixion, and had no further doubt that he was speaking to Jesus, risen in physical form from death (John 20. 24-29). Was it an hallucination, a concocted fiction to rally supporters, a case of hypnosis – affecting Thomas and a couple of dozen or so others also present? I have heard these and many other possibilities seriously canvassed, but my own judgement is that the man was sensible, knew what he was doing, and was convinced of the truth by his own unfuddled senses. If that makes me a fool and a dupe, so be it. I stand by my faith.

If we accept that the events our Biblical witnesses report actually happened, if only just once, can we then ever dismiss the idea that the miracles were possible because there was a supernatural element, something outside the limits of matter's built-in blueprints, involved? We do not need a natural system for a miracle. We *do* need a Divine intervention in this material world which is, as we know, constant and broadly predictable. Jesus, we Christians believe, walked the world as God Incarnate, the Word in human form which lived among us. If an all-powerful God cannot readjust the normal workings of his own Creation to impress the special nature of his presence within it upon people, what limits would we place upon his power, and why would we so limit him? As the Creator of all things visible and invisible, God is the guarantor of Creation's properties, structures and workings, and also of the constancy of these same attributes as commonly perceived from day to day. Yet as omnipotent – all powerful – God can surely act outside the laws of his Creation if he will. Thus miracles are just that – God effecting one-offs. For us to try and encompass God's abilities within human terms is to miss this point completely.

And we speak, in this context, as if we really know what we are. But we do not. We are aware of ourselves – which state we call consciousness – and we know that we can think – cf Descarte's *"Cogito ergo sum",* which is held to prove nothing by modern philosophical standards. It seems we really have no absolute way of knowing anything; we are at best approximations, the experience of our own minds. Fine, but what are our minds? We have argued that they do not seem to cease when the material brain dies, so where and what are they? At this point we are stuck; we cannot even work out and define a good approximation, as we can with Tyrrell's brick.

This brick, of course is material, and thus provable in the lab. The subjective qualities of consciousness and mind are not. Yet we know that we are ourselves and exist in time and space from day to day. We are, so far as we know, the only species to consider ourselves and Creation around us as a subject of interest in itself, as opposed to purely from the viewpoint of food, drink and any other necessary resources. We are in Creation, and have evolved as the 'fittest' part of that Creation to understand it in material and abstract terms. We do so by philosophy – the term derives from the Greek *philospohia* = love of wisdom – of which Natural Philosophy, science in all its branches and disciplines, is a part. Philosophy of a more abstract nature seeks to examine why things are as they are, usually in term of human capacities and relationships. The fact that 'Why?' questions raise themselves should alert us to the proximity of religion – Latin *religare* = to bind together. This suggests a tying up of loose ends into a coherent view of "all things visible and invisible" as the good old 'catch-all' in the Christian Nicene Creed puts it. Arguably as much can be done by philosophy alone, although the Big Bang is then necessarily spontaneous.

Where I would suggest that religion is functionally 'useful' is that it provides a coherent and all-embracing structure to accommodate human awareness and its experiences; it can truly bind them together. Philosophy on its own tends to deal with only one 'box' of experience or knowledge at a time. To join up 'boxes' and their associated branches of knowledge in one system-of-everything is not an easy or satisfying philosophical task. It can be done, and I have no reason to suppose that those who claim to have done it are not telling the truth as they see it – subjectively. But will their personal and detailed philosophical world visions encompass the equally personal world visions of other people? And how will they deal with the detailed anecdotal evidence reported by people in contexts for which there is "no testable evidence whatever"? Would the man on the Clapham bus go along with everything that a world-renowned expert in one of the sciences tells him is true, even if it is outside his own experience? Possibly he will be a little unsure about what he is hearing overall. But to tell the Clapham bus passenger, "God loves you," is a different matter. It goes straight to the heart of his own subjective experience.

For a start, he can conceive God, subjectively and in relation to his own understanding, regardless of whether he believes in him or not. He knows what love is, even if he does not actually love anyone, or anything, or feel he is likewise loved. And he knows who he is. Therefore the sentence, "God loves you," is instantly intelligible, and is subjectively felt. He can understand straight away what he is being told.

In any case, love and altruistic care for one another seem to be unique to the human race. Certainly other species show aspects of caring for their own families or groups, and it is currently contended in some quarters that there is a bias towards caring for individuals of the same species discernible amongst the primates. Observations of behaviour which suggests as much are reported, and it may become accepted that this bias exists; time will tell. However, the primates exhibiting this behaviour cannot explain to us why they show what is termed 'compassionate behaviour' by observers, and so it is upon our own subjective interpretation of their actions that such ideas must rest.

Chimpanzees – or the subspecies of bonobo – share around 97% of our DNA and are therefore 'almost' human. But they are not human. Let us be clear upon this point. We and the chimps are descended from an ancient common ancestor, but we have become separate species; we do not inter-breed. Also the *homo* species appears to be the only one which has this quality of abstract compassion in its make-up. We deduce this from various skeletal remains of Neanderthal men and women whose bones tell us that they were unable to move easily and contribute to hunting and gathering, because of such disabilities as arthritis or the results of terrible injuries. Yet they continued to live with their families or groups, and were therefore necessarily supported by their companions until they died a natural death. They were then laid to rest with evidence of ritual and respect. It is all there in the archaeology. They contributed to the general welfare in some other way, maybe. We can speculate that they were 'home guards', fire-tenders, cooks, healers, craftsmen, and keepers of wisdom, but we have no evidence, other than that their fellows cared for them when they had become incapacitated. This suggests that *homo* is unique in what we can perceive as a sympathetic moral sense.

In turn this suggests that to have a large intellect is to need also some check upon what one does with it. It has been shown that other species have a 'pecking order' to ensure that the pack leaders, i.e. the breeders who are the 'fittest' in both physical and Darwinian senses of the term, have the best of the food. This priority enables them to feed well, survive, and pass on their own 'selfish' genes, rather than allow breeding success to their 'less fit' fellows. By contrast, man takes to looking after those who are no longer fit. He is kind to them. He conceives compassion. Perhaps he has a reason to do so in specific cases, but not as a principle of life. What emerges here is love as opposed to mere lust for breeding. It is unique in evolution. Some species pair for life, it is true, but there is no perception of altruism. Their genes look out for themselves, ultimately.

This concept of altruistic love transcends a logical intelligence. We know this in ourselves. We probe the mysteries of Creation, and God, by both rational and intuitive means. Love is best classed as intuitive, even with the evolutionary 'best breeding material' element within its unconscious composition. Our logical brains can grapple with questions raised by our perception of Creation and provide answers which are useful to us. Which suggests that there is no Divine block imposed upon what we can consider. We are evolved and equipped to make the best of our circumstances. We are able to weigh information and choose what course to take. We are also responsible for the results – pollution and degradation of Creation and ourselves amongst them. So it follows that we should love ourselves, our species, and the rest of Creation around us, to our best overall advantage. We may also project that love still further upon a conceived loving Creator, from whom our unique capacity to love at all would seem to derive. This does not prove that God exists, but the perception of a love-based morality in our lives certainly mitigates the brutality of life as it would be lived with our huge intelligence at the sole disposal and direction of our 'selfish genes'.

Judaism codified the basic requirements of civilised society as The Law, which is also called The Ten Commandments. Christianity has adopted them, and Islam is conversant with them. Let us examine them in the context of present Western culture.

26. The Ten Commandments

For the government of the Jews following their exodus from Egypt, God gave Moses the Ten Commandments as principles for personal and, by extension, social conduct. This is our tradition, and our civilisation and culture have their roots deeply embedded in it and nourished by it. To quibble over whether or not these commandments were actually laid down by God is to evade their import. What are they? Let us look at them. (cf Exodus 20. 1-17 for context)

I am the Lord your God ... Worship no god but me.
This is the concept of The One; the Total, Absolute, and Ultimate; the Prime Cause. To this concept we must hold fast. To settle for anything less is to create '…isms' in the human mind by power of the human brain. The human brain is not Total, Absolute and Ultimate, so its creations are necessarily second best. Have we not seen enough of '…isms' applied by various regimes in the Twentieth Century to grasp the point that man is not too good at reinventing the business of Creation? Quite apart from Nationalism, Communism, Terrorism, Welfarism, and other political schemes, we are acquainted with Materialism and a host of allied 'quick fixes' and selfish short cuts which risk dominating us. We need to employ the transcendent aspects of God as a yardstick for our own values and aspirations.

Do not make for yourselves images…
Hold fast to the concept of The One. To put any man-made object, material desire, or philosophical objective on a par with God, and to relate to it or refer to it by way of expediency, is to lapse into the self-worship of the brain. The brain is part of Creation and will die. Its perceptions are expressed in the markers upon the plotting table; they are not, and cannot be, universal. Neither can the concepts our minds build from them. Thus they are skewed at the outset and are less than the attributes of The One and, again, are second best accordingly.

To centre one's life upon the pursuit of material gain is likewise a debased expression of one's humanity.

Do not use my name for evil purposes…

His uniqueness or 'otherness / other-than-worldliness' – i.e. the features of God transcending human understanding – set God apart in the scheme of things. To attach to God human motives and attributes for selfish human purposes degrades God and his uniqueness. This likewise diminishes the spiritual status of whoever presumes to do so. God is not a psychological lever, or a spiritual stick for beating our philosophical or political enemies. He is to be spoken of solely in his capacity of holiness. We ourselves cannot achieve anything near such holiness, as we need to recognise. God is to be taken seriously. That much understood, we may still make known God's word lightly, or speak of our human condition in relation to God with humour. There is no necessary and obligatory connection between devoutness and dreariness, and we are all blessed and refreshed by the gift of laughter.

Observe the Sabbath and keep it holy…

Give yourself time off, a day for re-creation, a time apart from normal daily work. By the tradition of *Genesis,* this should be every seventh day. It is to be used for our health – spiritual, psychological, and physical. To pause, regularly, from the round of physical survival is necessary to the whole well-being of the individual. Recall, also, when enjoying recreation that it is God who requires it so, for we have evolved to need it and benefit from it.

Respect your father and your mother…

People lived and dealt with life before we were born. Their experience of life is longer than our own. Heed it. Do not try to reinvent the world. It must evolve. We ourselves are the inheritors of our culture; we can never have gained enough wisdom to reinvent the patterns of life and start again from an arbitrary 'Year 1'. Look at the false values and horrible legacies left by those who have tried to do this. We must make sure our children appreciate the point, and evolve life in their own generation with due perspective and regard for the inheritance upon which they build, – which we must take pains to pass to them in good condition.

Do not commit murder.

Killing in order to get our own way is not a legitimate act. We presume too much in the process.

Do not commit adultery.

Adultery presupposes a commitment properly known as marriage. Any breach of this is betrayal; of our partner's trust, of our own integrity and, in consequence, of our commitments made to God and our fellows in respect of the married state. Adultery undermines the institution of marriage, which is the bedrock of the family. A family is based upon the love and shared disciplines of life in a household. Within the family there is structure, support, love and loyalty – a culture suitable for the proper raising of children, which process itself necessitates discipline, and from which they in turn learn self-discipline. To undermine the family state by yielding to the very real temptations of expedient sexual thrills is crass selfishness. Selfishness in any context is sinful, and the damage suffered by all parties when adultery breaks marriage, family and household, and corrupts society by extension, is sin – impure and all too simple.

Do not steal.

The material goods of this world are tenable according to the established rules governing our culture and society. Respect for these rules keeps harmony, social cohesion and co-operation. Anything which undermines them, such as theft, is a breach of trust damaging to our fellows, our wider society, and to our worth as a part of it all. It diminishes our integrity, and implies a contempt for our fellows and their own integrity and worth. In this way it separates us further from the Total, Absolute, and Ultimate standards of behaviour – 'Love your neighbour as you love yourself' – which are embodied in God.

Do not commit perjury.

Truth is the goal of all religion and philosophy. Total, Absolute and Ultimate truth is God. There can be no greater truth. Truth as we can know and usually demonstrate it is an attribute of Creation and of our evolved ability to conceive and formulate it in the context of our lives. It dignifies the human condition. To knowingly speak or do less than is true to our best belief, is to degrade ourselves and insult God. Common sense, however, suggests that the 'white lie' told, for example, to encourage someone who is seriously ill, or to prevent some greater evil, is permissible if the judgement of the individual speaking it suggests its wisdom. It should be the lesser of two plain evils. We have judgement, and moral responsibility for using it well. Regard for truth should always guide us in its exercise.

Do not covet...

This is a moral 'catch-all'. It is possible to lead our lives without murdering anyone. We may never steal, or even 'fiddle' a tax return or something such. It is, however, impossible not to see some desirable material object and wish, however fleetingly, that it was our own. Likewise we may wish that we were as accomplished, good looking, healthy, or in some other respect as well-endowed as some other individual. Making such comparisons is a natural human status check. It is also a temptation to envy. Where this temptation is allowed to overwhelm moral sense, and envy turns to jealous hatred, then our outlook is badly skewed and our judgement damaged. Sin is then rampant. Socially there are very great temptations for a certain type of politician to play upon the covetousness of the electorate and 'spin' promises of a 'better, more equal, and more just society' at the expense of some section of it whose status is set up to be envied. Appalling crimes have been justified this way in the last couple of centuries, and the evil is still present amongst us.

It is fair to say that these ten principles for living underpin Western society. That they should have been formulated in the Levantine Bronze-Age shows how fundamental they are to the human condition at its most basic and simple. Traditionally they were given to Moses by God; their simplicity and the power of their far-reaching implications may be held to underscore a more than human wisdom as their inspiration. The pettifogging and nit-picking legalist regulations which follow them in *Exodus* merely serve to throw their grandeur into higher relief.

Jesus simplified them, but without modification, still further; (Matthew 22. 37-40) "...'Love the Lord your God with all your heart, with all your soul, and with all your mind.' This is the greatest and most important commandment. The second most important commandment is like it; 'Love your neighbour as you love yourself.' The whole Law of Moses and the teachings of the prophets depend on these two commandments."

So there it is. In more down-to-earth terms we may read it as recalling to us that *Homo Sapiens* is not the author of Creation, but merely the part of it 'fittest' on an insignificant and peripheral planet to view and attempt to understand the whole. The greater concept of God transcends our piffling and rather grubby cosmic backyard, and epitomises and embodies all our greatest attributes. By choice, for nothing but God can check and restrain God who is Almighty, he wishes to have a relationship with us for our good. The constancy of his goodness, as opposed to caprice or vindictiveness, is the ever-present attribute of God. God does not mollycoddle his worshippers and ignore everyone else. His Creation and its laws are common to all. Yet he is known to those who seek him and enter into relationship with him. We cannot be anything like God in knowledge, morality or achievement, but despite our inevitable shortcomings he – his Holy Spirit – sustains us and assures us of his love. Therefore those who know God love him.

By reflection of God's love for his Creation we ought to love our fellows, for we are all God's creatures. Therefore, for the sake of God's love, we should extend to our fellows the same levels of courtesy and support which we would hope to receive from them. Yet to do so does not condemn us to a doormat existence at the whims of the uncouth and unbelieving. In New Testament Scripture, originally written in Greek, the word used for Christian love is *agape,* which means 'unconquerable good will'. This is to be the Christian approach to humanity, not some sort of mental and emotional soppiness. Therefore we are entitled to explain clearly why we adopt a certain standard of behaviour, and to urge and require our fellows to adopt it likewise in their dealings with us, to mutual advantage. Our laws presuppose this.

Equality before God consists of every created soul's potential to turn to God in loving relationship. This is understood to be what God wishes, and every conscious soul which repents its imperfections – and we are all imperfect by comparison with the Absolute, Total, and Ultimate attributes of God – and turns to him in faith by its own freewill may approach God *post mortem.* If the conscious soul chooses not to acknowledge God, then it remains *post mortem* at the distance from God at which its conscious life upon Earth has set it. All souls have potentially equal worth in God's sight. But in material terms we are not equal in every way. Our DNA is different, and our physical condition, environment, and life experiences to date all combine to make us highly individual. Thus it is truly said that no two people are alike, let alone exactly equal. For purposes of social cohesion, however, the convention has been established that all are (or should be) equal under the law of the land. This promotes fairness in the dealings of one person with another individually and collectively, and eliminates any *de jure* class which is beyond the law.

Part of Great Britain's legacy of empire has been to implant this convention of equality before the law in many parts of the globe. Its Christian roots are not always apparent in the context of other cultures, and it can cause difficulties accordingly – as with the individual's status under the Indian caste system, for example. In totalitarian States it tends in any case to be observed only so far as is politically expedient. But it is to individuals that God speaks, not to nations. And nations are ruled by governments comprised of individuals. It is their moral integrity which supplies the quality – or lack of it – of the rule they deliver. It follows, therefore, that religion must address itself to all people, and set the standards by which society views itself and conducts its business. If religion behaves as though it is an optional social distraction to be indulged in as and when tooth-and-claw scrabbling for material advantage can be relaxed a little, it has contributed nothing to the general good. It needs, therefore, to be a vocal and visible public conscience in society.

Yet Christianity has tended of late to ignore its role in forming the social conscience. I am not suggesting that nations should be ruled by theocracies; this has been tried now and then and proved disastrous as the power-struggles of politics have corrupted and degraded the underpinning beliefs of faith. Religion's role is to form and support the culture of people generally, presenting to them standards of thought, integrity, and subsequent behaviour which clearly define right from wrong, and divide acceptable conduct from the unacceptable. The development of individuals' souls for them to be acceptable to God in eternity is religion's aim. Each one of us has the choice of following the path of Faith or rejecting it. But if that path is never spoken about, if its course is never mapped out and put before us unless we happen to turn up at the church of St Goldilocks in the Woods at 9.30 AM, precisely, on Sundays – and only Sundays – how shall we know that it exists?

In its more formal and organised Anglican garb Christianity nowadays almost creeps along, silently, hoping to cause no offence to anyone, not even to sinners. By contrast, much good work is done by Christians, as individuals, charitable groups, or organisations, in alleviating distress in a multitude of forms. The world would be worse off if this were not so, and Christians are required to be charitable; the concept is based upon the Latin *caritas* = affection, which is in turn derived from *carus* = dear. This is rather different from the common understanding of 'charity', which is usually taken to mean 'cash hand-out, or a spontaneous action to improve the material condition of the less fortunate'. Which gets things done when there is a sudden need somewhere – as consequence of an earthquake, for example. It is spontaneous; Jesus never said anything about proceeding by way of five-year-plans to some sort of material paradise. An *ad-hoc* meeting of needs is the general idea.

There is a public perception, as a result, that Christianity's purpose lies in 'being good' by making material provision for 'victims' in conditions of great newsworthiness. Whilst there is nothing wrong with this in terms of necessary relief or help given, Christianity's 'PR image' is that it is concerned principally with what the Bible terms 'works'. Accordingly, to be 'caught' by 'the Church' is perceived as being forever condemned to helping with coffee mornings, bazaars, or appeals to raise cash – for charitable purposes, or merely to stop some particular church building's roof leaking. It is, actually, little appreciated that the State does nothing directly to support even the architectural gems of our great cathedrals, let alone help a small Victorian brick church in an anonymous suburb. So the church, and fund-raising, and 'being good' to 'victims', have all become lumped together in the public perception of what the church does and must, therefore, exist to do.

Fine, but does not our government provide the same 'goodness' to 'victims' much better? After all, it has greater funds to start with; just look at the way we are taxed! Its 'aid' efforts are always proclaimed by the Media – government employs thousands of 'spin doctors', of course – and so it is made obvious that it is 'concerned' at all sorts of unpleasant events and calamities. What can the congregation at St Goldilocks in the Woods do by comparison? Is the concern of this congregation even 'relevant'?

I have emphasised 'being good', 'victims', and 'concern', and added that publicity is given to them by spin doctors. They all relate to 'works'. So far – so good, we might think, and fail to notice that the goodness of those 'works' derives directly from the traditional Christian concept of charity which is underpinned by faith. Faith expressed in 'works' is a matter of Christian altruism. It is not some sort of points-system whereby the Christian can say, "OK, God. I've done this, that, and t'other thing, all of them good and highly laudable by the standards you have set. Therefore I am a remarkably good fellow, and you must accordingly let me into heaven. Indeed, y'know, in time they may even make me a saint." (cf Luke 18. 9-14) One does 'works' because one has faith, and that's it; no Brownie-points, no quid-pro-quo. It is by virtue of one's belief that one has 'worked' in the first place. St Paul puts it this way (Ephesians 2. 8-10) "For it is by grace that you have been saved, through faith – and this is not from yourselves [i.e. by something you have invented], it is the gift of God – not by works, so that no one can boast [i.e. get the spin doctors to make him look 'good', 'concerned', 'caring', and generally saintly]. For we are God's workmanship, created in Christ Jesus to do good works..." Again, in his letter to the Romans, "Therefore, now that we have been justified through faith, let us continue at peace with God through our Lord Jesus Christ, through whom we have been allowed to enter into the sphere of God's grace where we now stand... God demonstrates his own love for us in this – while we were still sinners, Christ died for us." (Romans 5; 1,2, & 8).

Unfortunately the materialism and secularism of the present age have corrupted even the concept of 'works', and have added an entirely selfish public relations element to it to create what has become known as 'political correctness'. Despite being much derided, 'PC' concepts have insidiously corrupted our thinking, our institutions, and our moral outlook. PC is a force for evil in its capacity to kill Christian standards of common sense, compassion, choice, and freedom. I want to show how it does this, and demonstrate the damage it has wrought to us all.

27. The Curse of 'Political Correctness'

I have just described 'political correctness' as evil. No doubt most people are irritated and amazed by its nonsense, but can it really be evil as opposed to just plain silly?

There was once a man called Horatius Cocles, a political thug on the streets of ancient Rome. The gang he was in had just thrown out some other political toughs and was enjoying the spoils of victory when its opponents made a bid to reverse matters. Horatius and his mates decided to offer resistance against the odds, and the poet Macaulay puts it thus:

> *Then up spake brave Horatius, the Captain of the gate,*
> *"To every man upon this Earth death cometh, soon or late..."*

But Macaulay wrote before Political Correctness became a sort of obligatory public religious practice. Consider the two lines of verse above from the PC viewpoint – 'Then up spake...' Ah! But should not Lars Porsena and Tarquinius Superbus (the villains of the piece) have been given their 'right to reply'? 'Brave Horatius...' Better not say 'brave' – it implies moral inequality, and might offend those who are 'disadvantaged' in the courage department. 'The Captain...' Grief! A title! This is hierarchy! Elitist! Horrid! Hateful! It ought to be 'Comrade Horace, the elected gateperson...' Not that this should imply, of course, that he was in any way responsible for the gate, or accountable if it went missing or if the wrong people came in through it. This would have been an office of public trust, after all, and its holder accordingly not be expected to be accountable to anyone. We must do away with the gate, too. Gates, when shut, *exclude* people. 'To every *man*...' Shriek! Faint! This is sexist muck. How can one allow it? 'Upon this earth...' implies other states of being for which there is "no testable evidence whatever", so the term should be banned in the interests of eliminating fantasy and superstition. 'Death cometh...' Well, we don't talk of death, do we? It *traumatises* people. And of course 'soon or late' should have been 'sooner or later', for we must uphold standards of literacy. Further, the old forms of English, i.e. 'Spake' and 'Cometh' are why all the churches are empty, don't y'know. People can't understand archaic English in this modern age, when only inclusive, meaningful, open-ended, accessible and relevant subjects – and stuff – comprise the national curriculum in schools.

The sentiment is killed with the poetry. And this is just what PC achieves; the reduction of life, sense, and the vastness of the human spirit to a denial of humanity and the eradication of individual responsiveness to it. Along with the individual's response there vanishes the individual's freedom to make choices from a range of proper alternatives, let alone to take personal responsibility for their results. Admittedly I have accentuated the PC outlook in relation to these lines, but I stand by the smug, twisted, rigid, self-righteous, intolerant, dictatorial pettiness of the PC-style comments. Superficially they appear to show a concern for the sensibilities of the underdog, but a closer examination reveals a nasty self-adulation and control-freakishness. The PC promoter is really saying, "Look at me and admire me for being good. And mine is the only point of view which is valid." This is worship of oneself, which is blasphemy. And selfishness equates with sin in any case. This is why I resist PC.

To get away with this sham morality the PC exponent has hijacked some of the basic Christian / Classical essentials of Western civilisation, and subtly perverted them. This is why PC, whilst detectable, often seems difficult to argue against and expose in all its blighting hypocrisy. It apes the genuine concerns of humane people, but promotes its own self-centred materialist version of them.

The hallmark of PC is its calculated self-regard. It is saying, "Look at me being good!". Its sole purpose is to project its own appearance of 'goodness', on its own terms, and to make sure that it is admired on the same basis. The whole point of PC is self-promotion, in other words; Public Relations, nothing more. It will not bear comparison with any true compassion or concern. So to try and avoid detection, PC strives to make consideration of any viewpoints but its own unthinkable. It pursues this end by shouting down alternatives, because it dares not allow an examination of them. There must be no non-PC options to choose from.

I have suggested that an entirely proper Christian concern with 'works', unsupported by sufficient explanation of 'faith', has left the way open for PC to impose its own standards upon people's charitable intentions. But let us look at what Jesus said about charity (Matthew 6. 1-4) "Make certain you do not perform your religious duties in public so that people will see what you do. If you do these things publicly, you will not have any reward from your Father in heaven. So when you give something to a needy person, do not make a big show of it, as the hypocrites do in the streets. They do it so that people will praise them. I assure you, they have already been paid in full. But when you help a needy person, do it in such a way that even your closest friend will not know about it. Then it will be a private matter. And your Father, who sees what you do in private, will reward you."

Christian reticence about 'faith' perhaps owes its origins to these injunctions. Let us not become confused by the term 'reward', either. We could call it spiritual development, by God's grace, with equal truth; there is no 'points system' involved, remember. If one's relationship with God is sound, one behaves accordingly.

To be able to PC-posture as a doer of good, one needs a beneficiary for one's PC-goodness. Thus a supply of 'victims' is absolutely essential to PC. (Interestingly enough, PC will not allow that anyone could be a victim of PC itself!) No demanding burdens of proof of 'victimhood' are needed. Anyone will do. To PC, once there is a 'victim' it follows that there must be a 'victimiser'. Therefore if one should declare oneself a victim, or be appointed one by a PC exponent, one must necessarily demand some form of material compensation from the 'victimiser' – i.e. the pre-judged 'guilty party' of one's choice. Upon that basis the 'guilty party' must then either yield and make reparation, or go to the trouble of proving his innocence. Under no circumstances may the usual legal presumption of innocence until guilt is proved be allowed to apply. Witch trials once proceeded on this same basis. But PC cannot be a witch-hunt in its own interest, can it? It only wants to make the world a better place – by eliminating everything that is not entirely and absolutely PC.

Nor does there have to be an identifiable 'victim' to satisfy PC's need for one. A notional or abstract 'victim' will fill the role very nicely in order for the PC exponent to be able to pose, posture, and preen himself whilst crying aloud, "Look at me being good, everyone!" Instances of this approach are legion. For example, it is recognised that smoking tobacco is a cause of lung cancer, not to mention other respiratory ills. This is common knowledge, backed by scientific proof. Therefore, if one chooses to smoke, one knows that one runs the risk of various illnesses, lung cancer included. One has made one's informed choice so one should logically take responsibility for the consequences, including medical treatment if one falls ill. This approach is entirely accepted and understood in the context of insurance. If one chooses to compete in motor cycle races, one's insurers will require a high life insurance premium in order to cover the increased likelihood of paying a large sum to one's widow if one is killed whilst racing. This is logical and just.

But, of the 'goodness' of its heart, PC seeks to prevent anyone from thinking this way. It proclaims a 'Right to Life'. It does not trouble itself to define 'right' or 'life', or the circumstances in which one's expectation of continuing to live might reasonably cease. This 'right to life' is in fact just one of a vast array of amorphous, notional, and downright imaginary 'Human Rights' which are asserted by PC to cater for its own purposes. No one has a 'right' to anything. Rights are cultural concepts, and history shows that they vary in nature and application over the years. They are usually to the advantage of the individual, as opposed to the convenience of the State, and have been hard-won and carefully exercised. Rights do not come with the biological process of being born. Further, rights have a tendency to require responsibilities of individuals in return. So if I want to own my own goods or property, without the State or anyone else taking them away from me at whim, I must live in a socially responsible way according to laws which apply equally to me and all others in the State. I therefore owe it to society to live according to law, and I owe it to my fellow citizens to ensure that the law works fairly for us all.

PC finds such ideas irksome – along with all choices and responsibilities, correct and incorrect social conduct, and duties to oneself and to one's neighbours. These merely inhibit PC. So it proclaims a blizzard of 'Rights', and defies the individual to challenge them. This is in keeping with its guilty-until-innocence-is-proven impositions upon common sense fairness in human relations. And it might be difficult for someone to question such a claim as a 'Right to Life', especially if the hosts of PC were shouting him down in every way provided by our media-ubiquitous age. Thus the idea of a 'Right to Life' becomes established as an unquestioned fact, ripe for PC exploitation. To be 'good', we – meaning by implication society as a whole – must *eliminate* absolutely everything that might possibly be harmful to potential 'victims', and so threaten their 'Right to Life'. "Look at us being good! We are protecting potential victims from every conceivable danger which we think may befall them somehow!" is the cry. So 'we' supposedly choose to restrict, regulate, repress, regiment, and often ban outright any activity which might conceivably produce a 'victim'. And how PC loves to ban things! Simply to inform people of perceived risks and let them make their own judgements about them is anathema to it. If people are free to make choices, they might not choose PC. So – no choices; ban them! By order!

But can we not evaluate the degree of risk an activity involves, and either decide – freely and of our own choice – to participate in it, or to ignore or shun it? If the activities of others are offensive to us, can we not arrive at an understanding with them by which they will only undertake such activities in ways or at locations where they will not interfere with our own lawful and quiet enjoyment of our lives? Is this not a free and fair way of behaving? Are people different in some way from ourselves not to be tolerated, and an equal toleration of us be expected from them in return? In short, why do we allow PC to use the spurious concept of 'rights' to tyrannise us into the restrictions of a one-size-fits-all code of behaviour on PC's terms? If someone chooses to race a motorcycle, is not the responsibility for any risk to his life and limbs his own? Why deny it to him? Likewise if someone wishes to smoke sixty cigarettes a day, who holds a gun to his head to force him to do so? If he smokes of his own free will, can he be a 'victim' by any definition other than one concocted by PC for PC purposes?

In all aspects of life there are risks. The sensible course for every individual to take is to evaluate the risks he faces, and take reasonable steps himself to reduce them. Risks cannot be eliminated, but it is certainly possible to manage them and keep them at a level which is acceptable to individuals using their own judgement and, accordingly, to the society they comprise. In loving one's neighbour as one loves oneself, one is putting such philosophy into practice. It is only if one wishes to exhibit a false kind of love towards one's neighbour that one tells him, "It occurs to me that by smoking – and I do not myself smoke, as you must surely have observed – your health may be affected by the fumes. Thus, for your sake, I am going to stop you and everyone else from smoking, in any place whatsoever. Isn't that good of me? Am I not wonderful?" This is the PC approach. It is restrictive, repressive, and denies the individual his freedom of choice and responsibility.

PC is at its vilest when it seeks to warp young minds. It tries to train youngsters to accept that in a world full of PC restrictions they have no option but to comply, because PC is 'good' and therefore its activities are all for their 'good'. There is an insidious attempt to create a PC-regulated citizen. Different standards of achievement, for example, must be eliminated, because to be talented or to excel in some way is 'elitist'. And those who are not talented or able to achieve their ambitions are designated 'victims' of some sort of PC-contrived 'injustice'. PC insists that we are all 'equal' in every way. This 'diminishes' us, to use PC's own concept against it. A school's football team may be photographed but, for equality's sake, its members' faces must be blanked out in the published picture, so that those who were not selected for the team do not feel 'diminished' or 'excluded'. (This is an actual example of PC.) Also, PC conceives that it might come about that a pervert will see the photograph and obtain some peculiar pleasure from looking at it. How 'good' it will be to prevent him from seeing the faces of its members! So therefore those of us who consider that all this is just vile PC nonsense have automatically revealed ourselves as elitist and perverted. How 'good' PC is to point this out to us! Otherwise we might have committed PC 'crimes' we never knew existed. How unspeakably bad that would have made us.

To work, to discover and develop talents or skills, to achieve some distinction in sport or anything worthwhile, is the way in which a child develops as an individual. It requires self-discipline, effort, and responsibility for organising oneself, and these attributes have to be learned-by-doing. It also pre-supposes that one has some goal in view and is ambitious to attain it – such as being selected for the school's football team. The child has been, of course, horribly perverted by the school for seeking a role in a competitive sport in which there will be winners and losers; concepts anathema to PC. According to PC there should be no such distinctions in any facet of life, for losers are 'victims', even in sports. But, regardless of PC, one is responsible for one's own efforts to attain one's ambitions, and for one's behaviour in the process. Accordingly one must be taught suitable approaches and disciplines. This is all part of growing up.

But wait! What about one's 'rights' in relation to 'discipline'? A child is, according to PC, equal in 'rights' to an adult. Thus if a teacher justly rebukes an unruly child, that child is 'diminished', 'traumatised', 'marginalised', 'excluded', and all the other PC terms useful for producing its stock capital of 'victims'. But children are not born knowledgeable or virtuous. Millennia of civilisation have concurred that the child is not the equal of its parent, the pupil not the equal of the teacher, the apprentice not the equal of the skilled craftsman, and so on. The child's proper position is that of an apprentice adult and citizen. Until it has been taught how to fulfil its roles as adult and citizen, it cannot be said to have full 'rights' in either category.

Yet, roughly weekly, we come upon Media reports of teaching careers ended, and decent people's lives ruined, because some unhappy teacher has required a five-year-old to sit down, be quiet, and pay attention, and has then been charged with infringement of that unruly infant's 'rights'. The rights of other pupils to be educated in a safe, organised, calm and structured environment have never been violated by the obnoxious child's disruptive behaviour, of course. But all that matters to PC is that the unruly child has had its 'rights' denied. And since children are no more stupid than the rest of us, it is easy enough for a child to make up in spite an allegation of 'denied rights' against a teacher, and be believed implicitly. Thus many teachers try to avoid insisting upon correct behaviour, and the child grows to maturity believing that it can do as it likes. A universal upsurge of bullying within schools, and anti-social behaviour outside them, is one self-evident result.

Who of my own generation has not at some time separated a couple of nine-year-olds, beside themselves with the fury of tempers lost, fighting in the street? Having been physically separated and calmed down, did they not then usually walk off together a few minutes later as the best of pals once more? Was not intervention by an adult, as a citizen who was mature, experienced, educated, authoritative, and able to speak a few pithy words of wisdom, the best outcome in such cases? Did the combatants not perceive how foolish they had been and, so, learn how to settle their differences better in future? Yet PC would term such intervention 'child-abuse'. So these days few people would care to risk the PC-legalised consequences of intervening. It follows that bad and violent behaviour in public are sanctioned by default. Those guilty of it perceive it as normal and personally advantageous, and society as a whole is brutalised. Heaven help any adult if he has to try and prove to a PC-minded magistrate with political ambitions that he is not a brutal, paedophilic, child-molester, before he can even obtain a hearing to justify his support of public-order in such a case! Yet should not adults uphold social courtesy, law, and order, and teach the young in the process?

Worse, PC prevents even direct 'Good Samaritan' action. My neighbour's ten-year-old daughter had the misfortune to sit upon a wasp during her lunch break at school. Because at that time only the Headmaster and a male teacher were present there, she was sent home by taxi – because the two men needed to give one another anti-paedophile alibis if they had driven her themselves, and they could not leave the school unattended. (So what about the solo taxi driver, if such a dirty-minded precaution has to be taken in the name of PC?) In short, two grown men, both fathers, dared not risk spraying an analgesic upon her bottom. Their justification for this moral cowardice? It might have been deemed indecent, and she might have had an allergic reaction to the spray. In the event there was no one at her home to tend to her, and she had to sit outside, in pain and shock, for a couple of hours before anything could be done to ease her distress. Such are the typical fruits of the climate of fear that PC brings about. And this is just one example. A perverted self-censorship, engendered by fear – sheer fear, and no sentiment more noble or justifiable – of PC-inspired consequences, suppresses the humane behaviour that our Christian / Classical culture has striven for a couple of millennia to develop. The Good Samaritan's conduct has been twisted into the new PC-promoted standard of evil.

Why on earth have we allowed PC to corrupt and ham-string our culture, laws, and civilisation in this way? Possibly because we do not know enough about the nature of true goodness, which comes from God, and the horrors of unfettered evil, which have their origin in the selfishness of human desires – and genes, of course. We need to become better acquainted with both. Without proper principles to guide their conduct, people will tend to turn blind eyes, keep quiet, and suffer convenient deafness in order to avoid what may prove troublesome to themselves. Did no one in Germany actually notice Jews disappearing from their normal places of residence and resort between 1935–1945, for example? Had absolutely everyone been conditioned to believe that, somehow, 'the government was taking care of it', it was 'all for the best', or that 'they deserve it, really', and so accept the Holocaust as a proper piece of policy whose hour had come? Or was there a pervasive fear of the consequences of acting in accordance with God's laws? The question is pertinent; it concerns a particular state of mind in such circumstances. If one de-humanises the 'enemy' – e.g. he is 'elitist' – then he is no longer human, and as such he does not matter as one does oneself. So do to him as you like; and make sure you are seen to be doing what you think is expected of you, for this course of action is safest for you and yours.

But all people matter. We are part of one Creation, sons and daughters of God.

To stand against evil is not always easy; no one said it was supposed to be. It can be downright dangerous – let us not fudge the issue. Jesus gave some advice on the subject, "I am sending you out like sheep among wolves. Therefore be as shrewd as snakes and as innocent as doves. Be on your guard against men; they will hand you over to the local councils and flog you… On my account you will be brought before governors and kings as witnesses [i.e. knowledgeable in the Gospel teaching, and therefore capable of justifying yourselves in God's terms] to them and to the Gentiles. But when they arrest you, do not worry about what to say or how to say it. At the time you will be given what to say. For it will not be you speaking, but the Spirit of your Father speaking through you." (Matthew 10. 16-20)

Of course, it helps to know right from wrong to start with.

28. The Necessity of Truth and Toleration

I have damned PC as evil, and tried to show its corrupting effects. I have given, too, a view of the fear it engenders. PC is the very opposite of Christianity, both in concept and application. As Christians we are told, "Love God, and your neighbour as yourself." Everyone will respond to this in his own individual way, and be responsible to God for what he does or does not do. But PC denies altogether the individual, choice, responsibility, and God, leaving a spiritual void surrounded by threatening fears. It is evil and worthless.

We have seen that the main word for love in New Testament Greek is *agape,* which translates as 'unconquerable goodwill'. The Greeks had other terms for love, too, and it is useful to know them and their shades of meaning. For love in the context of family affection, they spoke of *storge*; "A child loves and is loved by those who brought him into the world," says Plato, using the derivative verb *stergein.* Another term for close, warm, love and affection was *philia.* "Whom the gods love dies young," is a cheery quotation from Meander employing the verb *philein* which can also mean to fondle, caress, or kiss. *Eros* describes sexual love, a passion rather than affection or a companionable relationship. It does not occur in the New Testament. So the Greeks had a word for it, and *agape* is that word when Christians are dealing with Creation. We do not have to pretend to have any illusions about our neighbour; he is as we perceive him – and we may heartily loathe him, for perfectly justifiable reasons. We must nonetheless treat him with courtesy, as we would wish to be treated ourselves. We could explain to him why we were so engaged, and try and encourage him to modify his own behaviour, using means appropriate for the purpose. But goodwill towards him must underpin the action we undertake. And he has no claim upon us for *philia, storge,* or *eros,* whatever he may care to suppose.

We are once more dealing with words, as we did in the case of 'Paschal Lamb', 'field', 'energy', 'force', and so on. To cope adequately one needs to know the context in which the word is employed, the meaning normally given to it in that context, and the correct understanding and assumptions which follow. Much may depend upon getting the meaning right, especially if poisons or explosive materials are involved. A breadth of knowledge is desirable, and I again invoke the Natural Philosopher as culturally most likely to have it. We have just dabbled a little in Greek. But is it widely appreciated that four equivalent words for love exist in New Testament Greek, each with its own subtle shade of meaning? I doubt it. Does such an appreciation help us deal with the requirement to love one's neighbour as oneself? I should say so! Knowing this, does Christianity accordingly make better sense to people only vaguely acquainted with it? Quite possibly, if only because a reasonable requirement makes more sense than an apparently weird dogmatic demand. People are not stupid and in need of full-time 'nannying'; that condescending presumption is part of the PC evil. Tell them the truth, simply and clearly, and they will soon make up their own minds.

"What is truth?" asked Pontius Pilate (John 18.38). I confess to a sneaking sympathy for Pilate. He had a rotten job, was not the brightest of men – the Jews ran rings around him politically – and he had the sort of wife who pestered him whilst at work (Matthew 27. 19). Long ago I shared an office with a chap whose wife phoned him two or three times a day, on average, to moan about her own affairs and to interrogate him about what he was doing, offering loads of fatuous advice in the process. He was a most unhappy man. I tend to see Pilate as a like sufferer. What he in fact meant by truth was probably 'practical certainty' – something around which he could form, and then anchor, his views about life. For truth is something reliable which will not change its characteristics or melt away, even if some truths are of necessity provisional and awaiting confirmation or amendment. It is the quest for the truths about Creation which properly employs Philosophers, Natural Philosophers amongst them. We have already said as much.

Religion ties together and bundles up the package of truths – again as we have stated. It embraces the concept of Total, Absolute, and Ultimate Truths, epitomised in God, The One. In terms of material perceptions there is for God's existence "no testable evidence whatever". Yet God is known throughout Creation, "…so something must be going on". *Homo Sapiens* persists in experiencing anomalies in Creation, the 'spooky bits', for which there is currently "no testable evidence whatever". One day there may be, once science has found it out. *Homo Sapiens* also persists in striving for some form of society where abstract and non-natural-selective concepts such as justice, compassion, and truth itself are not only valued but are the norms of behaviour, "…so something must be going on". In short, the religious package is also part of the natural scheme of things. It requires an orderly Creation, in which its orderliness can be perceived and understood. If religion were not around in the background, it would have to be invented to fill out Creation's material shortcomings – to paraphrase Voltaire's comment about God. We have already noted that atheist political regimes do as much, with concepts such as Reason, or the personification of The Glorious Worker. Regardless of whether or not we are believers, it would seem that the human psyche is 'hard-wired' (an awful expression!) to embrace religion, Scientism included.

The Natural Philosopher is capable of taking up such approaches to Truth, and working with them in both their physical and transcendental aspects. It is, I believe, important that this approach is taken, and that our culture does not break up into 'factions', each denigrating and obstructing the work of all the others. It is often argued with dubious justification, by Prof. Dawkins for example, that this is exactly what religions have always done. The various gods worshipped have been an important part of cultural identity, certainly – "We Romans honour the gods because they bring us success…" But our Western civilisation is very much based upon Christian / Classical concepts, which is why it values truth and bridles at over-much dogma. To live within a nation which is part of the mainstream of this civilisation does not demand that all citizens embrace its beliefs. Toleration of other points of view has long been regarded as a hallmark of its civilised status, in fact, in times before PC. We should strive to maintain this practice of toleration. It allows all points of view to be expressed and examined, which process widens mental horizons to general benefit.

But claims about religious and doctrinal intolerance are valid in other parts of the world. It would be illegal for me to take a Bible into Saudi Arabia, for example, although if I were to pray quietly and inconspicuously in my own house there I might hope to be ignored. For several Christians to gather for worship would certainly create problems, however. Which is in itself a problem, for the concept of community is part of Christianity, and Jesus explicitly stated, "When two or three come together in my name, there am I with them" (Matthew 18.20). The particular interpretation of Islam currently dominant in Saudi Arabia derives from the Wahhabi movement, and is a markedly puritanical version of Moslem practice. It is, nonetheless, just as susceptible to adaptation and change as any other human interpretation of a religion's creed. So it follows that the current Wahhabi strain of Islam may as easily be rejected by future generations, just as the dogmatic intolerance of the Spanish Inquisition was removed from Roman Catholicism.

A wide-ranging reading of history, such as our Natural Philosopher would have undertaken, shows the adaptability of the human race to the perceived needs of any period of its existence. Its outward religious practices likewise prove capable of adjustment to the prevailing culture, without altering the essential basics of the Faith. As 'The People of the Book', as Islam terms it, Islam, Judaism and Christianity have their revelation of God, The One. This, potentially, is our shared basis for tolerant and courteous co-operation. The creation of dogmas is a human undertaking, in the sciences too, and all dogmas change with the better insights and enlightenment afforded by the course of time. Truth, in its total, absolute, and ultimate forms is what should be sought. Points of view about it are merely provisional, and this is usually understood.

For despite the assertions of Prof. Dawkins and allied dogmatic atheists, there is no necessary reason why people who worship according to the beliefs of one religion should wish to eliminate all who do not share them. In this respect Dawkins has confused religion with PC. Intolerance amongst mankind is most noticeable in political terms, in fact. Where any deviation from dogma will cause a regime to forfeit its self-proclaimed legitimacy to hold power, especially in some totalitarian People's Perpetual Paradise, a ruthless persecution of those dissenting from the views of the Great Leader of the day is both logical and necessary – from his point of view, at least. We see this exemplified most markedly at present in North Korea, but any regime based upon a self-proclaimed '…ism' will embody the same basic principle. Where to deviate from the '…ism' is to suffer a messy death – often accompanied by one's family – there is an obvious incentive to profess blind and bigoted orthodoxy, therefore. These strictly material considerations can be what bigoted atheism confuses with religion; their underlying principles are not unknown in the vicious groves of Academia, either.

Yet Scriptural requirements for religious intolerance can also be cited. We read (Matthew 12. 30-32) "He who is not with me is against me, and he who does not gather with me scatters. And so I tell you, every sin and blasphemy will be forgiven men, but the blasphemy against the Spirit will not be forgiven. Anyone who speaks a word against the Son of Man will be forgiven, but anyone who speaks against the Holy Spirit will not be forgiven, either in this age or the age to come." Blasphemy against the Holy Spirit means denial of God's primacy and omnipotence, incidentally. In the Koran we can read (Surah 3.115) "As for the unbelievers, neither their riches not their children shall in the least protect them from God's scourge; they are the heirs of the Fire, and there they shall remain for ever." (Surah 109) "Say: 'Unbelievers, I do not worship what you worship, nor do you worship what I worship. I shall never worship what you worship, nor will you ever worship what I worship. You have your own religion and I have mine." (Surah 3.118) "Believers, do not make friends with any but your own people. They will spare no pains to corrupt you. They desire nothing but your ruin. Their hatred is evident from what they utter with their mouths, but greater is the hatred which their breasts conceal. We have made plain Our revelations. Strive to understand them. See how you love them and they do not love you. You believe in the entire Book."

From a literal interpretation of such quotations as these it is possible to 'prove' intolerance to any atheist's satisfaction. Fundamentalists of both Christian and Islamic traditions could well join him in his view of the matter, whilst the basically ignorant, who still like to present themselves as informed and thus able to produce instant opinions, will go along with whoever is shouting loudest at the time. Without their particular input, how could TV and radio reviews of the latest news be padded out? But the point which they will all probably miss is that Scripture is not like a chemical process which will work according to the built-in blueprints of the elements involved in it because it can do nothing else. Scripture is open to interpretation, by people with free will. Depending upon what they make of it, it will form the basis for their beliefs and actions. And if those who are referring to these quotations, which are only extracts from far larger works known as Bible and Koran, are well versed in their respective Faiths, they will know that there is much more to God's revelation through Scripture than a few carefully selected lines. For example, God speaks of the breadth and diversity of his human Creation; Jesus says, "Do not let your hearts be troubled. Trust in God; trust also in me. In my Father's house there are many rooms; if it were not so, I would have told you." (John 14.2) Many rooms... many souls... of may individuals... each with his / her own relationship with God... based upon their own culture and religion, and not having to sit some sort of examination for orthodoxy according to a prevailing man-made '...ism' before admission to God's 'house' is granted. "Trust in God..." therefore. That is the message; not petty quibbling over transient, human-contrived dogmas.

We live in a disturbed age, mentally and spiritually. Perhaps it appears all the worse because our global communications make everything that happens seem to be taking place on our own doorsteps. We have not evolved to take such information overload in our mental stride, nor to have our daily range of thoughts stretched to embrace the import of events upon a global scale. One 'coping strategy' lies in over-specialisation, the very opposite of the breadth of view epitomised in the Natural Philosopher. Jesus told his disciples, "You will hear of wars and rumours of wars, but see to it that you are not alarmed. Such things must happen, but the end is still to come. Nation will rise against nation, and kingdom against kingdom. There will be famines and earthquakes in various places." (Matthew 24. 6,7) Consider what news of such events could have meant within the experience of quite ordinary people in first century Palestine, and compare it with our own TV images, radio reports, www blogs and the like. Never before have we been exposed to so much detail about our own species.

This has its effect upon our perceptions of life. The historian David Lowenthal has put it this way (*History Today* June 2006) "In the popular mind, both what was and what will be have shrunk, not in actual length and volume but in how these are grasped and felt... Disowning our Enlightenment legacy, we cease revering ancestors or welcoming descendants. The past, formerly guide and mentor, degenerates to domestic pet. The future, once embraced as a friend, becomes a fearsome foe... The Enlightenment invented faith in progress. Savants saw continual improvement. Science increased knowledge, nature was being tamed, diseases cured, prosperity rising, civic order spreading. Salvation was no longer exclusive to the hereafter; human advance augured paradise on Earth... And the gains of science magnified human responsibility... Until lately the future was a technofreak utopia. Science, social engineering, and giddy speed begat cornucopian prophecies... The archetypical future was a city of gleaming, tightly clustered towers with helicopters fluttering about their heads... [But] glittering streets in the sky became jerry-built crime-filled slums... Far from welcoming what lies ahead, we ignore it as risky if not ruinous... End-time preachers herald the horrors limned in the Book of Revelations. Worse still, it's all our own fault... today's envisioned endings stem from our own follies, eroding nature's fabric, polluting the planet beyond recovery, perfecting weapons that invite mass annihilation...

"The future that concerns young people today is tomorrow, next weekend... Few envisage becoming grandparents, even parents. Heedless of future millennia, they are reluctant to plan for their own lives, let alone for potential offspring... The bourgeois ideal of life as a career yields to career's older meaning: a helter-skelter dash towards no particular destination... Loss of faith in progress; the demise of job security; the dawning conviction, without precedent, that our children will be worse off than we (a conviction they share); fear that coming calamities are unavoidable and insoluble; growing doubt that science has the skill or statesmen the will to cure social malaise or environmental ruin."

Whatever we may think of the purple prose, the outline is stated clearly enough, and we can recognise in it elements of that '3 AM feeling'.

One word Lowenthal does not use is 'overpopulation'. It is an unfashionable word, unmentionable in PC circles. Which is odd, for there is any amount of solid material evidence for its effects upon Creation. We are told that there are – in 2009 – about 6,000,000,000 (6bn) humans upon Earth; in 1955 there were about 3bn of us. The same sources calculate that by 2050 we shall be 9bn all told – half as many again, in other words. Look around you and add 50% more people to those you see. It has been calculated by economists that for everyone in 2008 to enjoy roughly the same standard of living that the average European takes for granted, an *extra* 2.4 Earths would be needed. By 2050 this will be an extra 4 Earths. We do not have them, of course. Nor can we nip out and buy them. We have our battered old planet with its finite resources of water, food potential, and energy production. And that's it.

So do we all sit around passively waiting for the lights to dim and blink out, the food to disappear from the shop shelves, petrol to vanish from the garages, and transport to cease running, all as a prelude to a brief period of violent social mayhem followed by the starvation and death of urbanised billions? Or do we face a few facts and use our brains and our free will? How to reduce our numbers and the material demands we make of Earth seem to me to be the only important questions facing the human race at the moment. We can work out ways to do it humanely, justly, and compassionately, seeking a sustainable way of life, or we can let the 'selfish gene' have its way for as long as resources support it in eliminating, by its self-justifying methods, the 'less fitted' to survive. Humane ways, carefully adopted, could enable our civilisation to evolve along new lines. But the selfish-gene option logically leads to small, mutually hostile, groups competing for subsistence, and starting a new and survival-centred culture from scratch for the 'best fitted'. We have a choice, as ever, but not too many years in which to make it. The social turmoil and low-scale fighting amongst growing groups of selfish genes expressing themselves under the pressure of populations in contest for dwindling resources are already discernible, we may argue. Prof. Dawkins' theories can very adequately project the increased violence and destructiveness of the behaviours which will develop from these beginnings.

We need our Natural Philosopher to guide, weigh and balance, the options available. It does not at all follow that because some legitimate scientific process will work well in a particular situation, it should automatically be adopted. What needs to be considered is the quality of any particular process in relation to its outcome. This, in turn, implies value judgements. They tend to involve choices, the 'Why?' questions, whereas much science is purely utilitarian, proceeding along paths laid down by the built-in blueprints of its laws. The more widely-informed judgement of the Natural Philosopher is needed to help sort out ethical courses to take. We are, let us recall, only the most intelligent species upon one planet, in one Creation. I would then add that we are responsible to God for what we do. But even the most dogmatically materialistic atheist might appreciate his responsibility towards his neighbours-as-himself. We have no automatic right to survive as a species. The Selfish Gene starts to embarrass itself at this point, I think.

People have told me, in various ways, "I don't need Divine revelation in order to… service an engine, dig my garden, balance my books, pull a tooth, make a box, repair a gate, teach Serbo-Croat…" or any other activity. They have a point, so far as it goes. Yet if they were religious their beliefs would automatically be expressed in the development of their own personalities. In the way in which they led their lives, in their relationships with those around them, it is possible that their faith would show itself. I would suggest that an individual's life can be calmer, more stable, settled, and complete if it is based upon a religion – or a consistent and altruistic philosophy – than if it is governed by merely reacting to every circumstance which appears most advantageous to it at the time. The timescale in consideration is not 'tomorrow' but eternity. I also believe that Divine inspiration, the 'nudging' of the Holy Spirit, affects my unconscious mind and makes me an instrument in furthering God's kingdom. This is not fanciful. Science indicates, as we have noted, that the unconscious is the source of our decisions. The results of our decisions then shape our lives, and thus provide the basis for our further – unconscious – assumptions, the view we take of Creation. The process reinforces itself.

The quality of decisions made on our behalf by our Great Leaders, both nationally and globally, is coming under scrutiny beyond the usual infuriated outpourings which enliven the letter columns of the better newspapers, too. Vacuous, platitudinous vapourings on the subject of climate change are a case in point. Our Great Leaders have at their disposal the best scientific advice available, yet seem incapable of using it. Consequently I find scientific journals publishing rants about 'The Failure of Democracy...' and the like. Now, I tend to agree with Sir Winston Churchill's remark to the effect that democracy is an awful system, but the best one which has yet been devised. I also reflect upon the poet Dryden's line "The most may err as grossly as the few..." (*Absalom and Achitophel*). Therefore I jib at glib and narrow-minded rants demanding the 'primacy of science' in government and in all decision-making. I reflect that 'science' was done by Trofim Denisovich Lysenko, and Dr Mengele. Who would be required to decide whose 'science' is the ideal type for such a 'primacy'? What might happen if no one agreed with the resulting decision? This science-knows-best genre of article or letter-to-the-editor usually calls also for 'radical reform of democracy' – but into what? – and 'urgency' in decision making. Perhaps such writers would endorse Lowenthal's "...doubt that science has the skill or statesmen the will to cure social malaise or environmental ruin." But if all that this school of thought wants is instantly effective governance, it may as well impose a dictatorship and martial law and have done with it. The result will be very effective, but will it bring about the right decisions and actions, as opposed to those which will work, *pro tem*? The 'primacy' is Truth, not science, anyway. Science can only contribute its own knowledge to truth; knowledge deriving from other disciplines, insights, and inspirations is also needed to encompass truth properly. Our Natural Philosopher would be unequivocal upon this point.

There are also right courses of human conduct and wrong ones. Good and Evil are absolutes, not just expedient notions for the promotion of selfish genes' advantages. They are moral absolutes, as Religion knows. Politics often seeks to subvert them – PC, for example – or slide around them. Where PC succeeds, good is 'spun' as merely a better form of evil, whilst evil is brushed away as an unfortunate outcome of misapplied good. They are nothing such. They are concepts with distinctive qualities, and we serve no honest purpose by fudging the difference. Honesty and dishonesty themselves are warped by ignoring Truth, too. Without discriminating clearly between them society cannot function, for trust between people is weakened and the selfish cynic sets the standards of behaviour.

Also, tolerance of other viewpoints is essential to enable us to complement our own views. I will heed anecdotal evidence, even if I am not clear about what has given rise to its claims. Someone tells me he has seen a ghost, or a flying saucer? Fine; that is the interpretation he has put upon his experience. Let us proceed from there; I rule nothing out, *a priori*. So let me juggle ideas around it. If 'twistor space' turns out to exist, and has properties along the lines which will retain a ghost or so in its light networks, it will prove useful. If there is nothing in it, come the crunch, I can still post it up as a blind alley to warn me and others to look elsewhere. By such means the truths of Creation will be teased out. I will not find the attributes of 'twistor space' set out for me in the Bible, Koran, Upanishads, or any other religious traditions, however. To seek it and test its properties, if found, we need the disciplines of science, applied by minds and mortal brains. For this is where and how we stand in Creation.

We are creatures of stardust, living upon, and by, the debris of stars which have run their courses. Our material selves are composed of atoms which must respond to the dictates of their built-in blueprints, yet we ourselves have consciousness and choice. We recall the outcomes of the choices we make, and project the knowledge so gained into future choices required of us, thereby acknowledging responsibility for their outcome. We know that 95% of Creation is at present unknown to us. We are also uncertain about many attributes of Creation with which we deal daily, e.g. time, gravity, and a host of matters about ourselves – dreams, sentiments, creativity, consciousness itself. Then there are good indications that within Creation are the 'spooky bits', those features of experience for which there is "...no testable evidence whatever", but where we are left with the legitimate conclusion that "...something must be going on". There is no point in trying to ignore these. There is every reason to try and discover the truth about them, and about ourselves in relation to them. We have not evolved our large brains in order to give way to despair and neurosis, rather than setting them to work for our benefit. We must pursue Truth.

Also each one of us stands, as I believe, in a unique relationship with God. There is no built-in blueprint for religious belief by which believers must form uniform ranks like atoms in a crystal. We are just as we are, often a serendipitous and scruffy bunch. There is an individuality about religious belief, as well as the responsibility for what we do about it. Large amounts of *agape* are also required. Part of the business of being human is to strive to know Truth. It is an essential part of all considerations of Creation, and of our place in it. The search for it gives rise to the 'What?', 'How?', and 'Why?' questions with which I started.

So there I leave it. I trust in God. I seek to bring about his kingdom, according to the Christian culture which has nurtured me into old age. I am happy to share my beliefs with others. The 'spooky bits' of life interest me greatly for what they tell of the humanity I share with all mankind. They stir my curiosity, and I am obliged to search for answers – and pass on my conclusions to others to consider in the light of their own experiences. Hopefully we may together advance towards a more perfect grasp of Creation's truth.

And if I half-wake at 3.00 AM I entrust myself, body, mind and soul, to God – and go back to sleep again.

A M D G

Index

a-priori	21, 44
afterlife	144, 150
agape	233, 247
amygdala	93
anaesthesia	162
anecdotal evidence	56, 143
angel	148
anomalies	20, 21
apparitions	189 - 198
apports	206
atheism	78, 124, 150
'atmosphere'	191
Atonement, day of	88
Augustine, St.	38
Bede, The Venerable	144 - 153
Big Bang, the	26, 28 - 33, 52
bigotry	78
biophotons	136
birthmarks	156, 158
blueprints, built-in	30, 51
Buddhism	62, 79 - 80
bulldozer	24
brain	93 - 100, 101 - 109, 138, 141, 149, 154, 162, 170
brain-scans	129
Carr, Prof. B	170
chaos theory	43
Charman, R	129 - 130
Chatura	121, 154
choice	41, 51, 108, 239, 241, 243, 254.
Church	69
Christian altruism	51 - 57

Christianity 155
civilisation 4
Cockell, Jenny 159, 212, 216
cognition 103-104
Colossal Crunch 37 - 38
Confucius 87
consciousness 93, 98 - 100, 110 - 120, 162, 179
Creation 17 - 18, 39
crisis apparitions 153, 171
culture 108, 147, 191, 220, 245

Darwin, C 14, 49, 227
David, King 67
Dawkins, Prof. R 49, 200, 249, 254
Dayananda 121, 151, 154, 173
deliverance ministry 184
dentistry 162 - 169
discovery 14
dissociation 125, 216
dimensions 133
distance viewing 142
dogmatism 22
dreams 176
drugs 102, 107
Drycthelm 144

Earth, end of 35
Eden 13
EEG imaging 129
Ego 69
emotion 174, 181 - 188, 191
end-of-life experience 152
endorphins 167
energy 179
Episodic Controller 115
equality 221, 242 - 246
extra sensory perception 118
evolution 3, 14
expectation 124

faith	9, 52, 124
fear	183, 189 - 198
free-will	41 - 48, 52, 108, 201
free radicals	132
Galileo	12
gallery	113, 190
Gamaliel	87
genes	49, 168, 255
ghosts	101, 135, 189 - 198
Gilgamesh	17
Goal-Directed Controller	115
God	14, 17, 19, 25, 44 - 48, 52, 58 - 70, 108, 149, 183, 199 - 207, 233, 247 - 258
gods, invented	60 - 70
gold	148
Gospel	67, 223
Grace	90
gravity	19
Habitual Controller	115
Hawking, Prof. S	12
Haynes, JD	42, 115
hallucinations	139, 144
heaven	148, 202
Herod the Great	89
Hinduism	87
hippocampus	94, 107
Holy Spirit	67 - 70
Hoyle, Prof. F	32
Hubble telescope	34
hubris	40
hypnosis	159, 161 - 169, 211 - 219
Id	69
imagination	96
intolerance	199 - 207, 250 - 252
Islam	63 - 70, 87

jazz	111
Jesus	66 - 70, 148, 223, 246
JHWH	71
Josephus, Flavius	89
juggling	107

Kagan, Prof. J	120
Karma	154, 155
Kingdom of God	86 - 92
knowledge	40

lap-top computer	139
Law, The	77, 86
Libet, B	41 - 42, 115
libido	69
life	52
light	131 - 137, 152
London cabbies	107
love	86, 101, 226, 247 - 258

Manning, M	210
McGrath, Prof. A	200
meditation	97 - 100, 107
mediums	203, 209
MEG imaging	129
memory	94 - 100, 157, 216
mental baggage	176
Mesmer	167
mind	83, 99 - 109, 124 - 128, 138, 150, 160, 162
miracles	44, 224,
Montefiore, Bish. H	146
morality	160, 229 - 137, 239
Moseley, Dr. L	116
Moses	72, 86, 229
motherhood	180 - 188
multiverse	38
music	152

near-death-experience	118, 144 - 153
Nemesis	40

neural circuits   95, 107
New Age   154
noise, anomalous   186

orbital frontal cortex   94
Ossowiecki   135
out-of-body-experience   138 - 143

Patrick, St.   65
Paul, St.   82, 88
Pavlovian Controller   115
People-of-the-Book   63, 250
philosophy   8
photography   197
photon-field   132
physics   170
placebo effect   163
plotting table   112
'political correctness'   54, 238 - 246
poltergeist   179 - 188
post-mortem mind   119, 121, 137, 138, 141, 144
prayer   183
pre-frontal cortex   108

prejudice   54
prophets   72 - 77, 86, 203
psychic spying   177
psychokinesis   187
psychophore   126 - 127, 158
psychosomatic effects   161

quantum mechanics   45

random event generator   187
reincarnation   121, 135, 154 - 160
religion   7, 248
remotely-sensed psychokinesis   188
'Robert Webbe'   210

Sabbath	88, 230
Sanhedrin	87
scapegoat	89
scepticism	24, 204 - 207
science	8, 19, 56, 91
scientism	54, 117, 135, 153, 197
Scole	205
Scripture	146
Self	69, 110
senses	93
Sheldrake, Dr. R	118, 127, 171
sin	89
sleep	125
soul	124 - 128, 217, 233
'spooky bits'	5, 223
stars, life cycle	34
steady-state universe	32
Stevenson, Prof. I	126, 135, 161
stigmata	161
stimuli	162
stress	1, 80, 180, 216
stroke	141
subconscious	69
survival, of fittest	227
synapses	95
systems, physics	43 - 48
technology	3
telepathy	129, 136, 173, 204
temperature fluctuation	182
Ten Commandments	72, 229 - 237
time	21, 96 - 100
Titus	88
tolerance	6, 250 - 251, 257
trance	169
Trinity, the	65
truth	56, 153, 248 - 258
'twistors'	133
Tyrrell, GNM	103

'ubiquitous They'   5
unconscious   115, 255
universe   11, 30 - 59

Vespasian   88
victimhood   240
Voyager space probes   33

Wallace, A R   14, 49
weather   43
Western culture   47
will   160